Oxford Resources
for Cambridge

exam success

Cambridge IGCSE® & O Level

20th Century History

Revision Guide

Second Edition

Peter Smith
Neil Smith
Ray Ennion

OXFORD
UNIVERSITY PRESS

Great Clarendon Street, Oxford, OX2 6DP, United Kingdom

Oxford University Press is a department of the University of Oxford. It furthers the University's objective of excellence in research, scholarship, and education by publishing worldwide. Oxford is a registered trade mark of Oxford University Press in the UK and in certain other countries.

British Library Cataloguing in Publication Data
Data available

978-1-38-20-56526

10 9 8 7 6 5 4 3 2 1

Paper used in the production of this book is a natural, recyclable product made from wood grown in sustainable forests.

The manufacturing process conforms to the environmental regulations of the country of origin.

Printed in India by Manipal Technologies Limited

Acknowledgements

This Student Book refers to the Cambridge IGCSE® History syllabus published by Cambridge Assessment International Education.

This work has been developed independently from and is not endorsed by or otherwise connected with Cambridge Assessment International Education. IGCSE® is the registered trademark of Cambridge Assessment International Education.

The publisher and authors would like to thank the following for permission to use photographs and other copyright material:

An extract from *Special Providence: American Foreign Policy and How it Changed the World* by Walter Russell Mead published by Knopf in 2001. Reproduced with permission of Alfred A. Knopf, an imprint of the Knopf Doubleday Publishing Group, a division of Penguin Random House LLC.

Cover: William G. Vanderson / Fox Photos / Getty Images. Photos: p4: Everett Collection Historical / Alamy Stock Photo; p8: Historic Collection / Alamy Stock Photo; p10: Chronicle / Alamy Stock Photo; p19: Peter Newark Military Pictures / Bridgeman Images; p26: Vorwärts, reproduced in May 3, 1924; p30: World History Archive / Alamy Stock Photo; p32: Pictorial Press Ltd / Alamy Stock Photo; p35: Public Domain; p40: Pictorial Press Ltd / Alamy Stock Photo; p44: Hulton Archive / Stringer / Getty Images; p64: TopFoto; p82: Universal Images Group North America LLC / Alamy Stock Photo; p89: The History Collection / Alamy Stock Photo; p108: INTERFOTO / Alamy Stock Photo; p114: Shawshots / Alamy Stock Photo; p126: Shawshots / Alamy Stock Photo; p134: Bettmann / Getty Images; p140: Universal History Archive / Getty Images; p151: Everett Collection / Shutterstock; p154: Everett Collection / Shutterstock; p157: Pictorial Press Ltd / Alamy Stock Photo; p165: Niday Picture Library / Alamy Stock Photo.

Artwork by Aptara Inc., and Q2A Media.

Every effort has been made to contact copyright holders of material reproduced in this book. Any omissions will be rectified in subsequent printings if notice is given to the publisher.

Although we have made every effort to trace and contact all copyright holders before publication this has not been possible in all cases. If notified, the publisher will rectify any errors or omissions at the earliest opportunity.

Links to third party websites are provided by Oxford in good faith and for information only. Oxford disclaims any responsibility for the materials contained in any third party website referenced in this work.

FSC
www.fsc.org

MIX
Paper | Supporting
responsible forestry
FSC® C043100

Contents

Introduction

Engaging exam practice and revision guidance for the latest Cambridge IGCSE® and O Level History syllabus. Use alongside Cambridge IGCSE® & O Level Complete 20th Century History textbook or as a stand-alone resource to encourage grade improvement and maximise performance in examinations.

This Exam Success Guide:

- Brings clarity and focus to exam preparation, equipping students to reach their full potential

- Has complete coverage of key points in the latest syllabus to build knowledge and confidence for exams

- Raise grades with worked examples, exam-style questions, and exam tips

Key revision points are included as follows:

- Key ideas: at the start of every chapter. This summarises key things you need to know for each topic.

- Recap: each chapter recaps key content and theory through easy-to-digest chunks and visual stimulus.

Recap

Clemenceau's priorities were the defence of France and the return of land previously lost to Germany; he wanted action regarding the territories of Alsace-Lorraine, the Saarland, and the Rhineland. He also wanted Germany harshly punished and prevented from waging war again.

- Apply: targeted revision activities are written specifically for these guides, which will help you to apply your knowledge in the exam paper. These provide a variety of transferrable exam skills and techniques. By using a variety of revision styles you'll be able to cement your revision.

Apply

Prepare a table with three columns, one for each of the "Big Three" leaders at Versailles. List each leader's main ideas about how to prevent the recurrence of a major conflict.

Answers to the Apply questions are available in the digital version of the book.

- Review: throughout each chapter, you can review and reflect on the work you have done, and find advice on how to further refresh your knowledge. This will include references back to the Student Book.

- Exam tips: include particular emphasis on content and skills where students commonly struggle. The tips give details on how to maximise marks in the exam.

> **Exam tip**
>
> It is important that you provide arguments and evidence to support the view presented in the statement, and then present arguments and evidence that challenge this view. Your conclusion should comment on the extent to which you believe the statement is correct.

- Raise your grade: can be found at the end of each chapter. This section includes answers from candidates who didn't achieve maximum marks and advice on how to improve answers.

Raise your grade ↑

1. Describe German territorial losses as a result of the Treaty of Versailles.   **(4 marks)**

Germany lost a lot of land as a result of the Treaty of Versailles and therefore became much smaller.

To answer question 1, the student only provides a single general comment. 1 mark awarded. Two points with specific examples would improve the answer. For example: Germany lost land to France as a result of the Treaty of Versailles, including Alsace-Lorraine, which it had gained in 1871, and Eupen and Malmedy to Belgium. Land was also given to the League of Nations to administer, including Danzig and Germany's colonies.

Plan your answer

- This question is asking you to provide two features of German territorial losses as a result of the Treaty of Versailles.

- You must also give supporting examples for each point you make.

- Germany's territorial losses after the war were in Europe, such as East Prussia, which was given to the new state of Poland, and also further afield because it lost colonial territories, such as Togoland, as well.

How will you be assessed?

Candidates for Cambridge IGCSE® History take three components: Paper 1 and Paper 2, and either Component 3 or Paper 4.

Candidates for Cambridge O Level History are required to take two papers: Paper 1 and Paper 2.

Paper 1

Compulsory

For both the Cambridge IGCSE® and O Level, candidates have two hours to complete this paper and 60 marks are available.

For IGCSE, Paper 1 makes up 40 per cent of the overall marks.

For O Level, Paper 1 makes up 55 per cent of the overall marks.

Paper 2

You have 1 hour and 45 minutes for this paper and 40 marks are available.

Your teacher will know well in advance which option you will be taking for this paper.

For IGCSE, Paper 2 makes up 33 per cent of the overall marks.

For O Level, Paper 2 makes up 45 per cent of the overall marks.

Candidates taking Cambridge IGCSE® History are also required to choose one of the following:

Component 3

This is the coursework option.

There are 40 marks available for Component 3, which makes up 30 per cent of the overall marks.

or

Paper 4

This is the written paper option, and the alternative to the coursework option. Paper 4 requires you to answer one question from a choice of two on any of the topics that you have covered. Each question is divided into two sub-questions. Part a) questions require candidates to write about an event or feature of a period, while part b) questions require candidates to discuss the significance of an event or person within a particular period.

You have 1 hour for this paper, and 40 marks are available.

Paper 4 makes up 30 per cent of the overall marks.

1 How far was the Treaty of Versailles fair?

You need to know

- What the United States, Britain, and France wanted to achieve at Versailles
- The main terms of the Treaty of Versailles
- How far each of the "Big Three" was satisfied with the peace settlement
- The impact of the peace treaty on Germany and other defeated countries up to 1923
- Attitudes at the time towards Versailles

Background: The peace treaties of 1919–23

The First World War resulted in the deaths of almost 10 million people, cost more than any previous war in history, and destroyed four empires. It led to the creation of several new nations in Europe and the Middle East, triggered a revolution in Russia and, perhaps indirectly, led to the rise of the Fascist government in Italy in 1922, and then the Nazi regime in Germany in 1933. In January 1919 delegates from 32 countries were invited to meet in Paris at the Palace of Versailles. Each nation present wanted a settlement that would last. The defeated nations and Soviet Russia were not invited to attend.

At the Paris Peace Conference, which began in January 1919, five treaties were drawn up and referred to collectively as the Versailles Settlement. The main one was the Treaty of Versailles, which dealt with Germany; the other treaties dealt with Germany's allies: Austria, Hungary, Bulgaria, and Turkey.

While representatives from 27 nations participated in the peace conference, proceedings were dominated by three men: Prime Minister Georges Clemenceau of France, Prime Minister Lloyd George of Great Britain, and US President Woodrow Wilson.

What the United States, Britain, and France wanted to achieve at Versailles

Clemenceau, Lloyd George, and Wilson approached the peace conference determined to prevent the recurrence of a major conflict; however, they differed over the methods they believed would successfully achieve this goal.

Clemenceau's priority was to secure the defence of France and the return of land lost to Germany in 1871. He believed the best way to achieve these goals was to punish Germany harshly and make it impossible for Germany to wage war again.

Lloyd George believed that a "just and firm" peace that did not create a desire for revenge in Germany, along with the economic revival of Europe and Germany, would be the best way to prevent war. However, he also wanted a share of Germany's colonies to strengthen Britain's global position.

Wilson wanted a fair and lasting peace, with the Fourteen Points as the basis (see the Student Book, page 5), that would increase future international cooperation and encourage nations to negotiate rather than use violence as a tool to settle their differences.

> **Recap**
>
> Clemenceau's priorities were the defence of France and the return of land previously lost to Germany; he wanted action regarding the territories of Alsace-Lorraine, the Saarland, and the Rhineland. He also wanted Germany harshly punished and prevented from waging war again.

> **Recap**
>
> The Fourteen Points addressed the key areas to be settled after the war, including disarmament, self-determination, the League of Nations, and territorial disputes. (See the Student Book, page 5.)

1

Worked Example

What did Lloyd George hope to achieve from the peace settlement of 1919–20? (4)

Lloyd George hoped to make Germany pay for starting the war and thought Germany should pay compensation to the Allies. He therefore insisted that he chair a committee at Versailles to investigate how much Germany should pay.

He also hoped to maintain the dominant position of Britain's navy, which was essential to the protection of Britain's colonies and for trade within the British Empire, and he therefore supported restricting Germany's navy to 36 ships.

Worked Example

Why did Clemenceau and Wilson disagree over how to treat Germany? (6)

Wilson and Clemenceau disagreed over the issue of reparations. Clemenceau wanted to impose a very high level of reparations that would not only compensate the invaded countries for the destruction caused by the war, but would also prevent Germany from being able to wage war in the future. Wilson objected to reparations and only accepted that Belgium should be compensated for war damage because, he argued, the invasion of neutral Belgium was illegal.

They also disagreed over disarmament: in his Fourteen Points, Wilson stated that he wished to see nations' armaments reduced to a level necessary only for national defence, but Clemenceau disagreed, arguing instead for the permanent disarmament of Germany. He believed this was essential to protect France from future German attacks.

Recap

As well as their desire to prevent a future conflict, the leaders were heavily influenced by public opinion in their own countries. In France and Britain, the strongest feeling was that Germany should be made to pay for starting the war, while many people in the United States were very reluctant to see their country become involved in the affairs of European states again.

Apply

Prepare a table with three columns, one for each of the "Big Three" leaders at Versailles. List each leader's main ideas about how to prevent the recurrence of a major conflict.

Exam tip

To answer a question like this, you should provide two of Lloyd George's aims for the peace settlement, with a supporting detail for each.

Exam tip

The key to success with this type of question is to provide two fully explained reasons.

Key fact

The Peace Settlement 1919–20 refers to all five of the peace treaties signed with the defeated powers after the First World War. They were the treaties of:

- Versailles (with Germany)
- St Germain (with Austria)
- Trianon (with Hungary)
- Sèvres (with Turkey)
- Neuilly (with Bulgaria).

What were the main terms of the Treaty of Versailles?

The treaty was not negotiated with Germany and its terms were presented to the German delegation at the peace conference in May 1919. The following points were included in the main terms.

- Germany must take full responsibility for starting the war (the War Guilt Clause).

- Germany must accept liability for the damage caused by the war and therefore pay reparations to the countries directly affected by the war (a figure later set at £6.6 billion).

- The Rhineland must be demilitarised.
- **Anschluss** was forbidden.
- Disarmament: The German army was limited to 100 000 men, conscription was banned, the navy was limited to 36 warships, and Germany was forbidden from possessing any tanks or air force.
- The loss of territories in Europe was addressed. Land was given to France (Alsace-Lorraine), Belgium (Eupen and Malmedy), Denmark (North Schleswig), and to new states: Poland (West Prussia, Posen, and parts of Upper Silesia) and Lithuania (Memel). The Saarland would temporarily be administered by the new League of Nations for 15 years after which a **plebiscite** would be held to decide its future. Danzig became a free city administered by the League of Nations.
- Germany's colonies became mandates of the League of Nations.

Key term

Anschluss—the term given to the unification of Germany with its neighbour, Austria.

Key term

Plebiscite—a vote on a single issue in the manner of a referendum. Plebiscites were held after 1918 in areas of uncertain nationality to establish which country the populations wished to be governed by.

> **Worked Example**
>
> Describe the military restrictions placed on Germany as a result of the Treaty of Versailles. (4)
>
> The size of the German army was limited to 100 000 men as a result of the Treaty of Versailles and the army was not allowed to possess any tanks or heavy artillery.
>
> Restrictions were also placed on Germany's navy. No submarines were allowed, while the number of warships was limited to 36. In addition, Germany was not allowed either a military or naval air force.

Exam tip

You only need to describe the main restrictions, with supporting details. You are not being asked to analyse whether they were fair or not.

Why did all the victors not get everything they wanted?

Clemenceau, Lloyd George, and Wilson were pleased with some aspects of the Treaty of Versailles, but each was significantly unhappy with other aspects. This is perhaps understandable given the differences between the aims of the "Big Three". It was also a complex process to devise a peace settlement that sought to both identify and punish the country responsible for starting the conflict and put in place features to prevent the outbreak of a similar war in the future.

In summary, Clemenceau was most pleased with the:

- return of Alsace-Lorraine to France
- imposition of reparations on Germany
- weakening of Germany's military
- increased security for France as a result of the demilitarisation of the Rhineland.

However, he was less pleased with the:

- United States' refusal to create an Anglo–American Treaty of Guarantee to deal with Germany if it became aggressive again
- Saarland coming under the control of the League of Nations and not being given to France.

Lloyd George was most pleased with the:

- extension of the British Empire through the transfer of Germany's colonies to the League of Nations; several would be mandated to Britain to manage

- fact that Germany wasn't completely destroyed economically by the Treaty of Versailles, meaning it could play a part in the economic future of Europe.

He was less pleased that many German-speaking people were not ruled by Germany and found themselves in other countries, for example, in Poland or Czechoslovakia.

Wilson was most pleased that:

- the creation of a new League of Nations was included in the treaties

- the principle of self-determination resulted in the creation of new countries out of the defeated old empires of Europe

- some degree of disarmament took place after the war.

However, he was less pleased that:

- self-determination did not apply across the whole of Europe

- the treaty was much harsher on Germany than Wilson envisaged in his Fourteen Points

- ultimately, the United States never approved the treaty as **Congress** did not ratify it when it voted on it in November 1919 and again in March 1920; as a result, the United States did not join the League of Nations.

Recap

While the US President has the constitutional power to make and sign treaties, the president cannot ratify a treaty until two-thirds of the US Senate has voted to approve it. This is why Wilson had to carry out an intensive lobbying campaign in the autumn of 1919 to ensure that public opinion would force the Senate to approve the Treaty of Versailles.

Key term

Congress—the main law-making institution in the United States.

Source 1

THE ACCUSER

March 22, 1920

Fig. 1.1 *An American cartoon from March 1920*

Worked Example

Why was the cartoon in Source 1 published in March 1920? Explain your answer using details of the source and your own knowledge. (7)

This cartoon was published in March 1920 because the cartoonist wished to criticise the refusal of the US Senate to approve the Treaty of Versailles in a vote taken that month. The US Constitution requires the Senate to approve any foreign treaty with a two-thirds majority before the President can ratify it. The Senate had failed to approve it in November 1919 and had again failed to do so in March 1920. The cartoonist appears to be suggesting that by "killing off" the treaty, the Senate is effectively endangering the rest of humanity and future world peace. Should a future conflict occur then humanity would be able to accuse the US Senate of being partially to blame, hence the title of the cartoon: "The Accuser". By rejecting the treaty, the Senate prevented the United States from joining the new League of Nations, undermining President Wilson's attempt to develop international cooperation and create a lasting peace.

Exam tip

It is very important to refer to the context in which this cartoon was published and how it will affect both the message and purpose of the source.

Worked Example

"Prime Minister Clemenceau of France was the most satisfied of the 'Big Three' with the Treaty of Versailles." How far do you agree with this statement? Explain your answer. (10)

Clemenceau was probably the most satisfied of all the "Big Three" with the Treaty of Versailles. He would have been highly satisfied that Germany was harshly punished and that France's security seemed to have been assured. Germany had to accept the War Guilt Clause and pay a large amount of reparations, most of which went to France. Germany was also punished by losing its colonies, some to France, such as Togoland, and by losing a considerable amount of land in Europe, such as Danzig, which became a Free City. France's security seemed assured because of the extent of disarmament Germany had to accept, with an army of 100 000 volunteers and no air force or tanks. Furthermore, the west bank of the Rhineland had to be completely demilitarised.

Clemenceau was also highly satisfied because both Lloyd George and Wilson were unhappy with key elements of the treaty. For example, both objected to the scale of reparations. Lloyd George was keen to see Germany develop as a trading partner for Britain. Wilson believed the Germans would resent the reparations, possibly leading to future conflict.

However, Clemenceau was not satisfied that France's permanent protection from German aggression wasn't guaranteed: the United States would not agree to a Treaty of Guarantee against German aggression. Certain territories taken from Germany could be returned in the future, such as the Saarland, and Allied occupation of the Rhineland would end after 15 years.

It could also be argued that Lloyd George was the most satisfied as he wanted a moderate peace to allow the European economy to thrive and that was essentially achieved at Versailles. While Germany was punished, it was not broken up or de-industrialised, as Clemenceau wanted. In addition, Britain's interests were largely enhanced by gaining new colonies, such as Palestine, and by the removal of the German navy as a threat to British naval interests.

Many historians would disagree that Clemenceau was the most satisfied of the "Big Three". The treaty was closest to Lloyd George's aims before the peace conference and considerably strengthened Britain's position in the world.

Exam tip

It is important that you provide arguments and evidence to support the view presented in the statement, and then present arguments and evidence that challenge this view. Your conclusion should comment on the extent to which you believe the statement is correct.

How did the Treaty of Versailles impact on Germany up to 1923?

German reaction to the Treaty of Versailles was hostile almost from the point it was presented to Germany. These were Germany's main criticisms.

- It did not believe the War Guilt Clause was fair as it disputed that it was solely to blame for starting the conflict in 1914.

- The extent of disarmament was a severe blow to national pride: for decades the German military had been a symbol of German strength and prestige.

- Germany claimed to have agreed to an armistice in November 1918 on the basis that the peace would be based on the Fourteen Points. However, the eventual treaty appeared to be much harsher than Wilson's original plan.

- The peace settlement appeared to be inconsistent. For example, self-determination was provided for some nations' people, such as Poles, but not for many Germans.

- Furthermore, the peace settlement was imposed on Germany.

- Germany claimed that it was unable to pay the amount of reparations demanded and refused to pay any more at the end of 1922.

The Treaty of Versailles, and the wider effects of the war, had a significant effect on Germany, with political, economic, and social unrest plunging the country into chaos by 1923.

Worked Example

Why did many Germans believe that the Treaty of Versailles was unfair? (6)

Many Germans believed that the Treaty of Versailles was unfair because they felt it wrongly blamed Germany for starting the war. As a result, they strongly objected to the War Guilt Clause. They argued that Serbia and Russia contributed greatly to the start of the conflict through their provocation of Austria, and Germany was merely coming to the assistance of its neighbour and ally in the summer of June 1914.

They also believed it was unfair because they were not given the opportunity to discuss or negotiate the terms of the treaty. They argued that Germany's agreement to an armistice in November 1918 was on the basis that the war would be brought to an end and negotiations would follow; especially considering Germany had agreed to Wilson's conditions to remove the Kaiser from his throne and Germany had not itself been invaded. However, the treaty was a dictated peace, which was decided upon by the victors at Versailles and presented to the German delegates as something that they would have to accept.

Exam tip

To score highly on this question you need to provide two fully explained reasons why many Germans believed that this treaty was unfair.

Worked Example

How far would you agree that the Treaty of Versailles was an unfair treaty? (10)

On the one hand, there is a strong argument that the Treaty of Versailles was unfair. First, it appeared that Germany was being punished twice over for the damage that was caused during the war. The treaty stated that Germany would have to pay reparations to the victorious powers for war damage, for example the rebuilding of Ypres in Belgium, which had been virtually destroyed during

Exam tip

You should provide a balanced response, ideally giving two arguments for each side, and a conclusion evaluating how far you agree with the statement.

four years of fighting. When the final amount of reparations was agreed upon—£6.6 billion—Germany argued that it was not able to pay this amount. The very resources that Germany would need to pay for the reparations (coal, iron ore) were not available to the Germans as the Saarland was under the control of the League of Nations and Upper Silesia was given to Poland.

The treaty was also thought to be unfair because Germany appeared to have been treated differently from other nations. While the principle of self-determination was used to create new nations for Poles and Czechs, many Germans were left under the control of foreign governments, for example in the Sudetenland in Czechoslovakia. The principle of disarmament was applied to the defeated nations, but this was not applied to the other nations at Versailles.

However, one could suggest it was not unfair because the experience of Russia at the hands of Germany in March 1918 indicated that Germany would have imposed a treaty that was harsh, if not more harsh, on the Allies if it had won the war. The Treaty of Brest-Litovsk required Russia to give up approximately 1 million square miles of its territory to Germany, Austria, and Turkey, losing around 30 per cent of its population in the process and 90 per cent of its coal mines.

Furthermore, one of the more controversial aspects of the Versailles Treaty, the War Guilt Clause, was fair because German militarism and support for Austria in the summer of 1914 were the main cause of the war. If Germany had not given Austria a "blank cheque" in its dispute with Serbia and then implemented the Schlieffen Plan, there would not have been a war in Europe.

Worked Example

Describe how Austria and Hungary were treated in the Paris Peace Settlements. (4)

Both Austria and Hungary were forced to disarm as a result of the peace settlement in 1919. Both countries were forbidden from conscripting men to their armies, and while Austria could have an army consisting of 30 000 men, Hungary was allowed an army of 35 000 men.

New countries were also created from land taken from Austria and Hungary. Czechoslovakia, Romania, and Yugoslavia were all created using land taken from Austria and Hungary.

Apply

Some believed that the Paris peace treaties were unfair. Others believed that the treaties were not harsh enough. Consider both views. For both viewpoints, write three bullet points, giving a supporting example for each point.

Exam tip

The 4-mark description question is an introductory question. The answer needs to present two points, each with a supporting detail or example.

Could the treaties be justified at the time?

Opinions in the years immediately following the peace treaties broadly divided into three viewpoints.

- **The treaties were too harsh:** Some, like Lloyd George, feared that the treaties would stir up such resentment in the defeated countries, especially Germany, that Europe would be plunged back into war. Others, such as British economist John Maynard Keynes, argued that the scale of punishment would prevent Germany's economy recovering, which would impact on the prosperity of the rest of Europe.

- **The treaties were not harsh enough:** Many people in France feared that the Treaty of Versailles merely brought France a temporary respite from German aggression and thought that Germany should have also been broken into smaller states and had its industrial capacity completely destroyed. In Italy, Prime Minister Orlando was heavily criticised for not demanding that extra territory should be taken from Austria and given to Italy.

- **The treaties were fair:** President Wilson argued that the treatment of the defeated nations was appropriate for their roles in starting and sustaining the war. Edward M House, one of the American diplomats at Versailles, acknowledged that it was not a perfect peace settlement, but probably the best that could have been achieved given the circumstances.

Source 2

"Wilson's principles survived the eclipse of the Versailles system and they still guide European politics today: self-determination, democratic government, collective security, international law, and a League of Nations. Wilson may not have gotten everything he wanted at Versailles, and his treaty was never ratified by the Senate, but his vision and his diplomacy, for better or worse, set the tone for the twentieth century. France, Germany, Italy, and Britain may have sneered at Wilson, but every one of these powers today conducts its European policy along Wilsonian lines."

A historian writing about President Wilson in 2001.

Source 3

At the Peace Table

—*From Hvepsen, Christiania.*

C**LEMENCEAU** (to the German delegates): "Take your seats, gentlemen!"

Fig. 1.2 *A view of the peace talks from an American newspaper*

See the Raise your grade section for a question on this source.

Source 4

"To those who are saying that the treaty is bad... I feel like admitting it. But I would also say that empires cannot be shattered and new states raised upon their ruins without disturbance. To create new boundaries is always to create new troubles. While I should have preferred a different peace, I doubt whether it could have been made."

Extract from the diary of Edward M House, an American diplomat, June 1919.

Worked Example

Look at sources 3 and 4. How far do these sources disagree? Explain your answer using details of the sources. (7)

Sources 3 and 4 disagree in their main message. Source 3 suggests that the peace settlement is extremely harsh on the defeated powers, as represented by the spikes on the chairs and handcuffs on the table. Source 4, in contrast, suggests that the "Big Three" came up with as good and fair a peace as was possible given the impact of the war on Europe.

However, the sources do agree that the treaties were not essentially fair. Source 4 implies that the author acknowledges that he would have preferred a better treaty, and even suggest he agrees with those who say it was a "bad" treaty, which agrees with the main message and details of source 3.

In conclusion, the sources mostly agree that the peace treaties were not fair, although source 3 states this more explicitly and does not consider the context in which the peacemakers found themselves.

Exam tip

You should explain how the two sources agree and disagree on either the details or main message, and provide a judgement on the extent of agreement.

Source 5

"The Treaty contains no provisions for the economic rehabilitation of Europe; nothing to make the defeated Central empires into good neighbours, nothing to stabilise the new states of Europe, nothing to reclaim Russia; nor does it promote in any way a compact of economic solidarity amongst the Allies themselves; no arrangement was reached at Paris for restoring the disordered finances of France and Italy or to adjust the systems of the Old World and the New."

Extract from The Economic Consequences of the Peace, *by J M Keynes, 1919. Keynes participated at the peace conference as part of the British delegation.*

See the Raise your grade section for a question on this source.

Worked Example

Study source 5. Are you surprised by this source? Explain your answer using details of the source and your own knowledge. (8)

This source is surprising as Keynes was a member of the British delegation at Versailles and so would have been involved in writing the peace treaty. Furthermore, the treaty did not contain clauses to support the economic rehabilitation of Europe as reparations were to be used to compensate countries for the damage done during the war, and they were not set so high as to destroy Germany's economy completely.

However, it is not surprising as Keynes left the British delegation before the treaty was signed because he was so critical of how Germany was being treated. It is also not surprising because the peacemakers intended to punish the defeated Central Powers and were not concerned with rehabilitating them. The loss of land and extent of disarmament are good examples of this.

On balance, the message of the source is not surprising considering the harsh way in which the treaties dealt with the Central Powers after the war.

Exam tip

Base your response on the specific content of the source and relate it to what you know of the event being described.

Source 6

"The criminal madness of this peace will drain Germany's national life-blood. It is a shameless blow in the face of common sense. It is inflicting the deepest wounds on us Germans as our world lies in wreckage about us."

Extract from a speech made by a member of the Reichstag, 1919.

Source 7

Fig. 1.3 *A cartoon from a British newspaper, May 1919*

See the Raise your grade section for a question on this source.

Review

1. Describe how the peacemakers at Versailles attempted to achieve disarmament of the defeated powers. [4]

2. Why would President Wilson have been pleased with the terms of the Treaty of Versailles? [6]

3. Study sources 4 and 7. How far do these two sources disagree? Explain your answer using details of the sources. [7]

4. Study source 3. Are you surprised by this source? Explain your answer using details of the source and your knowledge.   [8]

5. "German opposition to the Treaty of Versailles was unjustified." How far do you agree with this statement? Explain your answer.   [10]

6. Who would have been happier with the Treaty of Versailles, Wilson or Lloyd George?   [10]

7. Study all of the sources in the chapter. How far do they provide convincing evidence that the Paris peace treaties 1919–20 were unfair? Use the sources to explain your answer.   [12]

For further information, review this section in the Student Book.

Raise your grade ↑

1. Describe German territorial losses as a result of the Treaty of Versailles.   (4 marks)

Germany lost a lot of land as a result of the Treaty of Versailles and therefore became much smaller.

To answer question 1, the student only provides a single general comment. 1 mark awarded. Two points with specific examples would improve the answer. For example: Germany lost land to France as a result of the Treaty of Versailles, including Alsace-Lorraine, which it had gained in 1871, and Eupen and Malmedy to Belgium. Land was also given to the League of Nations to administer, including Danzig and Germany's colonies.

Plan your answer

- This question is asking you to provide two features of German territorial losses as a result of the Treaty of Versailles.
- You must also give supporting examples for each point you make.
- Germany's territorial losses after the war were in Europe, such as East Prussia, which was given to the new state of Poland, and also further afield because it lost colonial territories, such as Togoland, as well.

Mark scheme

1 mark for each relevant point, plus an additional mark for supporting detail; maximum 2 marks per point.

2. "The 'Big Three' set out to cripple Germany at Versailles." How far do you agree with this statement? Explain your answer.   (10 marks)

On the one hand, this statement is correct. The French Prime Minister, Clemenceau, was intent on revenge on Germany for starting the war and inflicting terrible damage on France. He wanted to ensure that Germany was in no position to ever wage war and threaten France again. He wanted to cripple Germany militarily by permanently disbanding most of its armed forces and economically by imposing extremely high reparations, with the figure specified in the treaty so Germany could not negotiate a lower amount later. He also wanted Germany's industrial base either given to the League of Nations or placed under French control, to prevent Germany from ever developing into a military power in the future.

The British Prime Minister, Lloyd George, was very aware of the British public's demand to make Germany pay for the war and so he started the peace talks arguing for a high level of reparations that would cripple Germany and act as a deterrent for future aggressors. He also wanted to cripple Germany's navy, ensuring British naval supremacy, so took possession of most of Germany's military and merchant ships.

President Wilson did not intend to cripple Germany, and instead hoped to create a fair and lasting peace. He wanted to make his Fourteen Points the basis of the Versailles settlement. These were more concerned with removing the issues he believed had contributed to the start of the war, such as secret treaties and naval rivalry, and introducing a new international association, the League of Nations, through which countries could resolve differences.

On balance, although Wilson had different intentions, as Clemenceau and Lloyd George did set out to make Germany pay heavily at Versailles, it can be argued that most of the "Big Three" intended to cripple Germany.

This response stays focused on the question and provides a reasonably balanced argument with a clear judgement on how far the statement is correct. Relevant factual supporting detail is also provided. However, a further argument that the "Big Three" did not set out to cripple Germany is required. The student could perhaps point to Lloyd George's shift in position closer towards Wilson's viewpoint once the conference had started and the desire for a rebuilt Germany to act as a trading partner for Britain, and as a bulwark against Soviet communism. 9 marks awarded.

Plan your answer

- This question requires a balanced response, with clearly laid out arguments for each side, and using relevant supporting information for each argument.

- To get full marks, it is essential to provide a concluding judgement responding to the "how far" element of the question.

- For this particular question, you should analyse the motives of Clemenceau, Lloyd George, and Wilson, considering how far they wished to "cripple" Germany. While the positions of the French and American leaders were clear, you would be wise to identify those aspects of Lloyd George's position that support the "cripple Germany" argument and those that challenge it.

Mark scheme

Level 1:	general answer lacking specific contextual knowledge (1 mark)
Level 2:	identifies AND/OR describes reasons (2–3 marks)
Level 3:	gives a one-sided explanation (4–5 marks) or one explanation of both sides (4–6 marks)
Level 4:	explains both sides (7–9 marks)
Level 5:	explains with evaluation (10 marks)

3. Study source 7 on page 10. What is the message of the cartoonist? Explain your answer using details of the source and your own knowledge. (8 marks)

The message of this source is that the peacemakers at Versailles do not appear to be concerned that future generations will be upset by the decisions made at Versailles. The peacemakers clearly believe that they have come up with a good peace treaty and Clemenceau only thinks it curious that someone who may be a child in 1919 would be upset by the treatment of the defeated powers at Versailles.

This type of question requires students to identify and explain the attitude of the cartoonist, something which this response does not fully do. A more developed answer would explain that the cartoonist is critical of the peace settlement and fears that the peacemakers have constructed treaties that may lead to a further conflict, possibly in 1940, as referenced by the use of "cannon fodder" in the title of the cartoon and the "class of 1940" weeping. 5 marks awarded.

Plan your answer

- This question requires you to identify and explain the main message and sub-message of a cartoonist.

- In the answer you need to state what the cartoonist thinks about the likely impact of the Treaty of Versailles.

- The cartoonist manages to suggest that the peacemakers are oblivious to the effects their actions may have on future generations of Europeans, represented by the child behind the pillar.

Mark scheme

Level 1:	describes or misinterprets the cartoon (1 mark)
Level 2:	identifies AND/OR explains valid sub-messages in the cartoon (2–4 marks)
Level 3:	identifies AND/OR explains the big message, but does not include the cartoonist's view (5–6 marks)
Level 4:	identifies AND/OR explains the big message and the cartoonist's view (8 marks)

4. Study sources 3 and 5 on pages 8 and 9. How far do these two sources disagree? Explain your answer using details of the sources.

(7 marks)

Sources 3 and 5 fundamentally agree that the post-war peace treaties were deeply flawed and likely to create resentment among the defeated powers after the war. These sources agree that the treaties seek to punish the defeated powers. Source 3 includes handcuffs on the table for the German delegation; source 5 suggests that there was nothing designed to make the defeated powers willing to work with the other nations after the war.

However, the sources also disagree. Source 3 suggests that the victorious powers are united and working together as they are helping to "serve" the meal as a team. However, source 5 suggests that the peace treaties didn't promote unity among the victors or encourage cooperation to deal with economic problems faced by countries such as France and Italy.

This response focuses on the question and provides an assessment of how the two sources both agree and disagree, including reference to the details of each source and the main messages of both sources. 7 marks awarded.

Plan your answer

- This question requires you not only to understand the sources but also to compare the extent to which their main messages and sub-messages agree.

- Consider the views of the author and the cartoonist on the terms of the Treaty of Versailles: do they agree, and if so, why? (This is the big message of each source.)

- Think not only about the big message but also the sub-messages—which particular aspects of the treaty the author and the cartoonist believe are the most significant.

Mark scheme

Level 1:	writes about the sources but makes no valid comparison (1 mark)
Level 2:	identifies information that is in one source but not in the other OR states that the sources are about the same subject (2 marks)
Level 3:	agrees or disagrees with sub-messages or other details (3–4 marks)
Level 4:	agrees and disagrees with sub-messages or other details (5 marks)
Level 5:	compares what the sources suggest about the Treaty of Versailles (6–7 marks)

2

How far was the League of Nations a success in the 1920s and 1930s?

You need to know

- The structures of the League and how organisational issues caused weakness
- The impact of the World Depression on the League of Nations
- The failures of the League in the 1930s, including the Manchurian and Abyssinian crises

Background: The League of Nations' aims, organisation, and power

The aims of the League of Nations were set out in the Covenant. They were to:

- achieve international peace and security
- promote international cooperation, especially in business and trade
- encourage nations to disarm
- improve living and working conditions for the people of all nations
- uphold and enforce the Treaty of Versailles.

The League of Nations was created through the peace treaties at the end of the First World War. It was based in Geneva, Switzerland. It started work in 1920.

At the League's inception there were 42 members. The League was originally made weaker by the absence of the United States, Germany, and Soviet Russia and by the withdrawal of certain countries, including Germany, Japan, and Italy, in the 1930s. Britain and France were the only major countries to remain members throughout the time of the League's existence.

Collective security was the intended means to maintain peace. There were three stages to this—moral disapproval, economic sanctions, and military sanctions. The League did not have an army of its own.

The 1920s proved to be a relatively successful period for the League, although even during this period it adopted the role of passive bystander. However, the League used agencies and commissions to address issues of disease, poverty, and exploitation and achieved a lot in the 1920s.

The 1930s saw the work of the League made more difficult by the World Depression. This decade also saw the League fail in its peacekeeping role in Manchuria and Abyssinia.

The organisation and structure of the League

The Assembly

- The Assembly met annually at the League's headquarters.
- All members of the League were represented.
- The Assembly considered matters of general policy and recommended actions to the Council.
- The Assembly fixed the budget.
- Every member of the League had one vote.
- Decisions had to be unanimous.

The Council

- The Council met four times a year and for emergencies.
- There were both permanent and non-permanent members of the Council.
- In 1920 the permanent members were Britain, France, Italy, and Japan.
- The non-permanent members were elected by the Assembly for three-year periods.
- In 1926 Germany became a permanent member.
- The number of non-permanent members increased from four in 1920 to nine in 1926 and 11 in 1936.
- Each member country had one vote.
- Decisions had to be unanimous.

The Secretariat

- All the administrative and financial work of the League was performed by the Secretariat.
- This work included organising conferences and meetings, keeping records, and preparing reports.

Agencies, committees, and commissions

- The Mandates Commission ensured that Britain and France acted in the interests of the people of the former colonies of Germany and its allies.
- The Refugees Committee assisted in the return of refugees to their original homes following the end of war.
- The Slavery Commission worked to abolish slavery around the world.
- The Health Committee began to educate people about health and sanitation, and started to deal with dangerous diseases.

The powers of the League

The League could take action in three ways to try to solve a dispute.

- **Moral condemnation:** The League could put pressure on a country guilty of failing to cooperate with the League's aims by rallying world opinion against that country.
- **Economic and financial sanctions:** Members of the League could refuse to trade with an uncooperative country.
- **Military force:** Armed forces from member countries could be used against an aggressor.

How successful was the League in the 1920s?

Why was the League able to achieve some successes in the 1920s?

- **There was no appetite for conflict:** People and governments did not want a repeat of the First World War, so there was a high level of goodwill towards the League.
- **Disputes were often between smaller countries:** They were willing to give the League a chance and readily accepted the League's decisions, an example of this being the dispute over the Aaland Islands.
- **Countries were rebuilding after the First World War:** They were in no position, economically or militarily, to enter into further conflict.

> **Apply**
>
> Using the information on the Assembly, Council, and Secretariat, draw a diagram that shows how the League worked.

> **Recap**
>
> The power of the League lay in the idea it worked collectively—nations together applying pressure through economic, military, or moral methods.

- **The League of Nations was new and countries were willing to give it a chance to be successful:** It was led by the victors of the First World War (except the United States). This gave the League some credibility.

Success in settling political disputes

Issue	Solution reached by the League
Sweden and Finland fought over the Aaland Islands (1921).	Territory was given to Finland.
There was a dispute between Germany and Poland over Upper Silesia (1921).	A plebiscite was held and the area was divided between the two.
There was a dispute between Turkey and Iraq over the province of Mosul (1924).	Agreement was reached, meaning that Iraq kept the territory and Turkey received a 10 per cent royalty payment each year on oil deposits.
Greece and Bulgaria fought over their borders (1925).	Greece was ordered to withdraw and pay Bulgaria £45 000 compensation.

> **Recap**
>
> During the 1920s the League proved successful at settling disputes between smaller countries and finding peaceful solutions.

Success in dealing with humanitarian issues

- **Refugees:** After the war around 400 000 prisoners and refugees were successfully returned to their homelands from Russia and Greece.

- **Health organisation:** The League helped Soviet Russia to prevent a typhus epidemic in Siberia; worked hard to defeat leprosy; and started an international campaign to exterminate mosquitoes, reducing the spread of malaria and yellow fever.

- **Transport:** The League made recommendations for the marking of shipping lanes and produced an international highway code for road users.

- **Economic and financial:** To deal with Austria's economic problems, the League devised a plan that stabilised the currency; and devised similar plans for Hungary, Greece, and Bulgaria.

- **Social issues:** 200 000 slaves in British-owned Sierra Leone were freed and the League challenged the use of forced labour on the Tanganyika Railway in Africa, reducing the death rate from 50 per cent to 4 per cent. The League also blacklisted large international companies involved in illegal drug selling.

- **Working conditions:** The League banned poisonous white lead from paint and recommended a limit on working hours for young children.

> **Recap**
>
> The League carried out humanitarian work at an extremely important time. The end of the First World War had created huge issues with shifting borders, scarcity of medical resources, and also lack of working relationships between governments.

> **Worked Example**
>
> Describe how the League of Nations tried to improve living and working conditions around the world (4).
>
> The League of Nations attempted to address working hours. Although it couldn't pass laws, the League recommended a reduction of the hours of work for children, for example. The League also established a Health Committee that attempted to address major challenges faced by member states. It worked hard to defeat leprosy, including setting up leper colonies. The League also tried to eliminate malaria—its attempts failed but the League did reduce the number of cases.

> **Exam tip**
>
> With a question like this, the aim is to identify specific actions the League took and add supporting detail. Aim to present three significant points.

What were the League's failures in the 1920s?

Failure to deal with aggressors

- Poland and Lithuania fought over Vilna (1920). Poland was clearly the aggressor but did not withdraw. The French would not act against Poland as they saw the Polish as a possible future ally.
- Italy and Greece had a dispute over Corfu (1923). In this case Mussolini went behind the back of the League to the Conference of Ambassadors, persuading it to change the League's ruling.

Failure to implement disarmament

- All attempts at international disarmament failed, despite the efforts of the Disarmament Commission. The French regarded disarmament as a threat to their security. This encouraged the Germans to argue that they had a right to rearm to protect themselves.

Agreements made outside the League

- There was limited faith in the League's ability to deal with any major challenge in the 1920s as the resolution of disputes was in relation to minor countries.
- France was the country most concerned about its security, making mutual assistance pacts with other countries, including Poland and Czechoslovakia.
- The Locarno Treaties of 1925 provided guarantees for the frontiers of north-eastern Europe.
- The Kellogg-Briand Pact had 65 signatories of countries renouncing war by 1928.

Recap

Failures with disarmament and also in dealings with major European powers such as France and Italy weakened the League and undermined its power. They also provided a hint of the problems it would face in the 1930s.

Worked Example

Describe two successes of the League of Nations in the 1920s. (4)

In 1919, Poland and Czechoslovakia fought over Teschen, an area rich in coal. In 1920 the League arbitrated on the dispute, splitting the area between the two countries. Although neither country was happy about the decision, they accepted it and stopped the fighting.

The League was able to settle a dispute between Sweden and Finland. This also proved successful.

Exam tip

The answer starts well and gives a good explanation of one success in the 1920s. However, it needs to include more detail on the dispute between Sweden and Finland over the Aaland Islands and the investigation the League led, which resulted in the islands staying with Finland.

The weaknesses in the League's organisation and membership

Membership

Three of the most powerful countries in the world were not initially members of the League.

- The United States refused to join.
- Germany was only allowed to join the League in 1926 after it had demonstrated its peaceful intentions.
- The Soviet Union was not invited to join the League because it was communist.

This reduced the ability of the League to take action against aggressive countries either militarily or by considering economic and trade sanctions. Britain and France were the only major powers who were members of the League throughout its existence, but they were both greatly weakened by the First World War. Britain was trying to maintain its empire, while France was primarily concerned with increasing security against Germany.

Also, several countries left the League once it had begun.

- Japan left in 1933 following criticism for invading Manchuria.
- Italy left in 1937 following the imposition of sanctions over Abyssinia.

Collective security

The League did not have an army of its own and so relied heavily on collective security.

- If military sanctions were to be imposed, member countries would be asked to contribute towards a fighting force. This created uncertainty as an appropriate army would be difficult to assemble, since member states would be reluctant to send their army to participate in a dispute in which they were not directly involved.
- In theory, collective security appeared to be a good idea for the preservation of peace, but often nations looked to the League to take action when they were not willing to take action themselves.
- The absence of the United States reduced the League's effectiveness as it was deprived of a powerful army and strong financial backing in support of sanctions.
- The League's Covenant demanded unanimous decisions in both the Assembly and the Council. This made it difficult to take decisive action against any country acting in a war-like manner.

The impact of the World Depression on the League

Countries found themselves under pressure to find new markets and raw materials. Often this was through colonisation or annexation, for example, Japan in Manchuria.

Reluctant to impose economic sanctions, countries wanted to maintain existing trade contacts.

Extremists came to power who were often nationalist in nature. They did not believe in democracy and ignored the authority of the League.

How the World Depression affected the League of Nations

League members lacked the means to deal with aggressors as there was no money to spend on armaments.

People lost their jobs and turned to extreme parties like the Nazis who promised solutions to the economic crisis.

Extreme nationalism brought with it militarism. Parties built up their armed forces and used aggression to achieve their aims, for example, the Nazi Party in Germany.

Fig. 2.1 *The effects of the World Depression on the League of Nations' effectiveness*

How successful was the League in the 1930s?

Faced with an economic slump from a declining export market for its silk, in part due to the global depression that had occurred, Japan invaded Manchuria in an attempt to find an answer to a need for food and raw materials.

Recap

Unanimous decisions were in place to prevent the League from being dominated by stronger, more powerful countries. This gave all members an equal say in the running of the League.

Apply

Create a table with one column for the successes of the League in the 1920s and one for its failures. Can you argue that the League was functioning well up until 1929 or did it already seem flawed?

Recap

Collective security was the intended means by which the League aimed to maintain peace. However, it depended on the willingness of the members of the League to work together to deal with aggression.

Collective security represented an idealistic approach. It was unrealistic to expect a nation to obey the rules of the collective security system, while at the same time failing to give the system the power to enforce the nation's will.

Response of the League to Japan's invasion of Manchuria

Action

- The League instructed Japan to withdraw, but was ignored and the invasion continued.

- A commission of enquiry was set up, led by Lord Lytton. This concluded that the invasion was not justified. The commission did not present its report until 1932, a full year after the invasion. The findings were considered by the League in February 1933 and were accepted by a vote of 42 to one.

- Japan responded by terminating its membership of the League.

Failure to introduce sanctions

- No European country wanted to cut back its trade with the Far East, especially as the United States would have taken over.

- Imposing military sanctions was less appealing, as this would have involved the sending of a naval task force to the other side of the world with little chance of success.

- Britain and France feared attack on their Far East colonies if sanctions were imposed.

- The League was Eurocentric in nature and did not see Asia as vital for Europe.

Results

- Japan demonstrated blatant aggression as Hitler and Mussolini watched with interest.

- The League looked weak when faced with aggressive action taken by a strong country.

- To avoid taking action, the League regarded Manchuria as a Japanese sphere of interest.

- As these events took place in East Asia, the League was less damaged. Some League members believed that if the aggression had been in Europe the League would have taken appropriate action.

Source 1

"Manchuria showed that the League was toothless. The failure of the League to stop aggression in Manchuria had grave consequences in Europe too. The lesson was obvious; there was no power in the world to stop a determined aggressor."

Extract from Essential Modern World History *by Steven Waugh, published in 2001.*

Source 2

THE DOORMAT.

Fig. 2.2 *A cartoon published in Britain's* Evening Standard *newspaper, 19 January 1933*

> **Recap**
>
> Japan's behaviour showeda flaw in the workings of the League— once Japan withdrew from the organisation, the sanctions the League could apply were rendered useless.

Worked Example

Read source 1 and look at source 2. How far would the cartoonist have agreed with source 1? (7)

I think the cartoonist would have largely agreed with the views expressed in source 1. The cartoonist shows Japan having walked over the figure representing the League of Nations, implying that it was not powerful enough to stand in the way of Japan. In a similar way, this view is expressed by source 1, which states that "Manchuria showed the League was toothless" and that "there was no power in the world to stop a determined aggressor", supporting the view expressed by the cartoonist. Both of these sources are referencing the events surrounding the Manchuria crisis, where Japan's aggression could not be stopped by the attempted sanctions of the League once Japan withdrew. The only part of source 1 the cartoonist might have disagreed with would be that source 1 indicates this was catastrophic for the League. The cartoon does at least suggest that the League is attempting to save face and therefore implying the event may not be as serious.

Italy's invasion of Abyssinia

- In October 1935 Italy invaded Abyssinia.

- Mussolini was looking for ways to boost his popularity in Italy following a period of economic recession and unemployment.

- Abyssinia's defences were relatively undeveloped—they were no match for the modern Italian army and air force.

Action

The League immediately condemned the unprovoked aggression of Italy and imposed economic sanctions that banned arms sales to Italy (but not Abyssinia), monetary loans to Italy, imports from Italy, and exports to Italy of rubber, tin, and metals.

Failures of the League

- The League failed to ban oil and coal exports to Italy as it was thought that the United States would not support this and the economic interests of League members would be affected.

- The League did not close the Suez Canal to Mussolini's supply ships for fear of reprisals against the British colonial possessions of Gibraltar and Malta.

Results

- On 9 May 1936 Mussolini formally annexed the whole of Abyssinia. The League watched helplessly.

- Britain and France showed self-interest—for example, it was reported that if coal had been included in the sanctions 30 000 British coal miners would have lost their jobs.

- The incident showed the League was powerless when its most important members failed to take effective action. They feared that Mussolini would ally with Hitler and so did not respond to the invasion.

- In November 1936 Mussolini and Hitler signed the Rome–Berlin Axis, showing that attempts by Britain and France to keep Italy on their side had failed despite their lack of action.

Source 3

"Economic sanctions against Italy were serious, but not a great problem. Banning the sale of weapons and rubber simply made Italy look for suppliers who were not members of the League. The biggest worry was a ban on selling oil. If that happened in 1935 the invasion of Abyssinia would have halted in a week."

Extract from Mussolini *by Denis Mack Smith, published in 1983.*

Source 4

"Could the League survive the failure of sanctions to rescue Abyssinia? Could it ever impose sanctions again? Probably there had never been a clear-cut case for sanctions. If the League had failed in this case there could probably be no confidence that it could succeed again in the future."

Anthony Eden, British Foreign Minister, speaking to members of the government about the crisis in Abyssinia, May 1936.

Apply

Compare the Abyssinian and Manchuria Crises. Consider the following questions. What similarities were there in how the League reacted? Was one of these crises more important than the other in exposing the weaknesses of the League? For each question, write a bullet list of information to use in your answer.

Worked Example

Read sources 3 and 4. Having read source 4, are you surprised by source 3? (8)

In one way I'm surprised by source 3, as Eden in source 4 seems to suggest that sanctions wouldn't have worked and that the failure of them may be the end of the League, whereas source 3 suggests that Italy would have been forced to pull out of Abyssinia if sanctions had been used to full effect.

However, I'm not completely surprised having considered the provenance of the source. It is written by the British Foreign Secretary who may be seeking to downplay the potential effectiveness of sanctions in the context of the crisis. He is explaining to the government a situation where ultimately Britain chose not to support action against Italy, in part due to the fear of Italy's reaction, thus undermining the credibility of the League. In contrast, source 3 is written after the event by a historian who will have had a chance to write about the incident with hindsight.

Exam tip

To answer this question, it is important to explain whether or not you are surprised based on the content of the sources, but you also must consider their provenance. Think about: Who wrote each source? When was each source written? How does this impact on whether you are surprised?

Review

1. Describe the methods available to the League to uphold its aims. [4]

2. Describe how the League of Nations tried to prevent future wars between nations. [4]

3. In what ways did the League of Nations lose credibility? [6]

4. Why was it difficult for the League to achieve its aims? [6]

5. Why did the League fail in Corfu? [6]

6. "The League of Nations was doomed to failure from the start." How far do you agree with this statement? Explain your answer. [10]

7. "The League of Nations failed because of Britain and France." How far do you agree with this statement? Explain your answer. [10]

For further information, review this section in the Student Book.

Raise your grade ↑

1. What was collective security? (4 marks)

Collective security is the idea that everyone works together to act as a deterrent against aggression. Its basis is that if everyone promises to act as one, if someone else attacks, any form of conflict is less likely.

The answer is good in the way it attempts to explain two issues relating to collective security. First, it offers a brief explanation of what collective security is, then it attempts to put this into context with further detail.

The answer could be improved by attempting to focus more on the League itself and offering less of a generalised answer. It doesn't speak of countries or members, and doesn't explain how collective security is an effective deterrent by other countries working together. 2 marks awarded.

Plan your answer

- The answer needs to have a clear focus on collective security and what it means.
- Once collective security is defined, a point is needed outlining how it works.
- The key to any question about collective security is the idea that its strength lay in all the members working together as a show of force.
- To answer this question, keep the focus on the League of Nations itself, don't talk in general terms.
- The question is not asking for specifics of how the League did or didn't act, so there is no need to give examples.

Mark scheme

1 mark for each relevant point, 1 additional mark for supporting detail; maximum 2 marks per point made.

2. Why did the structure and membership weaken the League of Nations? (6 marks)

The membership of the League of Nations caused real problems for the organisation. After feeling drawn into the First World War, the United States opted out of joining the League and was never a member. Russia, which had become the world's first communist state, didn't join the League until 1934 and Germany wasn't allowed to join until 1926 due to its role in the First World War. Even though Germany did join, it left the League in 1933. Other countries also left, such as Japan in 1933, Italy in 1937, and Russia in 1939.

The answer gives a lot of relevant information about membership issues that the League faced and the details presented are correct. However, the student doesn't explain why these countries either joining late or leaving the League posed a problem—there needs to be more focus on what this actually meant and how it weakened the organisation.

There is also no attempt to address structural weaknesses the League faced. The student could have mentioned that the structure as set out by the Covenant meant that the power lay in who the members were, and so by not including some key countries, the League was unable to act. 3 marks awarded.

Plan your answer

- There are two parts to address with this question—structure and membership.
- For a 6-mark question you need to identify and explain two reasons that help answer the question—so for this question, one explanation is needed for structure and one for membership.
- In terms of membership, it is important to think of who didn't join the League initially (Germany and Russia) and also consider who never was a member (the United States). These countries were major powers in Europe and would probably be at the heart of any conflict. Without them the League was weakened.

- In terms of structure, the League also had problems. It often required a unanimous decision to be reached.

- The League only met once a year and this meant decisions could take a long time to be made and might come long after the event they were referring to. The League's decisions therefore lacked credibility.

Mark scheme

Level 1:	general answer lacking specific contextual knowledge (1 mark)
Level 2:	identifies AND/OR describes reasons (2–3 marks)
Level 3:	explains ONE reason (4–5 marks)
Level 4:	explains TWO reasons (6 marks)

3. How far was the League of Nations a success? (10 marks)

The League of Nations' main successes came not from fighting but from helping to resolve the problems caused by the violence of the First World War. After the First World War many people were left homeless and the League helped to solve the large refugee problem. In the Treaty of Versailles, German and Turkish colonies were put under temporary control of Britain and France, and the Mandates Commission kept a close eye on them until it was felt that these countries were able to govern themselves.

Another success of the League was the work done to improve conditions for ordinary people. Workers were represented by actions such as the banning of poisonous white lead from paint and the limitations placed on the working hours for young children. A health organisation was also set up to help combat the spread of epidemic diseases. The League was also able to resolve disputes at times. When Finland and Sweden clashed over the Aaland Islands the League ruled that the territory belonged to Finland, but no weapons were to be kept there. Both sides agreed to this.

However, once the World Depression occurred, the League was unable to have the same impact as countries turned away from cooperation. As high unemployment and depression hit, self-preservation in countries led to the pursuit of selfish aims. In the face of emerging dictators in Italy, Germany, and Russia, the League was powerless due to inherent weakness.

The student addresses the "success" part of the question well, and in the first paragraph identifies and explains several different reasons why the League was a positive organisation in the 1920s. This is a good example of how to make points and then explain them—it shows the impact and the importance of the statements made.

However, the counter argument with focus on the failures is minimal. The second paragraph offers an explanation of the reasons why the League failed, and is quite an evaluative comment, but there isn't the same level of detail focusing on the League's weaknesses. Much more is needed on the failures of the League to make this less of a one-sided answer. 6 marks awarded.

Plan your answer

- While the question implies it is a one-sided statement, by asking "how far" it requires an evaluation of the level of success achieved by the League. The answer therefore needs to consider successes and failures.

- Specific examples of successes and failures need to be included.

- For the successes of the League the answer could include, for example, dealing with issues from the First World War, making recommendations regarding working hours, and establishing a health organisation that addressed the spread of disease.

- The League also solved some disputes, such as over the Aaland Islands, as well as administering plebiscites in various territories to decide whether or not they wanted to stay in Germany.

- When it comes to the League's failures, it is the events of the 1930s that need attention. Failures with Abyssinia and Manchuria showed the League to be weak, as did the lack of agreement on disarmament.

- To gain maximum marks you need to evaluate the evidence presented—so it is worth considering the significance of the material you choose to include. For example, does the fact that the League dealt with the issues post-war in the early 1920s mean it deserves credit? Or did the failure to halt the aggressive actions in the 1930s encourage others, such as Hitler, to pursue their territorial aims?

Mark scheme

Level 1:	general answer lacking specific contextual knowledge (1 mark)
Level 2:	identifies AND/OR describes reasons (2–3 marks)
Level 3:	gives a one-sided explanation (4–5 marks) or one explanation of both sides (4–6 marks)
Level 4:	explains both sides (7–9 marks)
Level 5:	explains with evaluation (10 marks)

3

To what extent was aggressive German nationalism responsible for the breakdown in international order in the 1930s?

You need to know

- The long-term impact of the Treaty of Versailles
- The results of the failings of the League of Nations in the 1930s
- Hitler's foreign policy and whether it led to the outbreak of war in 1939
- Whether appeasement was a legitimate policy to follow
- What was the importance of the Nazi–Soviet Pact?

Background: International peace in the 1920s and 1930s

In the 1920s the existence of the League of Nations, as well as a series of international agreements such as Locarno, brought a period of relative calm and stability. Some people were even suggesting that it was an age of peace and tranquillity.

Despite this, few were surprised that war broke out again in 1939. The 1930s was an age of increasing tension and conflict in Europe, as the economic crisis that resulted from the **Wall Street Crash** brought a return to strong nationalism and aggression across Europe.

The long-term effects of the Treaty of Versailles

The signing of the Treaty of Versailles in 1919, which imposed harsh conditions on Germany, fuelled resentment and nationalist sentiments. It left many in Germany determined to reverse the terms. The harsh terms of the Treaty had made life for ordinary Germans tough and while the newly established democratic government achieved some successes, the Weimar Republic faced numerous challenges, including economic difficulties, political instability, and social unrest.

Some Germans, particularly those on the political right, blamed the politicians who signed the armistice and the Treaty of Versailles for what they perceived as a humiliating defeat and the subsequent economic hardships. These "**November Criminals**", those seen as responsible for signing the armistice in November 1918 which ended the First World War, were blamed by those on the right. The German people, encouraged by the "stab in the back" myth, turned to the Nazi Party.

> **Key term**
>
> **Wall Street Crash**—the collapse of the New York Stock Exchange on 29 October 1929. The crash started the Great Depression and stock prices did not return to a similar level until late 1954.

> **Key fact**
>
> The "stab in the back" myth—that Germany had been betrayed by a group of weak, unpatriotic politicians—developed after the First World War. The myth gained popularity, giving rise to the thinking that if the war had not really been lost then the peace settlement was unnecessary and should be overturned.

> **Key term**
>
> **November Criminals**—the term was often used to criticise and vilify the politicians involved in the armistice, accusing them of betraying the country. It became a catchphrase employed by nationalist and right-wing groups, contributing to the broader atmosphere of discontent and anger that eventually played a role in the rise of extremist movements, including the Nazi Party led by Adolf Hitler. The term was a propaganda tool, rather than an accurate historical characterisation. The politicians involved in the armistice negotiations and the establishment of the Weimar Republic were acting within the context of the challenges and pressures of the time. The label reflects the divisive and polarised political climate in post-First World War Germany, rather than an objective assessment of the actions of those individuals.

The Nazi Party led by Hitler followed a foreign policy designed to destroy the hated Treaty of Versailles. Additionally, Hitler made aggressive demands such as **Lebensraum** and the destruction of communism.

The Great Depression brought militarist extremists to power. In Germany many people turned to the Nazi Party as the Nazis promised work and food. It was clear by the summer of 1936 that the League had failed and with it the idea of collective security. An alternative had to be found to preserve world peace. Britain and France turned to appeasement, while at the same time rearming as a matter of urgency.

It was clear that appeasement had failed when Hitler occupied Czechoslovakia in March 1939. The next country to be invaded by Germany would be Poland. Britain and France promised assistance should Germany decide to attack. When Germany did, and refused to leave, Britain declared war on Germany.

> ### Key term
>
> **Lebensraum**—the territory which a group, state, or nation believes is needed for its natural development, particularly relating to the post-First World War German concept of settler colonialism into eastern Europe.

Recap

The Paris Peace Settlement left many nations dissatisfied and wanting revisions to the treaties. Japan had wanted increased trading rights, for example, and Italy had expected to receive a greater share of the redistributed territories. The most dissatisfied nation was Germany. Most Germans wanted to reject the Treaty of Versailles as they did not agree with the territorial provisions, disarmament, war guilt, and reparations. This dissatisfaction stemmed from the "stab in the back" myth.

Fig. 3.1 *The "stab in the back"*

Recap

Although the Treaty of Versailles was harsh on Germany, it failed to completely disable the country militarily and economically. This gave Germany the opportunity to rebuild when the time was right.

Hitler promised to destroy the treaty and this promise assisted his rise to power. To carry out this promise would require the rise of Germany as a strong military nation. This was forbidden by the treaty.

Recap

Britain and France disagreed about how to treat Germany. The British thought the Treaty of Versailles had been too harsh and were prepared to make concessions; the French were afraid of Germany becoming strong again.

The impact of the League's failures in the 1930s

Issue	Actions	Consequences
Japan	Japan invaded Manchuria in 1931. A Special Assembly of the League was held and 40 nations voted that Japan should withdraw. Instead of withdrawing from Manchuria, Japan withdrew from the League.	<ul><li>It showed that the League was weak in the face of aggression by a great power, encouraging further acts of aggression.</li><li>Having withdrawn from the League, Japan moved closer to Hitler and then to Mussolini through the Anti-Comintern Pact.</li><li>The invasion of Manchuria encouraged Italy and Germany to think that their territorial ambitions were achievable.</li><li>The League had no power to force countries to obey.</li></ul>
Italy	When Italy invaded Abyssinia in October 1935, Abyssinia appealed for help from the League. The League took action by imposing economic sanctions.	<ul><li>The sanctions imposed failed to include essential commodities such as oil and coal and so were not hard-hitting.</li><li>Britain and France refused to support the action. Both countries needed Mussolini's friendship as they saw him as an ally against Hitler.</li><li>This showed countries were incapable of putting internationalism before national interests.</li></ul>
Disarmament	The League of Nations tried to persuade countries to disarm. At the Disarmament Conference of 1932–33 the Germans stated they would disarm if every nation disarmed. The French would not accept this.	<ul><li>Hitler walked out of the conference and Germany left the League.</li><li>The failure of the League led to intensive rearmament programmes for Britain and France.</li></ul>

Germany had left the League of Nations, signed treaties with Italy, Poland, and Japan, and also supported Franco in the Spanish Civil War. Although European conflict didn't seem imminent, Hitler had taken steps to prepare for a future war.

Apply

Study the information in the table. Make a list of the impacts for European peace based on the events that occurred.

Worked Example

Why was the League of Nations seen as a failure by 1936? (6)

The League of Nations was intended to create stability and preserve peace in Europe. However, by 1935 the League seemed massively flawed due to a series of failures.

Through its failure to handle the Japanese invasion of Manchuria, the League appeared weak and lacking authority. Japan invaded Manchuria in 1931 and after an appeal to the League by Manchuria 40 nations voted that Japan should withdraw. Japan walked out of the League and the League was powerless to act, making it appear weak in the face of aggression by a great power.

In a similar vein, the League also failed to deal with the Abyssinian crisis of 1935. When Italy invaded Abyssinia in October 1935, Abyssinia appealed for help from the League. The League took action by imposing economic sanctions. The sanctions were ineffective though. Britain and France refused to support the action and the sanctions imposed failed to include essential commodities such as oil and coal so lacked real impact.

By failing to address either of these issues, the League of Nations appeared to be weak and lacking credibility with countries when faced with a crisis.

Exam tip

For a 6-mark question, this is an excellent answer to use as a model: choose two good examples of the failure of the League and explain them fully. Adding a short summative sentence at the end, although not compulsory, shows a good understanding.

To what extent was Hitler's foreign policy to blame for the outbreak of war in 1939?

Hitler's foreign policy aims

Hitler had very clear aims for his foreign policy. They were outlined in his book *Mein Kampf* and evolved as he came to power in Germany. They included:

A desire for *Lebensraum* (living space): Hitler's primary territorial goal was to acquire more living space for the German people, which he believed could be achieved by expanding eastward into eastern Europe. This expansion was intended to provide resources, including agricultural land, and to create a racially homogeneous German-dominated territory.

Reversal of the Treaty of Versailles: Hitler sought to overturn the restrictions imposed on Germany by the Treaty of Versailles, which had ended the First World War. This included rearmament, remilitarisation of the Rhineland, and the reunification of ethnic Germans in places like Austria and the Sudetenland.

Destruction of communism: Hitler was strongly opposed to communism and the Soviet Union. He saw the Bolshevik movement as a major threat and sought to eliminate what he perceived as the Jewish-Bolshevik conspiracy.

Expansion and dominance in Europe: Hitler aimed to establish German dominance in Europe and create a continental empire under German control. This involved the subjugation and domination of other nations, especially in eastern Europe, to serve the interests of the German "master race".

Racial ideology: Hitler's foreign policy was strongly influenced by his racist ideology. He believed in the superiority of the Aryan race and sought to establish a racially pure empire.

What foreign policy actions were taken by Hitler from 1933–36?

1933	• Germany refused to pay any more reparations.
	• Hitler walked out of the Disarmament Conference and withdrew Germany from the League of Nations.
	• The rearmament of Germany began in secret.
1934	• A non-aggression pact was agreed with Poland in January. This ensured that if Germany decided to attack Austria or Czechoslovakia, Poland would not intervene.
1935	• A massive rearmament rally was held in Germany. Britain and France believed that a strong Germany was a buffer against communism.
	• Germany signed a naval agreement with Britain allowing Germany to have a navy up to 35 per cent of the size of the British navy.
	• A plebiscite was held in the Saar in accordance with the terms of the Treaty of Versailles. Over 90 per cent were in favour of a return to Germany. Germany regained its first piece of lost territory by legal and peaceful means.
1936	• Germany remilitarised the Rhineland. Britain and France made no effort to stop this.
	• Hitler and Italy signed the Rome–Berlin Axis.
	• The Anti-Comintern Pact committed Germany and Japan to hostility towards Soviet Russia. Neither Germany nor Japan would assist Soviet Russia if it attacked either country.
	• After the outbreak of the Spanish Civil War, Italy and Germany supported Franco's nationalists in the war. Britain and France decided not to become involved. Soviet Russia supported the Republicans.

Rearmament and the Four Year Plan

Hitler took several steps to rearm Germany in violation of the Treaty of Versailles, which had imposed restrictions on the size and capabilities of the German military after the First World War.

- **Reintroduction of conscription (1935):** In March 1935, Hitler announced the reintroduction of conscription, increasing the size of the German military. This move directly violated the Treaty of Versailles, which had limited the size of the German army.

- **Creation of the Luftwaffe (1935):** In 1935, Hitler announced the existence of the Luftwaffe, the German air force. The establishment of a new air force was another violation of the treaty, which had prohibited Germany from having an air force.

- **Remilitarisation of the Rhineland (1936):** The reoccupation of the Rhineland was followed by the remilitarisation of the region. German forces moved in, establishing a military presence in the area that had been off-limits according to the Treaty of Versailles.

Adolf Hitler's Four Year Plan was a series of economic initiatives launched in Nazi Germany with the aim of achieving economic self-sufficiency and preparing the country for war. The plan was introduced in 1936 and spanned a four-year period, concluding in 1940. There were several key aims to the plan:

- **Autarky (economic self-sufficiency):** The primary goal of the Four Year Plan was to make Germany economically self-sufficient, reducing its dependence on imported resources. This was seen as a strategic move to ensure that Germany could sustain itself even if cut off from international trade during times of conflict.

- **Military preparedness:** The plan aimed at accelerating the rearmament of Germany and building up its military strength. This involved expanding the production of weapons, equipment, and supplies necessary for war. The emphasis was on creating a robust industrial base capable of supporting a large and modern military.

- **Expansion of key industries:** The Four Year Plan targeted specific industries deemed crucial for military and economic purposes. These included the production of synthetic materials, such as synthetic rubber and oil, as well as the expansion of the steel industry and other heavy industries.

- **Agricultural self-sufficiency:** In addition to industrial self-sufficiency, the plan aimed to make Germany agriculturally self-sufficient. The government encouraged farmers to increase production and implemented policies to ensure a stable and secure food supply for the population.

- **Creation of a war economy:** The Four Year Plan marked a shift toward a war economy. Resources were increasingly diverted towards military production, and civilian industries were directed to support the rearmament effort. The plan laid the groundwork for the comprehensive mobilisation of the German economy during the Second World War.

While the Four Year Plan made some progress in achieving economic self-sufficiency, it did not fully achieve its objectives before the outbreak of the Second World War in 1939. The war ultimately became the driving force behind the German economy's complete mobilisation and many of the economic policies established during the Four Year Plan were further intensified during the conflict.

The Spanish Civil War

- The Spanish Civil War gave Hitler an opportunity to test his new military equipment. His Luftwaffe was tested and committed a ruthless assault on Guernica.

- Hitler saw the Spanish Civil War as an opportunity to fight against communism.

- He succeeded in establishing Mussolini as an ally. They formed the Rome–Berlin Axis.

Fig. 3.2 *Guernica, northern Spain, after a bombing raid, May 1937*

Worked Example

Did Hitler's actions from 1933–36 reflect more an attempt to achieve equality with Britain and France than they were steps on the road to war? (10)

It can be argued that the actions taken by Hitler and Germany in the 1930s were an attempt to bring Germany more into line with Britain and France. This can be seen by the decisions in 1935 to introduce conscription and begin rearmament. It could be argued that Hitler was simply looking to restore Germany's status as a European power and exercise the same control over his country as other states.

However, the extent to which this is true can be questioned. In isolation these activities might be seen to be restoring Germany's power, but the other actions Hitler took in this period seemingly indicate he was preparing the country for an impending war. The support of Franco's nationalist forces in Spain shows Hitler wanted to test his newly formed air force's capacity in conflict. The treaties with Italy, Poland, and the Soviet Union were an attempt either to form alliances or agree non-aggression pacts with potential rivals, ensuring that if the opportunity arose any attempt at seizing territory would be straightforward.

Exam tip

This is a tricky question, demanding that you offer a consideration of both arguments in the statement. You need to find evidence of the view that Hitler was looking to achieve equality with Britain and France and evaluate this; and then consider the opposing view, which is that Hitler always had war in mind.

What this answer does well is to develop the two sides of the argument and give specific actions that indicate the view. There isn't a conclusion though, and there should be in an answer of this length.

What happened from 1936–39?

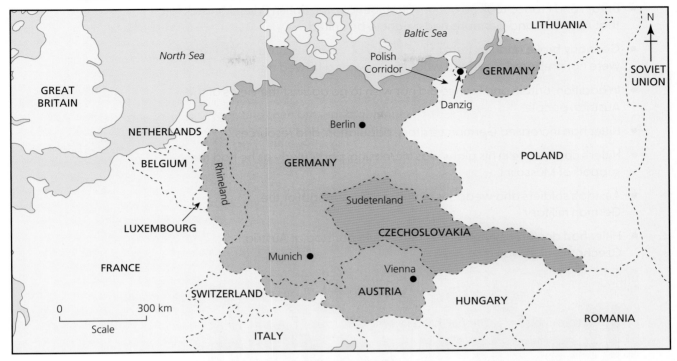

Fig. 3.3 *Map of central Europe after the Austrian Anschluss (1938)*

Anschluss with Austria, 1938

Reasons for union with Austria

- Hitler was born in Austria and he had stated in *Mein Kampf* that he felt the two countries belonged together as one German nation.

- One of Hitler's aims was to form a "Greater Germany" that would include all German-speaking peoples. Austria had the largest number of German speakers outside Germany.

- Many in Austria supported the idea of union as their country was economically weak after it had been reduced in size by the Treaty of St Germain.

- Union with Austria was an opportunity to break the Treaty of Versailles further, as it had forbidden Anschluss.

Events

- In early 1938 Hitler encouraged the strong Nazi Party in Austria to provoke unrest. The Nazis staged demonstrations and started riots encouraging union with Germany.

- Hitler forcefully told the Austrian Chancellor Schuschnigg that political union was the only way to sort out the problems. Hitler persuaded Schuschnigg to agree but then Schuschnigg changed his mind, ordering a plebiscite to be held among the Austrian people.

- Hitler was furious, ordering Schuschnigg to withdraw the plebiscite and resign. At the same time Hitler ordered invasion plans to be drawn up.

- The new Austrian leader, Seyss-Inquart, asked Germany to send troops into Austria to restore law and order. On 12 March 1938 German troops invaded and two days later Austria was made a province of Germany.

- On 10 April, under the watchful eye of the Nazis, 99 per cent of the Austrian people voted for Anschluss.

Results

- Britain and France took no action. Chamberlain, the British Prime Minister, felt that Austrians and Germans had a right to be united.

- Germany broke another term of the Treaty of Versailles. Britain and France were not prepared to defend what they saw as a flawed treaty.

- In addition, Britain and France did not wish to go against the views of the Austrian people.

- Hitler had increased German territory, population, and resources.

- Hitler's confidence in his plans was increasing, particularly as he had the support of Mussolini.

- Austria's soldiers and weapons increased the strength of the German military.

- Hitler had declared his intentions and would not stop at Austria. Czechoslovakia would be next.

Fig. 3.4 *Nazi poster for the Anschluss. The caption says: "The whole people say Yes!"*

Recap

Hitler had managed to break a key term of the Treaty of Versailles and increase the strength of Germany. It was the first step to creating a "Greater Germany" and, more significantly, showed that the Treaty of Versailles was dead.

Worked Example

What did Hitler achieve by the Anschluss? (4)

By joining together Germany and Austria in the Anschluss, Hitler had successfully broken the Treaty of Versailles and helped his development of a "Greater Germany". Through adding the country of his birth, not only had Hitler increased the size of Germany, he had also increased the strength of Germany through the wealth of its industry and also by adding Austria's soldiers and weapons to its own army. The Anschluss showed that the Allies were not willing to go to war over the Treaty of Versailles, which encouraged Hitler to break it further.

Exam tip

To answer the question, you need to demonstrate thorough knowledge of the Anschluss. This example answer would be improved by focusing more heavily on what Hitler achieved rather than adding narrative detail. In your answer, remember to use the key wording from the question—in this case, "achieve"—to show that you are focused on the question.

The Sudetenland, 1938

Reasons for the issue

- After the First World War, Czechoslovakia had been created by the Treaty of St Germain.

- The Sudetenland formed the border area between Germany and Czechoslovakia.

- There were 3.5 million Germans living in the Sudetenland area and many Sudeten Germans complained of discrimination by the Czech government.

- In 1938 Hitler demanded that Germany be given the Sudetenland. If this happened, Czechoslovakia would be defenceless against a German attack.

- The British Prime Minister, Chamberlain, wanted to find a peaceful solution to the problem rather than allowing Hitler to use force.

Events

Meetings took place between Hitler and Chamberlain in an attempt to resolve the situation. They resulted in the Munich Agreement.

Location and date	Matters discussed
Berchtesgaden, Bavaria, 15 September 1938	• It was agreed that areas of the Sudetenland where the majority of the population was German should be handed over to Germany. This was to be subject to the approval of the British, French, and Czech governments.
Bad Godesberg, Rhineland, 22 September 1938	• Hitler went back on the agreement and stated that unless the whole of the Sudetenland was given to Germany by 1 October 1938 there would be war. Chamberlain was appalled by Hitler's new demand. Europe was on the brink of war.
The Munich Conference, 29 September 1938	• This conference was attended by Chamberlain (Britain), Hitler (Germany), Mussolini (Italy), and Deladier (France). The Czechs and the Soviets were not invited. • Hitler gained what he had demanded at Bad Godesberg. The Czechs were forced to accept the agreement or face the full force of the German army on their own. • The following day, Chamberlain and Hitler signed a declaration promising that their countries would never go to war. Chamberlain returned to Britain saying, "I believe it is peace in our time." He received a hero's welcome.

Results

- Britain and France had abandoned Czechoslovakia. On 1 October 1938, German troops marched into the Sudetenland.

- In March 1939 Hitler took over the rest of Czechoslovakia. There was no resistance from the Czechs. Britain and France did not help.

- Poland would be Hitler's next target. Britain promised Poland it would guarantee Poland's independence.

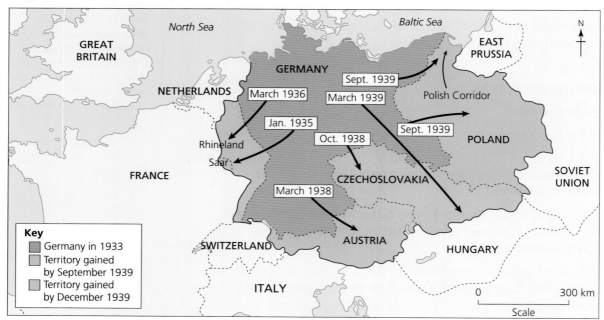

Fig. 3.5 *Map of Europe showing Hitler's territorial gains, 1935–39*

Source 1

"We have suffered a total and unmitigated defeat... You will find that in a period of time... Czechoslovakia will be engulfed in the Nazi regime... And do not suppose that this is the end. This is only the beginning of the reckoning."

From a speech made by Winston Churchill to the House of Commons in 1938. The speech was made soon after the Munich Agreement.

Source 2

"It was thanks to Mr Chamberlain's courage that a senseless war was avoided. As I wrote to him then: 'Millions of mothers will be blessing your name tonight for having saved their sons from the horrors of war.' I also wrote at the time: 'The day may come when we may be forced to fight Germany. If we have to do so, I trust that the cause may be one in which the honour and vital interests of Britain are clearly at stake.' This was not the case in September 1938."

From Sir Neville Henderson's account, published in 1940, of his time as British Ambassador to Germany from 1937 to 1939.

The Nazi–Soviet Pact

Reasons for the issue

- Ever since 1933, when Hitler came to power, Stalin had been concerned about the threat Germany posed. Hitler had openly stated his wish to crush communism and to gain land as *Lebensraum*.

- Stalin signed a treaty with France in 1935. The treaty stated that France would help the Soviet Union if Germany invaded the Soviet Union. However, Stalin was not sure whether France would come to his aid if needed.

- Stalin's concerns were increased by the Munich Agreement in 1938. He had not been invited to the conference nor had he been consulted. He concluded that Britain and France would allow Hitler to take land in the east.

- Discussion with Britain and France over the spring and summer of 1939 came to nothing.

Events

- On 23 August 1939 the foreign ministers from Germany and the Soviet Union signed a ten-year non-aggression pact.

- The clauses of the Nazi–Soviet Pact provided a written guarantee of non-aggression by each towards the other, and a declared commitment that neither government would ally itself to, or aid, an enemy of the other party.

- Secretly, Germany and the Soviets decided to split Poland between them. Stalin was interested in sections of eastern Poland and wanted the Baltic States that had once been part of Russia.

Results

- The two most ideologically opposed countries had signed a pact that made war seem inevitable.

- The pact gave Stalin time to build up his armed forces, which were weak following the Purges, as he realised that eventually Hitler would break his promise and attack the Soviet Union.

- The pact gave Hitler the confidence to invade Poland, knowing he would not have to fight a war on two fronts.

- Hitler did not believe Britain and France would go to war over Poland and he assumed that Anglo-French opposition would not be any more serious than it had been over Czechoslovakia.

The invasion of Poland

Fig. 3.6 *A cartoon satirising Germany's invasion of Poland*

Reasons

- Under the terms of the Treaty of Versailles, the "Polish Corridor" was given to Poland in order to provide an outlet to the sea and Danzig was put under the control of the League of Nations. Hitler wanted to reclaim this land.

- The demand to return Danzig to Germany was not unreasonable as its people were mainly German-speaking.

- The destruction of Poland was an essential preliminary to the invasion of the Soviet Union, the destruction of communism, and the acquisition of *Lebensraum*.

Events

- On 31 March 1939 a British–French guarantee was given, promising that Poland would receive support and assistance if attacked.

- On 1 September 1939 Germany invaded Poland.

- Britain and France issued an ultimatum to Germany for the army to be withdrawn from Poland.

- On 3 September 1939, as Germany had not responded to the ultimatum, Britain and France declared war on Germany.

Results

- It was clear that Germany was making a bid for European dominance and not just establishing the principle of self-determination for German-speaking peoples. Events in Czechoslovakia had shown Hitler's real aim of European dominance by force.

- Europe was at war.

Was the policy of appeasement justified?

Arguments for appeasement

- Many people agreed that the Treaty of Versailles was unfair and Hitler should be allowed to recover what was rightfully Germany's.

- The Soviet Union under Stalin was seen as a much greater threat than Germany. The British hoped that a strong Germany would stop the spread of communism.

- Britain and France were militarily weak and still coping with the Great Depression's impact. Appeasement would give time for rearmament.

- It was hardly surprising that Britain and France wanted to avoid war. Memories of the horror of the First World War were still vivid.

- There was concern that Commonwealth countries might not give support. Some thought that support would not come from the United States. Would Britain and France be able to survive?

Arguments against appeasement

- It was morally wrong. Other leaders had allowed Hitler to go unchallenged and abandoned Czechoslovakia to its fate. Appeasement was another word for cowardice.

- The British and French assumed Hitler was a rational politician and they could negotiate on equal terms. His ruthlessness was misjudged.

- Hitler took any concession as a sign of weakness and demanded more.

> **Apply**
>
> Create a timeline for 1933–39 of Hitler's actions in foreign policy. Mark on the line where you think France and Britain should have acted to stop Hitler. Would you have acted sooner than France and Britain did over Poland? Why?

- The opportunity to stop Hitler was missed. Had resistance been shown to Hitler in the Rhineland he may well have withdrawn. Although it gave Britain and France time to start rearmament, it also gave Germany the opportunity to grow more powerful.

- The policy alarmed the Soviet Union. Hitler made no secret of his wish to destroy communism and expand eastwards. Stalin was convinced that Britain and France would not stand in his way. As a result, the Nazi–Soviet Pact was signed.

Review

1. In what ways did Hitler build up his armed forces before 1936? [4]

2. What measures had Hitler taken by 1938 to prepare Germany for war? [4]

3. What was Anschluss? [4]

4. What was the Nazi–Soviet Pact? [4]

5. What happened in the Saar in 1935? [4]

6. What actions had Hitler taken by 1936 to prepare for war? [4]

7. Describe events in 1938 relating to Czechoslovakia. [4]

8. Why did Britain and France not want to go to war with Germany? [6]

9. Why did some people argue that appeasement was the wrong policy? [6]

10. Why did Stalin agree to the Nazi–Soviet Pact? [6]

11. Why did Hitler become involved in the Spanish Civil War? [6]

12. Why was the Munich Agreement (1938) important? [6]

13. Why did Hitler's demands over Czechoslovakia not lead to war in 1938? [6]

14. Why did Britain and France end their policy of appeasement? [6]

15. "Hitler achieved his foreign policy aims." How far do you agree with this statement? Explain your answer. [10]

16. "Hitler was an opportunist rather than a planner." How far do you agree with this statement? Explain your answer. [10]

For further information, review this section in the Student Book.

> **Apply**
>
> Looking at the arguments surrounding appeasement, which of them would have appealed to:
>
> - a senior member of the armed forces
> - a mother who had lost her son in the First World War?

Raise your grade ↑

1. What was the Munich Agreement? (4 marks)

The Munich Agreement was a settlement reached by Germany, Britain, France, and Italy that allowed Germany to annex the Sudetenland, an industry-rich area of Czechoslovakia. In line with Hitler's aims of uniting German speakers within a "Greater Germany", he had laid claim to the area as there were some 3 million native Germans living there. The agreement was drawn up to avoid war—Hitler had made it clear he was prepared to take the area by force and France and Britain, despite the fact that France had an alliance with Czechoslovakia, wanted to avoid war.

The student makes two well-developed points—first, defining what the agreement was; second, explaining why the agreement was needed. 4 marks awarded.

Plan your answer

- Answers to "What?" questions require two good points about the topic in the question, which are then explained.

- A question like this needs a focused answer. Don't be tempted to include extra information just because you know it.

- The Munich Agreement was signed in September 1938 and relates to the agreement reached with Germany by France and Great Britain over the future of Czechoslovakia.

- Hitler's claim was over the Sudetenland area of Czechoslovakia and the German speakers who lived there.

- The agreement was seen as preserving peace in Europe at the time, and was greeted with great celebration in France and Great Britain.

Mark scheme

1 mark for each relevant point, an additional mark for supporting detail; maximum 2 marks per point made.

2. Why did Britain and France allow Germany to remilitarise the Rhineland in 1936? (6 marks)

Britain and France allowed Germany to remilitarise the Rhineland as there was strong feeling that the Treaty of Versailles had been too harsh on Germany. There was a genuine feeling of empathy for Germany and so when it moved into the Rhineland, rather than a massive public outcry, significant portions of the public and government accepted this as a fair action. Anthony Eden, the British Foreign Secretary at the time, remarked that it was just "Gerry going into his own backyard".

In this answer the reasoning is good, and certainly the Treaty of Versailles is a key reason why Britain and France reacted as they did, but for a 6-mark answer there needs to be another reason identified and explained. The quote at the end is correct—although it was actually said to Eden and he reported it in Parliament—but an explanation of what it meant would improve the answer. 4 marks awarded.

Plan your answer

- The answer to this type of question needs to include two well-developed reasons for the event.

- There are various reasons why Germany had legitimate cause to remilitarise in 1936. These included the idea that the Treaty of Versailles was out of date and the fact that the Rhineland was part of Germany and so Germany should be allowed to do as it chose.

- The decision also formed a wider part of the policy of appeasement—Britain and France were looking to buy themselves time to rearm and at the same time avoid conflict.

- There is little doubt that the context is also important—in 1936 Hitler's demands didn't seem unreasonable, nor did any European country have an appetite for war so soon after the effects of the Great Depression.

Mark scheme

Level 1:	general answer lacking specific contextual knowledge (1 mark)
Level 2:	identifies AND/OR describes reasons (2–3 marks)
Level 3:	explains ONE reason (4–5 marks)
Level 4:	explains TWO reasons (6 marks)

3. "The Spanish Civil War was more important to Hitler than the remilitarisation of the Rhineland."
   How far do you agree with this statement? Explain your answer.   (10 marks)

The Spanish Civil War was certainly important to Hitler in the 1930s, as it allowed him the opportunity to test his new military equipment in a war zone for the first time. By offering support to Franco in his fight against his own people, Hitler was able to see how the newly developed Luftwaffe would fare in conflict, as well as sending heavily armoured divisions as support.

Involvement in the Spanish Civil War also gave Hitler a chance to fight communism and paint communists as a natural enemy. This was something that would help later when fighting the Soviet Union.

However, it can be argued that by remilitarising the Rhineland, Hitler also greatly benefited.

Not only did the action win the support of the generals within Germany, it was a clear contravention of the Treaty of Versailles. It did not draw a significant reaction from Britain, France, or the League of Nations.

It was also part of Hitler's wider plan to regain military strength and territory, and would therefore have aided his popularity in his own country.

The candidate has attempted to explain both sides of the argument and does offer a balanced view. There is good material included and some depth to knowledge. However, evaluation is lacking: the student identifies and explains issues, but there is no sense of how important these issues are. Their importance could have been covered after the point about the Treaty of Versailles, for example, explaining how this had an impact on the future. 7 marks awarded.

Plan your answer

- The question is asking for a judgement about the importance of the Spanish Civil War to Hitler in relation to his attempts to militarise Germany and prepare for a future war.

- The war was important as it allowed Germany to test elements of its military, such as the air force, in an actual war zone.

- The importance of this war though needs to be balanced against the importance for Hitler of the remilitarisation of the Rhineland. This was the first territorial break of the Treaty of Versailles by Hitler, and it showed for the first time his aggressive intentions.

- It was also the first chance for France and Britain to respond to Hitler's actions.

Mark scheme

Level 1:	general answer lacking specific contextual knowledge (1 mark)
Level 2:	identifies AND/OR describes reasons (2–3 marks)
Level 3:	gives a one-sided explanation (4–5 marks) or one explanation of both sides (4–6 marks)
Level 4:	explains both sides (7–9 marks)
Level 5:	explains with evaluation (10 marks)

4

Why did the wartime alliance collapse, 1945–49?

You need to know

- Why the United States–Soviet Union alliance began to break down in 1945
- How the Soviet Union gained influence in eastern Europe
- How the Soviet Union gained control of eastern Europe by 1948
- How the United States reacted to Soviet expansion
- What the Berlin Blockade was and what its consequences were
- Who was the most to blame for starting the Cold War: the United States or the Soviet Union

---

Background: Tensions between the Soviet Union and the United States in 1945

By the end of 1944 it was becoming obvious that Germany was going to lose the war and the Soviet Union was going to play a greater part in world affairs. By this time, ideological differences and tensions between the United States and the Soviet Union were re-emerging.

The United States, the Soviet Union, and Britain set up two conferences in 1945 at Yalta and Potsdam. At the conferences it was evident that there were major differences over the future of eastern Europe. The Soviet Union believed that the west wanted the recovery of Germany, which would make it a threat in the future, while the United States suspected the Soviet Union of trying to spread communism to as many countries as possible. The Soviet Union was now regarded by the west as the main threat to peace. The United States followed a policy of **containment**, introducing the Truman Doctrine and Marshall Plan in an attempt to prevent the expansion of the Iron Curtain.

> ### Key term
>
> **Containment**—the United States' government policy under Truman, based on the principle that communist governments would eventually collapse provided they were prevented from expanding their influence.

What were the reasons for a decline in US–Soviet relations?

- **Removal of the common enemy:** The threat from Germany was gone and therefore there was no need for the Allied cooperation that had been extensive during the war.

- **Ideological differences:** The United States followed a democratic, capitalist approach opposed to the communist ideology of the Soviet Union. This made it more difficult to build up trust between the two nations.

- **History of distrust:** Going back to 1918 and the intervention of the west in the Russian Civil War against the Bolsheviks, Stalin saw that it frequently tried to limit Soviet interests. He believed that the west had seen Hitler and the Nazis as the buffer against the spread of communism in the 1930s. In addition, Stalin was not invited to the Munich Conference.

- **The Soviet Union in world affairs:** By early 1945 it was obvious that the Soviet Union's sphere of influence was growing. Stalin was included with other European leaders in important conferences at Yalta (February 1945) and Potsdam (July 1945). Stalin made no secret of his desire to see communism spread to other countries, which worried the United States.

Fig. 4.1 *A cartoon showing Truman, Stalin, and Churchill discussing Europe*

Issues to be addressed at the Yalta and Potsdam conferences

What the challenges were	What was decided at the Yalta Conference, February 1945	What was decided at the Potsdam Conference, July–August 1945
What to do with a defeated Germany	• Surrender was to be unconditional. • Germany and its capital Berlin were to be temporarily divided into four zones. • Germany's eastern border was to be moved westwards. • War criminals were to be punished. • Germany had to pay reparations.	• The Nazi Party was to be banned. • Germany was to be denazified and war crime trials held. • The decision to split Germany and Berlin into four zones was confirmed. • Each country was to take reparations from its own zone.
What to do with countries formerly occupied by Germany	• Following liberation, these countries were to be allowed to hold free elections for people to decide how they were to be governed.	
The future of Poland	• A provisional government would form, comprising pro-Soviet Lublin Poles and exiled London Poles who had fled in 1939. • Poland's border was to be moved westwards into German territory. • Free elections were to be held.	• The Polish–German border was to be the Oder–Neisse Line formed by two rivers. • No agreement was reached over the future government of Poland.
How war against Japan could be ended	• Stalin agreed to intervene in the war against Japan after Germany was defeated. • In return, Russia was to receive land in Manchuria and territory that had been lost to Japan during the 1904–05 Russo–Japanese War.	• The Soviet Union wished to intervene in the war against Japan but this was refused by Truman.
How a lasting peace was to be maintained	• An organisation to be known as the United Nations was to be set up.	

Recap

The Yalta Conference put in place what would happen after the war. One key decision was to divide Germany into four zones.

The Potsdam Conference was the start of Cold War tensions and hostility. Little was agreed except to enlarge Poland and divide Berlin.

Apply

Consider the issues discussed at the Yalta and Potsdam conferences. Draw a mind map of the issues you think would be the most likely to cause tensions between the Soviet Union and the United States in the future.

Relations at the Yalta Conference had seemed good, and there had been plenty of agreement over the action needed, but the Potsdam Conference saw real tension and disagreement. What had changed?

In the United States: President Roosevelt died in April and was replaced by Harry S Truman. Truman was strongly anti-communist but inexperienced in international affairs. On the eve of the Potsdam Conference, Truman informed Stalin that the United States had successfully tested an atomic weapon.

In Britain: Churchill's Conservative Party was defeated in a general election. Churchill was replaced by Labour Party leader Clement Attlee.

In the Soviet Union: The Soviets had liberated eastern Europe and were installing sympathetic governments. They failed to hold "free" elections.

The results of the Potsdam Conference—from wartime alliance to the Cold War

The United States and the Soviet Union emerged from the Second World War as superpowers and were prepared to face each other head on.

Former British Prime Minister, Churchill, referred to an "iron curtain" dividing eastern Europe from western Europe, democracy from communism.

Stalin accused Churchill of trying to provoke war against the Soviet Union. The Soviet Union had been invaded from the west twice in 30 years. Stalin was determined to set up a "buffer zone" of protective states to ensure that invasion never happened again. His reply to Churchill's speech was robust.

Worked Example

What was agreed at the Potsdam Conference? (4)

There were several key agreements reached at the Potsdam Conference. The border between Poland and Germany was settled, as was the idea that Germany would be divided into four zones and each of these would be ruled according to the "4Ds"—denazification, demilitarisation, disarmament, and democratisation. It was also agreed that the Soviet Union would join the war against Japan, although due to the use of the atomic bomb by the United States, this was never needed as the war ended shortly after.

Source 1

"A shadow has fallen upon the scenes so lately lighted by the Allied victory. From Stettin on the Baltic to Trieste on the Adriatic, an iron curtain has descended. Behind that line lie all the states of central and eastern Europe. The Communist parties have been raised to power far beyond their numbers and are seeking everywhere to obtain totalitarian control. This is certainly not the liberated Europe we fought to build. Nor is it one which allows permanent peace."

Adapted from a speech by Winston Churchill, March 1946.

Source 2

"Mr Churchill now takes the stance of warmonger. The following circumstances should not be forgotten. The Germans made their invasion of the USSR through Finland, Poland, and Romania. They were able to make their invasion through these countries because, at the time, governments hostile to the Soviet Union existed in these countries. What can there be surprising about the fact that the Soviet Union, anxious for its future safety, is trying to see that governments loyal in their attitude to the Soviet Union should exist in these countries?"

Stalin replying to Churchill's speech, 1946.

What was the reaction of the United States to Soviet expansion?

The United States became committed to a policy of stopping the spread of communism. This was the policy of "containment". This was in response to the Soviet Union's actions in eastern Europe.

How was the Soviet Union able to gain so much power in eastern Europe by 1948?

- At the end of the war the Soviet Red Army remained in much of eastern Europe.

Recap

The change between the Yalta and Potsdam conferences was down to several factors—but all regarding trust issues between the United States and the Soviet Union. There was a new US President in Harry Truman, who was fiercely anti-communist; the emergence of the United States as a nuclear state; and also the Soviet Union's ambition in eastern Europe meant that the Cold War was about to begin.

Exam tip

To answer a question like this, focus on specifics. Address the question in the first few words—showing an understanding of what's being asked—then follow up with specific knowledge.

Apply

Read sources 1 and 2 (extracts from speeches by Churchill and Stalin). List the reasons why the two leaders' views differ so much.

Apply

Prepare a table showing what benefits the United States and the Soviet Union gained from the Yalta and Potsdam conferences.

- As agreed at the Yalta Conference, elections were held in eastern European countries. By 1948 all these countries had communist governments, achieved through rigged elections and intimidation.

- The countries now under Soviet control became "satellite" states. COMINFORM, an alliance of communist countries, formed in 1947.

- Only one eastern bloc country, Yugoslavia, rejected Stalin's leadership, although it remained communist.

Soviet troops remained after liberation.
New government formed in June 1945 dominated by "Lublin" Poles.
Opposition leaders arrested and murdered.
Rigged elections in 1947 gave communists 80 per cent of the vote.

Soviet troops remained after liberation.
Communists won 17 per cent of the vote in November 1945 elections.
Used secret police to discredit and persecute rival politicians and parties.
Rigged elections in 1947 gave communists control of a **coalition government.**
Social Democratic Party and Communist Party merged in 1948.

Soviet troops remained after liberation.
Soviets accepted a coalition government in 1945, accepting key positions for communists.
Rigged elections in 1946 gave the communists and their allies 90 per cent of the vote.

Soviet troops left after the war.
Post-war elections gave communists leadership of a balanced, coalition government.
Foreign Minister Jans Masaryk, a popular and non-communist politician, murdered in May 1947.
All non-communist members of the government resigned in February 1948, with communists filling vacant positions.

Soviet troops remained after liberation.
Initially joined a coalition with other parties.
Monarchy abolished in 1946.
New constitution in 1947 effectively destroyed parliamentary democracy.

Not liberated by Red Army.
Marshal Tito elected President in 1945.
Not prepared to take orders from Stalin.
Expelled from COMINFORM in 1948.
Accepted aid from the west.

Fig. 4.2 *Map of Soviet expansion 1945–48*

Map labels: N, ESTONIA, SWEDEN, LATVIA, DENMARK, LITHUANIA, SOVIET UNION, Berlin, EAST GERMANY, POLAND, WEST GERMANY, CZECHOSLOVAKIA, AUSTRIA, HUNGARY, ITALY, ROMANIA, YUGOSLAVIA, BULGARIA, Black Sea, ALBANIA, GREECE, TURKEY

Legend:
☐ Land taken by Soviet Union at the end of the Second World War
■ Soviet-controlled communist countries
☐ Non-Soviet-controlled communist country

0 ——— 400 km

The Truman Doctrine

Source 3

"I believe that it must be the policy of the United States to support all free people who are resisting attempted subjugation by armed minorities or by outside pressures. I believe that we must help free peoples to work out their own destiny in their own way."

President Harry Truman, March 1947.

The United States feared that the Soviet Union was attempting to spread communism around the world. If they did nothing, Greece and Turkey might be the next countries to fall to Stalin.

Key term

Coalition government—a government formed by multiple political parties promising to cooperate for the common good, reducing the dominance of an absolute party within that coalition. The usual reason for this arrangement is that no single party can achieve a majority in the parliament.

Truman persuaded the US Congress to provide aid in the form of arms and money for Greece and Turkey. In Greece, the communists were eventually defeated in 1949, following a civil war.

Marshall Aid

In June 1947, following a visit to Europe, the US Secretary of State George Marshall announced an economic recovery plan that provided aid to build up Europe's economy. This became known as the Marshall Plan.

Source 4

"The United States should do whatever it is able to do to assist in the return of normal economic health to the world. Without this there can be no political stability and peace. Our policy is directed not against any country or idea but against poverty, hunger, desperation, and chaos. Its purpose should be the rival of a working economy to permit the emergence of conditions in which free institutions can exist."

George Marshall, June 1947.

Source 5

Fig. 4.3 *A cartoon criticising the Marshall Plan*

To help war-torn Europe recover, the United States offered money, machinery, food, and technological equipment. In return, European countries would buy American goods and allow American investment in their industries. The offer was accepted by 16 western European states. Between 1948 and 1952 the United States gave $13 billion of aid.

Why take this action?

- Truman believed that countries suffering from poverty were vulnerable to the spread of communism. Many countries in Europe were struggling to cope with the after-effects of the Second World War and were facing economic collapse.

- In addition, if Europe became prosperous again it could become a trading partner for the United States.

How did Stalin react?

Stalin refused Marshall Aid for the Soviet Union and banned eastern European countries from receiving it. To counter the effects of the Marshall Plan, Stalin set up COMINFORM in 1947. This aimed to develop economic cooperation between communist countries.

What was the Berlin Blockade?

Fig. 4.4 *Germany in 1948*

Tensions over Germany

- Following the conferences at Yalta and Potsdam in 1945, the Allies had agreed to divide Berlin into four zones of occupation.

- Berlin, which was deep inside the Soviet zone, was also divided into four zones.

- The war had left Germany devastated and the Allies had different ideas about how to rebuild Germany.

- The United States and Britain wanted to help Germany recover quickly. The Soviet Union, however, wanted a weak Germany.

- Stalin was using German resources to rebuild the Soviet Union.

> **Recap**
>
> Stalin saw the United States' actions as an attempt to exert authority over Europe and he set up COMINFORM in return.

> **Recap**
>
> The United States offered financial aid to European countries. As well as supporting their recovery after the Second World War, the United States was aware that this money would tie the countries most at risk of falling to communism more closely to the United States, rather than establishing ties with Russia.

Causes of the blockade

Long-term causes of the blockade	Short-term causes of the blockade
• Within the Soviet zone, Soviet troops were able to control all access.	• In January 1947 Britain and the United States combined their zones to form "Bizonia".
• The Soviet Union believed the western allies had no right to be in Berlin. The western allies were seen as a threat as they had a base inside the Soviet zone.	• France joined a year later. Stalin felt threatened by this, fearing he was being forced out.
• The western allies needed to be there to prevent the Soviet Union fully controlling Berlin.	• West Germany began to recover with the help of Marshall Aid. In East Germany there was poverty and hunger.
• The west could spy on Soviet activity behind the Iron Curtain.	• In 1948 the western allies introduced a new currency into West Germany. Stalin refused to introduce it in the Soviet zone.

Stalin's motive

In June 1948 Stalin retaliated by blocking all road and rail links into West Berlin. Berlin was cut off from all supplies. Stalin increased the pressure by turning off all gas and electricity supplies. His aim was to force the other three powers to pull out of Berlin, making Berlin fully dependent on the Soviet Union.

The Berlin Airlift

- The airlift lasted for 11 months and involved nearly 300 000 flights.
- Cargo carried included coal, food, medicines, and petrol.
- Planes were landing in West Berlin at the rate of one every two minutes.
- Although they did not fire on incoming aircraft, the Soviet Union used obstruction tactics, including jamming radios and shining searchlights to temporarily blind pilots.

The Berlin Airlift was really the only solution available to the Allies. Other options, such as driving armed convoys through the blockade, would be highly provocative with a risk of war. However, pulling totally out of Berlin would render the Truman Doctrine an empty threat and mean countries would not trust the United States to stand up to communism in the future.

Stalin lifted the blockade on Berlin in May 1949 having failed to achieve his goal.

Worked Example

Explain why the Soviet Union blockaded Berlin in 1948. (6)

There were several reasons why the Soviet Union decided to blockade Berlin in 1948. Stalin became increasingly concerned that France, Britain, and the United States were planning to unify their three zones into a new West Berlin which would be in direct opposition to the Soviet Union's zone of influence. Blockading Berlin would be a way of forcing the west to reconsider these issues.

Secondly, Stalin was concerned by Marshall Aid and how western influence was spreading into the Russian-controlled sector of Berlin. Berlin was deep within the communist zone of Germany and by blockading the city he was able to restrict travel to the western zones and therefore limit influence. Marshall Aid also clashed with his idea for Germany. While the Allies wanted to rebuild the country in order to trade with it in the future, Stalin saw Germany as a source of raw materials to help rebuild his heavily damaged country.

Exam tip

For a 6-mark question you need to ensure that you not only give reasons why something happened, but also fully explain them. You gain 1 mark for each point you correctly make, but full explanation of that point scores more highly. The example given is a good answer as it develops two points in relation to the question.

The consequences of the blockade

October 1949
Stalin retaliated by turning the Soviet zone into the **German Democratic Republic**. This meant Germany was divided, with hostility between the two parts. East Berlin was part of East Germany. The division would last for 40 years.

May 1955
The **Warsaw Pact** was formed with eight communist countries unifying their armed forces under a central command. This was a direct response to the rearmament of West Germany and its incorporation into NATO.

May 1949
It was announced that the **Federal German Republic**, West Germany, had been formed by the merging of the zones of the western allies.

April 1949
The **North Atlantic Treaty Organization (NATO)** was set up. Membership included the United States.

January 1949
COMECON was set up with the intention of establishing stronger links for Soviet bloc countries over economic issues

Fig. 4.5 *A timeline of the consequences of the Berlin Blockade*

Who should be held responsible for the start of the Cold War—the United States or the Soviet Union?

In what ways was the United States to blame?

Beliefs

The United States saw the threat of communism as a direct challenge to its own interests abroad. Therefore, the actions taken by Truman looked to preserve American interests as well as protect the rights of citizens of other countries to access democracy. Its actions can be seen to reflect this—it can be argued that the true purpose of Marshall Aid was to provide a market for American goods and to ensure the preservation of a capitalist, free market system.

Actions

- The Marshall Plan promised aid to countries willing to stand up to the communist threat and therefore increased anti-communist sentiment.

- The creation of Bizonia and the introduction of a new currency into the western zones of Germany was a clear breach of the Potsdam Conference agreement and an attempt to impose a capitalist system.

- Truman was very aggressive in his dealings with officials from the Soviet Union and felt that as a powerful, atomic power the United States should be allowed to dictate terms at the Potsdam Conference.

- NATO was set up as a military alliance to defend its members against possible communist attack.

In what ways was the Soviet Union to blame?

Beliefs

The idea of communism was that it should be spread. It intended to impose its own system of government throughout the world. Stalin had a mistrust of the west. This led to concerns for Soviet security at the end of the war, which stemmed from historical fears about invasion from the west. These fears were caused by:

- the events of the Russian Civil War

- the belief that Britain and France encouraged Nazi Germany to expand eastwards during the late 1930s

Key term

The Warsaw Pact—a collective defence treaty signed between the Soviet Union and seven Soviet satellite states of central and eastern Europe in Warsaw, Poland, in May 1955, during the Cold War. Its members were the Soviet Union, Albania, Poland, Romania, Hungary, East Germany, Czechoslovakia, and Bulgaria.

Key term

NATO—the North Atlantic Treaty Organization—a military alliance of countries founded on 4 April 1949 to strengthen international ties between member states, especially the United States and Europe, and to serve as a collective defence against an external attack. It remains in existence today.

Key term

COMECON—the Council for Mutual Economic Assistance—an economic organisation that comprised of the countries of the eastern bloc under the leadership of the Soviet Union between 1949–91, along with a number of communist states elsewhere in the world.

Apply

Write short fact files about:

- the Potsdam Conference

- the Truman Doctrine

- the Berlin Blockade.

- the belief that the western allies deliberately delayed opening a second front in order to weaken the Soviet Union
- Britain refusing to share the German secret Enigma codes
- the secret development and testing by the United States of an atomic bomb.

Actions

- The creation of COMECON ensured that each eastern European country followed the Soviet model of economic policy.
- The establishment of COMINFORM was a clear sign that Stalin intended to undermine capitalist society.

For each event, how can it be argued that this was the start of the Cold War?

- Stalin did not abide by the agreements made at the Yalta Conference. He installed a communist government in Poland and went on to impose Soviet systems throughout eastern Europe.
- Stalin's actions over Berlin in 1948 were drastic and destroyed any remaining trust between the two sides.

Review

1. What decisions, in relation to Germany, were agreed at Yalta and Potsdam? [4]

2. What was the Berlin Airlift? [4]

3. Explain the importance of NATO. [4]

4. Why was the Truman Doctrine significant? [6]

5. Why was the Potsdam Conference significant? [6]

6. "It was the Soviet expansion in eastern Europe that caused the Cold War." How far do you agree with this statement? Explain your answer. [10]

7. To what extent was the failure of the Potsdam Conference the start of the Cold War? [10]

For further information, review this section in the Student Book.

Raise your grade ↑

1. What was the Iron Curtain? (4 marks)

The "Iron Curtain" was the name for the division of Europe into two separate areas from the end of the Second World War. The name was used by Winston Churchill and made sense as a term because not only was there division between east and west and so a "curtain", it was also "iron", as Stalin and the Soviet Union restricted access to the west and attempted to control the actions of those countries through the Warsaw Pact.

The answer does well to identify that it was Churchill who established the term and also offers a brief explanation of what the division did. The answer gives some explanation of why it is an effective term, picking apart the meaning and placing it in context with the Warsaw Pact. 4 marks awarded.

Plan your answer

- The question is asking for two points focused on a key term relating to the Cold War.
- In addition to stating two points, the answer needs to explain in detail what they mean.

- The term was first used by Winston Churchill to describe the boundary that developed between the east and west.
- Churchill was referencing the division between east and west Europe that emerged as the Cold War developed.
- The term also symbolised the way in which the Soviet Union blocked its territories from open contact with the west.

Mark scheme

There is 1 mark for each relevant point, an additional mark for supporting detail; maximum 2 marks per point made.

2. Why was the Truman Doctrine introduced? (6 marks)

President Truman was a fierce anti-communist who stated to Congress in March 1947 that he would try to counter the Soviet threat. Truman promised to send aid to Turkey and Greece because it was felt that without aid, both would inevitably fall to communism, with grave consequences throughout the region.

However, the Truman Doctrine was wider ranging than just aiming at these two countries and implied American support for other nations allegedly threatened by Soviet communism. The Truman Doctrine became the foundation of American foreign policy, and led, in 1949, to the formation of NATO.

This is a good example of an answer from a student who clearly knows a lot about the Truman Doctrine, but hasn't answered the question. Although a lot of information about the Truman Doctrine is presented, the student doesn't tell us why this policy was introduced. The answer needs to be focused on the reasons the United States felt the need to react in this way. 2 marks awarded.

Plan your answer

- As this is a "Why?" question, the answer needs to explain reasons why the United States introduced the Truman Doctrine.
- The answer shouldn't just list reasons why the United States acted, it needs to include two well-explained reasons in order to obtain a good mark.
- Truman wanted to support countries in eastern Europe who were at risk of falling to communism in the uncertain and challenging post-war period.
- As well as political motives, there were also economic benefits for the United States—the Truman Doctrine led to the Marshall Plan, which brought enhanced European trade for the United States.
- In the short term, the Truman Doctrine was introduced due to the fear of Greece falling to communism, as other eastern European countries had.

Mark scheme

Level 1:	general answer lacking specific contextual knowledge (1 mark)
Level 2:	identifies AND/OR describes reasons (2–3 marks)
Level 3:	explains ONE reason (4–5 marks)
Level 4:	explains TWO reasons (6 marks)

3. To what extent should the Soviet Union be blamed for the Cold War? (10 marks)

It can be argued that the Soviet Union was to blame for the Cold War because of the beliefs and actions of Stalin in the period following the Second World War. The Soviet Union was a one-party communist state.

After the effects of the war, the Soviets wanted to spread their control over eastern Europe. They did this by making other countries communist, suppressing free speech, and establishing control through the creation of the COMINFORM.

Stalin broke with what was agreed at Yalta and ignored the idea of free elections in eastern Europe.

Stalin also increased tension in Europe through his behaviour in Germany. By blockading Berlin from the west, he forced the drastic action of the Berlin Airlift and this made tensions worse.

The student has presented a lot of information that is relevant to the question, but the mark scheme shows that the answer needs to be wider ranging rather than just focusing on the Soviet Union.

There is no doubt that the actions of Stalin did lead to tensions between east and west, but this argument needs to be evaluated against the idea it was also the United States' fault that the Cold War broke out. The Truman Doctrine, the Marshall Plan, and the anti-communist stance of the United States meant that the Americans could also be seen being as responsible for this war. 5 marks awarded.

Plan your answer

- For the higher-mark questions, remember that first you need to evaluate the factor specified in the question and then evaluate another side to the argument.

- The answer to this question should not be a simple list of reasons why the Soviet Union was to blame for the Cold War, with some detail added. Instead, try to give a full explanation of how the actions of the Soviets can be seen as a contributing factor to the cause of the war.

- The Soviet Union's attitude to Germany post-war undoubtedly led to tensions—their aim of using German resources to rebuild their country was certainly very different from that of the western allies.

- As a communist state, the Soviet Union wanted to spread Soviet beliefs and ideology across Europe. This caused concern among the western allies, who feared their own interests would be compromised.

- To answer this question fully, you also need to consider issues other than the actions of the Soviet Union. For example, Winston Churchill's "Iron Curtain" speech was seen as very provocative, and it can be argued that the United States' use of aid through the Truman Doctrine also raised tensions.

Mark scheme

Level 1:	general answer lacking specific contextual knowledge (1 mark)
Level 2:	identifies AND/OR describes reasons (2–3 marks)
Level 3:	gives a one-sided explanation (4–5 marks) or one explanation of both sides (4–6 marks)
Level 4:	explains both sides (7–9 marks)
Level 5:	explains with evaluation (10 marks)

5

How far was the United States able to limit communist expansion?

You need to know

- The role of the United States and events in Korea, 1950–53
- The role of the United States and events in Cuba, 1959–62
- How the United States was involved in Vietnam, examined using:
  - the events of the Cold War
  - a particular focus on American involvement in Vietnam

Background: American concerns about communism

When the Second World War came to an end, the United States became increasingly concerned about the threat of communism, seeing it as a Russian attempt to dominate first Europe and then the world. This posed a challenge to American economic, political, and ideological interests.

Korea becoming communist in 1948 and China in 1949 led to concern that Asia would be engulfed by communism. To prevent this, the United States was willing to go to war. The spread of communism also threatened American interests in Cuba, while Vietnam presented a challenge to American influence.

Korea

Background to events in Korea

	1910	Korea had been controlled by the Japanese.
Division: The Japanese troops based in the north of Korea surrendered to the Soviet Union while those based in the south surrendered to the United States. A temporary dividing line was drawn up between the north and south along the 38th parallel of latitude (38° north). Free elections were to be held for a united, democratic Korea.	**1945**	
	1948	Elections: Separate elections were held. The south became the Republic of Korea, a capitalist dictatorship. In the north, now called the Democratic People's Republic of Korea, there was a communist dictatorship, supported by China and the Soviet Union.
25 June: North Korean soldiers, armed with Russian weapons, invaded South Korea.	**1950**	

Fig. 5.1 *Timeline summarising the background to events in Korea*

Worked Example

Why did North Korea invade South Korea in June 1950? (6)

The ruler of North Korea, Kim Il-Sung, wanted a united Korea under communist rule. He felt that, after the elections of 1948, the power the communists had established in North Korea would be great enough to take control of the South too.

North Korea also felt that it had powerful allies and therefore would be successful in invading the South. North Korea had support from Stalin's Soviet Union as well as Mao's China. With this support North Korea's armed forces, using weapons supplied by the Soviet Union, were stronger than the armed forces of South Korea. In addition, China had developed its own atomic bomb, making the Chinese more powerful. Kim Il-Sung's view was that this made an American response unlikely, as Korea was not a major American priority.

Exam tip

When answering a "Why?" question about the causes of a specific event, aim to explain two different reasons why the event occurred.

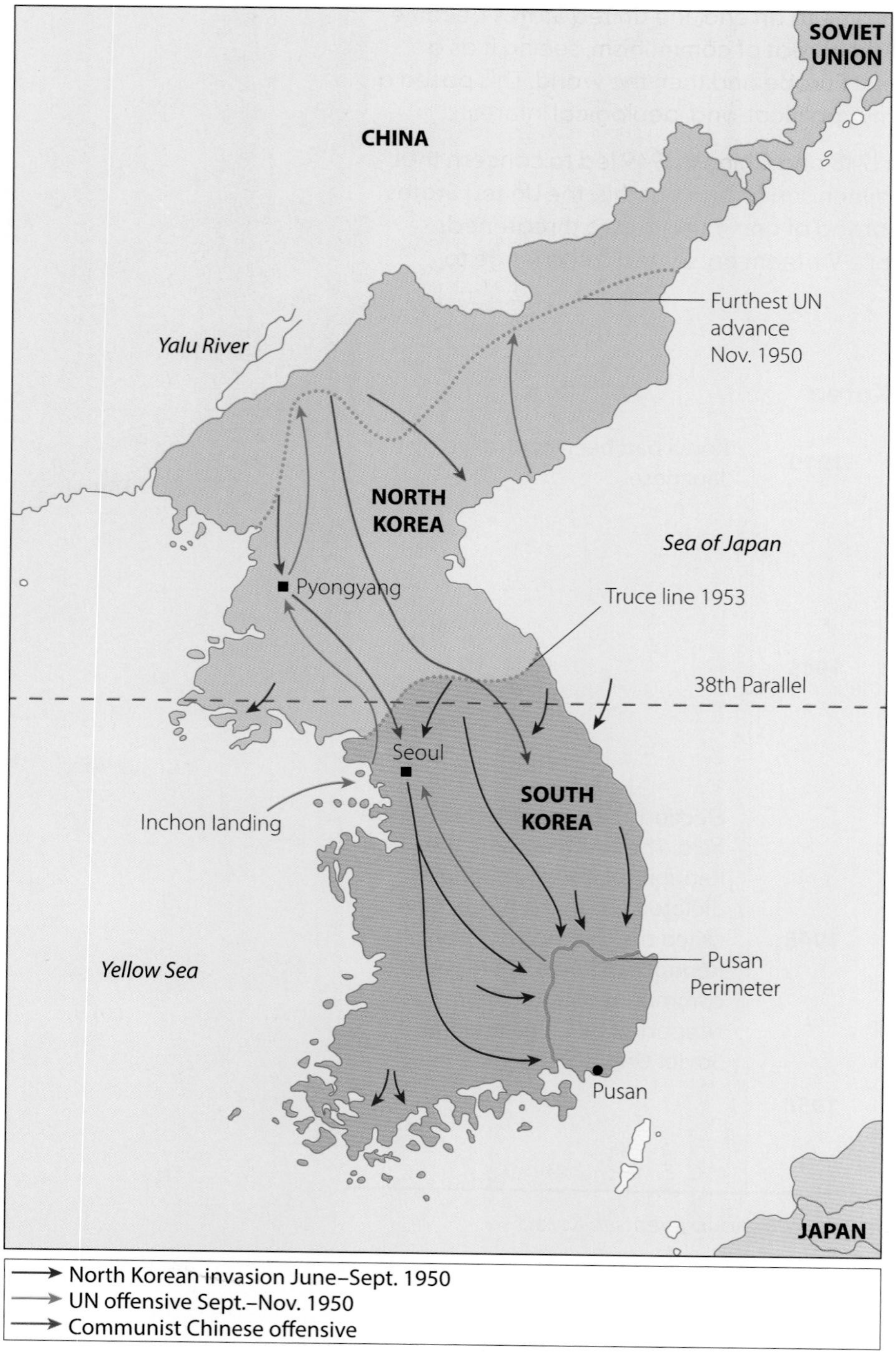

Legend:
→ North Korean invasion June–Sept. 1950
→ UN offensive Sept.–Nov. 1950
→ Communist Chinese offensive

Fig. 5.2 *The Korean War, 1950–53*

How did the UN and the United States become involved?

President Truman sent the US Seventh Fleet to try to prevent a Chinese attack on Formosa (Taiwan). He ordered General MacArthur to go to Korea with military supplies.

The United Nations Security Council met on the day that North Korean troops crossed the border into South Korea. An American resolution was passed at the United Nations (UN) demanding the withdrawal of North Korea. Its passing was made possible by the absence of the Soviet representative on the Security Council. At that time the Soviets were not present, as a protest against the United States' treatment of communist China.

As North Korea had no intention of withdrawing, a second American resolution was put forward on 27 June. A third resolution ten days later made clear how military forces were to be deployed.

Troops from the United States and 15 other countries were sent to assist South Korea. The UN forces were to be commanded by the American General MacArthur, who took his orders directly from Truman rather than from UN officials. Half the ground forces were Americans, together with over 90 per cent of the air forces and over 85 per cent of the naval forces.

Why did the United States become involved?

- The United States wanted to stop the spread of communism—it was determined to halt further communist expansion. The actions of North Korea were seen by the United States as part of Moscow's attempt to gain world domination.

- The Americans wanted to protect their interests. They feared that success in South Korea would encourage communist China to attack Formosa (the base of the non-communist Chinese). If South Korea and Formosa fell to the communists, Japan would come under threat. From the point of view of the United States, the fall of South Korea, Formosa, and Japan to the communists would represent a major shift in world power balance. The most effective way to prevent this was to oppose the North Korean invasion of South Korea.

Recap

The United States became involved because the Americans feared the spread of communism would threaten their own interests and make China more powerful.

The course of the war

In September 1950, UN troops landed at Inchon and forced the communists back into North Korea. UN troops invaded North Korea in an attempt to defeat the communists. In response, the Chinese leader Mao Zedong sent a large Chinese army to attack MacArthur's army.

In 1951 the UN army was forced to retreat to the South, followed by the communists. A UN counter-attack forced the Chinese and North Koreans back to the 38th Parallel.

There were disagreements between Truman and MacArthur over the course of the war. President Truman did not want a lengthy or costly war in Asia, but MacArthur wanted to carry on into China. He even suggested the use of the atomic bomb. Truman dismissed MacArthur in April 1951.

In 1953 a ceasefire was agreed that left Korea as two separate countries. Truman settled for communism being contained in North Korea.

Recap

American support meant that South Korea was able to resist North Korea's aggression. However, Korea would remain divided.

What were the results of the Korean War for the UN?

The UN had used military sanctions against an aggressor, showing that it was more purposeful than the League of Nations had ever been. The UN had failed in its objective of a "unified, independent, and democratic government" for Korea. The massive involvement and influence of the United States made it look more like an American action than one by the UN.

UN support for the American motion had only been achieved by chance. When the Korean War began, the Soviet Union was boycotting the UN Security Council and so there were no Soviet delegates to veto the UN decision.

Apply

Write a bullet list of the reasons why the Korean War developed.

What were the results of the Korean War for the United States?

- A total of 40 000 troops died.

- The American policy of containment had been successful as the spread of communism into South Korea had been prevented.

- Many American Republicans felt the United States had missed an opportunity to destroy communism in China. This feeling contributed towards the excesses of McCarthyism in the United States.

- American relations with China, as well as with the Soviet Union, were now strained, bringing a new dimension to the Cold War.

Worked Example

How great a threat was the Korean War to world peace? Explain your answer. (10)

It can be strongly argued that the Korean War did threaten world peace as it meant the Cold War had now spread to Asia and potentially could bring China, the Soviet Union, and other countries into full-scale conflict with the United States. At times, war seemed very likely to spread beyond Korea. In November 1950, American troops reached the border between Korea and China, and the Chinese launched a large-scale counter-offensive. If the war did move to mainland China, a growing power with a newly developed nuclear threat, then this would definitely threaten world peace.

The Korean War can also be seen to have threatened world peace as it increased mistrust between the Soviet Union and the United States. In the aftermath, the Soviet Union saw the United States as an expansionist country, and further deepened the growing Cold War tensions. On the United States' part, the fact that the Soviet Union gave arms to North Korea hardened the view that the Soviet Union was looking to undermine democracy in other countries and was a threat to the world interests of the United States.

However, it also can be considered that the Korean War was not a threat to world peace. The UN stood up to an act of aggression by North Korea that had been supported by two major powers. The UN moved quickly to respond to the invasion of Korea and many member nations offered troops and military and medical equipment in assistance. Ultimately, the invasion was unsuccessful and in 1951 the United States, the Soviet Union, and China started negotiations to end the war. Neither side wanted to make the crisis any larger and when it looked as if it might spread to China, Truman immediately scaled back American involvement and replaced MacArthur as commander.

Exam tip

To answer a question like this, it is important that you attempt a balanced answer—consider the question from both sides, rather than arguing for one particular viewpoint.

The United States and Cuba

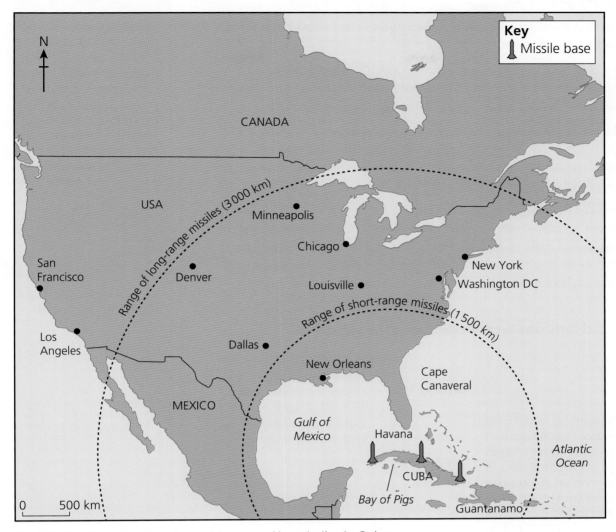

Fig. 5.3 *The threat to American cities posed by missiles in Cuba*

Background to events in Cuba

Cuba was important to the United States for a range of economic, military, and political reasons. The United States invested heavily in the Cuban economy, controlling the railways, telephone system, and tobacco plantations. Cuba was also a significant importer of American goods and Guantanamo Bay was an important US naval base. Cuba was a holiday island for rich Americans and the American mafia controlled much of the gambling, horse racing, and hotels in Cuba.

The United States was seen as corrupt by many in Cuba because of the interests it held there. This is an important reason why there was support for the new regime.

Why did tensions develop between Cuba and the United States?

In 1959 there was a revolution in Cuba. The unpopular President Batista was overthrown by revolutionary Fidel Castro. Castro promised to end American influence and control. The United States was worried by this, as it had supported Batista. The Americans feared Castro would turn out to be a communist. Castro negotiated trade agreements with the Soviet Union to export sugar and Khrushchev sent Castro advisers, military equipment, and economic aid.

Recap

Cuba was very useful to the United States as a trading partner, a holiday destination, and also a naval base. The Americans did not want their influence in Cuba to be reduced.

Apply

Draw a spider diagram showing the reasons why Cuba was important to the United States.

Worked Example

Why was the Cuban Revolution seen as a threat to the United States? Give two reasons and explain them. (6)

The Cuban Revolution was a threat to the United States as it threatened American interests within Cuba. The United States held a controlling interest in a range of industries and a communist takeover put these in danger.

Cuba was also a source of revenue for particular interest groups from the United States, such as the mafia, who made a great deal of money from controlling gambling and hotels within the country. Any communist revolution would also threaten these American interests.

The Cuban Revolution also was a threat to the United States because of any links that were established with the Soviet Union. As the Cold War developed, the Soviet Union seemed intent on supporting the spread of communism to other countries. With Cuba so close to the United States, any communist state established there with strong links to the Soviet Union would be a potential route of aggression.

Exam tip

The key to answering the question is to consider the level of threat to American interests that the Cuban Revolution posed. Consider how profitable Cuba was to the United States and what things might change after the event.

How did tensions worsen between the two sides?

	January 1961	In response to Cuban trade links with the Soviet Union, the United States banned all trade with Cuba and cut off diplomatic relations.
President Kennedy made weapons and transport available for an attempt to overthrow Castro. In this invasion 1500 Cuban exiles landed at the Bay of Pigs to find themselves faced with 20 000 Cuban troops armed with weapons supplied by the Soviet Union. The anticipated support from the Cuban people did not materialise and the exiles were killed or taken prisoner. The invasion was a dismal failure.	**April 1961**	
	June 1961	Khrushchev met Kennedy in Vienna. The United States was concerned that Kennedy was thought to be weak and would not back the containment policy with force.
Castro nationalised all American industries in Cuba.	**July 1961**	
	September 1961	Khrushchev publicly announced that he would provide arms to Cuba.

Fig. 5.4 *Timeline of events causing tensions to worsen*

Key fact

The Bay of Pigs Invasion was a disaster for the United States. The details of the attack were leaked and Castro was prepared for the attack. The Cuban exiles were met by 20 000 Cuban troops. The invasion forces immediately came under heavy fire and although some escaped into the sea, most were killed or captured. The supporting air strikes missed many of their targets and few, if any, Cubans joined the invaders.

Recap

The Bay of Pigs Invasion was a disaster for Kennedy, who was newly in post as President.

What was the Cuban Missile Crisis?

The United States became increasingly alarmed about the Soviet military build-up in Cuba and were worried that a nuclear attack might be launched from Cuba by the Soviet Union. In September 1962, Khrushchev told Kennedy that he had no intention of placing nuclear missiles in Cuba. This was proved to be false, causing tensions to heighten, when an American spy plane photographed the construction of nuclear missile sites in Cuba on 14 October 1962.

Why did the Soviet Union place missiles in Cuba?

Reason	Explanation
Placing missiles in Cuba would reduce the advantage held by the United States.	The United States had missiles in western Europe and had recently placed missiles in Turkey, which bordered the Soviet Union.
They would act as a deterrent.	Cuba was an ally of the Soviet Union. Missiles in Cuba would act as a deterrent against another attack. Cuba was the only communist country in the western hemisphere.
It would send out a message of strength to the United States.	Khrushchev was seen by some within the Soviet Union as not being strong enough in his dealings with the United States. Missiles close to the United States would give Khrushchev increased bargaining power.
The Soviet Union wanted a base close to the United States for its medium-range missiles.	Cuba was only 90 miles away from the United States. Medium-range missiles would be able to reach the United States.

Thirteen days

Once the United States had confirmed that the missiles had been placed in Cuba, Kennedy and his advisers met for 13 days and nights to try and find a solution to the crisis.

Key fact

EX-COMM—the Executive Committee of the National Security Council— was a body of government officials that advised Kennedy during the Cuban Missile Crisis. It was made up of members of the National Security Council, along with other advisers. The meetings were secretly recorded by Kennedy and the evidence from these tapes helps us understand this period of crisis.

	Tuesday 16 October 1962	President Kennedy is informed of the missiles in Cuba. A group of advisers called EX-COMM meet in secret to discuss the United States' response.
EX-COMM continues to work on a response to the crisis.	**Wednesday 17 October 1962**	
	Thursday 18 October 1962	Kennedy meets with the Soviet Foreign Minister. The minister denies the presence of missiles in Cuba. Kennedy does not reveal what he has discovered.
Kennedy decides to impose a blockade of Cuba. This decision is taken despite some members of EX-COMM favouring a show of force.	**Sunday 21 October 1962**	
	Monday 22 October 1962	In a live broadcast on American television, Kennedy informs the American public of the missiles and that he is going to impose a blockade. He asks Khrushchev to withdraw the missiles from Cuba.
Khrushchev replies, stating that there are no nuclear missiles in Cuba. He calls the blockade an act of piracy. Soviet ships sail towards the American blockade. If the blockade is ignored, the United States will fire on the ships. War seems certain to follow.	**Tuesday 23 October 1962**	
	Wednesday 24 October 1962	The Soviet ships reach the blockade. Kennedy stands his ground. One ship is allowed through, the others turn back. One crisis has been averted but the missiles still remain in Cuba.
Khrushchev admits to the existence of missiles in Cuba. Kennedy receives a letter from Khrushchev saying the Soviet Union will remove the missiles from Cuba if Kennedy agrees to lift the blockade and promises never to invade Cuba.	**Friday 26 October 1962**	
	Saturday 27 October 1962	A second letter from Khrushchev revises his proposals of the first letter. His new condition for the removal of missiles from Cuba is the withdrawal of American missiles from Turkey. In another development, an American spy plane is shot down over Cuba, killing the pilot. The advice to launch an immediate reprisal attack is ignored by Kennedy. Kennedy ignores the second letter but agrees to the demands made by Khrushchev in his first letter.
Khrushchev agrees to remove the missiles from Cuba. Conflict is avoided. Robert Kennedy informs the Soviet Ambassador that the United States will not invade Cuba and that the missiles in Turkey will be removed within six months.	**Sunday 28 October 1962**	

Fig. 5.5 *Timeline showing how the Cuban Missile Crisis unfolded, 16–28 October 1962*

Key fact

Robert Kennedy, President Kennedy's brother, served as Attorney General and was a key adviser while J F Kennedy was US President.

Apply

Draw a spider diagram that shows the successes and failures in Kennedy's response to the Cuban Missile Crisis.

Who won the Cuban Missile Crisis?

Countries	Positives	Negatives
The outcome for Cuba	Cuba remained communist, becoming a base for other communists in South America. Castro remained in power, keeping control of the American industries he had nationalised at the time of the revolution. Castro maintained the support and protection afforded to Cuba by the Soviet Union, although he was disappointed with the deal Khrushchev agreed with the United States.	Unable to trade with the United States and dependent on the Soviet Union, Cuba remained a poor country and isolated in the western hemisphere.
The outcome for the Soviet Union and Khrushchev	Khrushchev was able to say that he had acted responsibly by agreeing to remove the missiles from Cuba. Cuba was maintained as a communist ally in the western hemisphere. This was a significant achievement in the face of American action. The United States had agreed to remove NATO missiles from Turkey. As this was a secret agreement, Khrushchev was unable to take the credit.	Many in the Soviet Union felt humiliated by the fact that Khrushchev had been forced to back down and remove the missiles from Cuba. Khrushchev's reputation was tarnished and he was replaced as Soviet leader within two years. His critics believed he had not been forceful enough.
The outcome for the United States and Kennedy	The possibility of nuclear war had been avoided. Kennedy's prestige in the world increased. He was seen by the west as a tough negotiator as he did not back down over his naval blockade. Some of Kennedy's military advisers, who were critics of containment, thought he should invade Cuba to turn back communism. He avoided this high-risk strategy by standing up to these hard-liners.	Cuba remained a communist state close to the United States. Restrictions on trade between Cuba and the United States remained in force. The United States was criticised by some of its allies, including Britain. British newspaper articles were critical of the Americans' attitude that it was acceptable for them to have missiles in Turkey and other European bases but they complained about Cuba. The removal of missiles from Turkey had left some NATO members unhappy as technically the weapons were NATO missiles. The removal of the missiles was kept from the American public.

The aftermath of the crisis

Relations between the United States and the Soviet Union improved after the crisis. Both sides realised that brinkmanship had to be avoided in the future. The Cuban Missile Crisis was the nearest both sides came to conflict during the whole of the Cold War. They were now prepared to reduce the risk of nuclear conflict. A "hotline" telephone link was established between the Kremlin and the White House so that problems could be discussed. A Test Ban Treaty was signed in 1963.

Apply

Consider the effect of the Cuban Missile Crisis on the Soviet Union and on Cuba. Write a fact file focusing on how the crisis strengthened or weakened each country's position and the reputation of its leader.

American involvement in Vietnam

Background

Before the Second World War, Vietnam was ruled by France. In 1942 it was occupied by the Japanese. In 1945, following the defeat of Japan, the French returned, hoping to rule Vietnam. However, there was strong opposition to French rule from the Vietnamese, who wanted to run Vietnam themselves.

In 1954 the Battle of Dien Bien Phu marked the end of French involvement in Vietnam. Under the Geneva Peace Accords of 1954, agreed by the **Vietminh** and the French, the following terms were set:

- Indo-China was split into three countries: Laos, Cambodia, and Vietnam.
- Vietnam was temporarily portioned into two parts (north and south) at the 17th Parallel.
- Free elections were to be held in 1956.

These elections never took place because the United States feared the communists would win. The domino theory was introduced by the United States. It was thought that if one country became communist, others nearby would follow. Vietnam was therefore seen as a battleground against communism.

Fig. 5.6 *The domino effect*

In 1955 the Americans supported Ngo Dinh Diem to set up the Republic of South Vietnam. Diem was bitterly opposed to communism. The North, meanwhile, formed a communist government under the Vietminh. Clashes began between the South and the Vietcong—communist members based in the South who used guerrilla warfare.

Why did the United States become involved in Vietnam?

- Diem's government was weak and needed support. By 1963 the communist Vietcong controlled 40 per cent of South Vietnam.
- American policy was based on the idea of containment.
- President Eisenhower believed in the domino theory—if South Vietnam was allowed to become communist, then Laos, Cambodia, Burma, India, Thailand, and Pakistan would quickly follow.
- President Kennedy decided to increase the American military presence because he saw Vietnam as crucial to the Cold War. He wanted to look strong after the failed Bay of Pigs Invasion and the Cuban Missile Crisis.

> **Key fact**
>
> The Vietcong, or National Liberation Front (NLF), was the guerrilla force that, with the support of the North Vietnamese Army, fought against South Vietnam and the United States. The Vietcong was based in the south of Vietnam.

How did American involvement in Vietnam increase?

- **Aid:** After France had left, military and economic aid was offered to South Vietnam.
- **Advisers:** President Kennedy sent military advisers to support the South Vietnamese army. In May 1961, 500 were sent. In 1963, the number of advisers totalled 16 000.

> **Key term**
>
> **Vietminh**—a communist-dominated nationalist movement, formed in 1941, that fought for Vietnamese independence from French rule.

> **Key fact**
>
> Vietnam, along with Cambodia and Laos, was referred to as French Indo-China when ruled by the French. It was only when the French left that it officially became known as Vietnam.

> **Recap**
>
> The United States' involvement in Vietnam was similar to that in Korea—the threat of communism and the belief in the domino theory motivated the Americans to intervene.

- **The Gulf of Tonkin Incident:** In August 1964, two American warships were attacked by North Vietnamese gunboats while in international waters. This confrontation was known as the Gulf of Tonkin Incident. In response, the US Senate granted Johnson permission to give armed support to South Vietnam.

The timeline below summarises the main events of the Vietnam War.

Recap

In November 1963, President Diem was overthrown by a military coup. Later the same month President Kennedy was assassinated. His successor President Lyndon B Johnson was more prepared to enter into full-scale conflict in Vietnam than Kennedy had been. (See the Student Book, pages 110–11.)

	February 1965	Operation Rolling Thunder—bombing of North Vietnam started, with targets that included the Ho Chi Minh Trail.
The first American combat troops were sent to Vietnam.	**March 1965**	
	January 1968	Start of the Tet Offensive—a large-scale communist attack on major towns and cities in South Vietnam. Targets included the American Embassy in Saigon. Although the communists were defeated, the attacks were a major shock to Americans who had thought the war was almost won. The American media called it a defeat and public support for the war plummeted. Following the Tet Offensive, peace talks started. A ceasefire was not achieved for a further five years.
A group of American soldiers was searching for Vietcong. The soldiers landed by helicopter close to the village of My Lai. They failed to find any Vietcong so rounded up the inhabitants of the village and massacred them all, including infants. When news of the massacre reached the American people there was shock and horror. Numerous anti-war demonstrations followed.	**March 1968**	
	October 1968	Operation Rolling Thunder finished. More bombs had been dropped on North Vietnam than were dropped by the United States on Germany and Japan during the Second World War. Also in this month, the American policy of **Vietnamisation** was introduced by President Nixon.
President Nixon attacked Cambodia to prevent the Vietcong from using it as a base from which to attack American forces.	**1970**	
	1973	A ceasefire agreement was signed.

Fig. 5.7 *Timeline of the main events of the Vietnam War*

Key term

Vietnamisation—support given by the United States to strengthen the South Vietnamese army to allow the gradual withdrawal of American combat troops from the Vietnam War.

Were the military tactics of the United States or those of the communists the most effective?

Strategies used by the Vietcong during the Vietnam War

Strategy	Impact
Ho Chi Minh based the Vietcong guerrilla warfare strategies on the methods used by the communists to gain power in China. Features of Vietcong guerrilla warfare were as follows. • Guerrilla fighters did not have a base camp. • They did not wear a uniform, making it difficult to differentiate between villagers and Vietcong. • They used the element of surprise, carrying out attacks then quickly disappearing into the jungle, taking refuge in villages or their underground tunnels. • They ambushed American troops and set booby traps using trip wires and mines. • The closeness of fighting ("hanging on to American belts") negated the greater strength of American fire power.	• The morale of American troops, whose average age was only 19, was reduced. • The number of American casualties was increased. • Mistrust built between Vietnamese civilians and American soldiers, who were unable to distinguish between friend and foe.

Strategies used by the United States during the Vietnam War

Strategy	Impact
Strategic bombing: During the war the United States bombed Vietcong strongholds, supply lines, and key cities. Operation Rolling Thunder started in 1965. Bombing continued after Operation Rolling Thunder stopped in 1968.	• Supply lines were disrupted but not stopped. The system of tunnels and underground passages was not affected by the bombing. • South Vietnamese targets were still attacked. This was the area the United States was supposed to be protecting. • Extensive bombing of Hanoi (the North Vietnam capital) encouraged the start of peace discussions. • The financial cost of this bombing was huge.
Use of chemical weapons. The Americans developed "agent orange" and also used napalm.	• Agent orange was used to carry out defoliation of the jungle in South Vietnam. The chemical was dropped from the air and removed the leaves from the trees in an attempt to prevent the Vietcong hiding in the jungle. The Vietcong underground supply lines were not affected. • Napalm was often dropped on villages to destroy them. Thousands of innocent Vietnamese civilians received terrible burns and many died. This shocked the American people and meant that American troops lost any support from the villagers.
Search and destroy: In response to the guerrilla tactics of the Vietcong, the Americans carried out raids using helicopters. The helicopters would land near Vietnamese villages. The American forces would then kill hiding Vietcong fighters and set fire to the village.	• Although some Vietcong were killed, the impact was minimal. • The raids were often based on incorrect information, resulting in villages being destroyed and large numbers of innocent villagers killed. • American troops became unpopular with the villagers who then gave their support to the Vietcong.
Imposing strategic hamlets: Whole villages were moved to new sites enclosed by barbed wire.	• The Americans were able to control and check those who entered and left the village. • There was resentment from villagers who were forced to leave their homes to live somewhere else.

Worked Example

Describe the United States' tactics in Vietnam. (4)

The United States used a range of tactics in the war in Vietnam. In an attempt to combat the guerrilla warfare American troops faced, the United States used chemical weapons to try and limit the territory that the Vietcong could hide in. Agent orange and napalm were developed. Agent orange was used to bring about defoliation of the jungle in South Vietnam. The chemical removed the leaves from the trees in an attempt to prevent the Vietcong hiding in the jungle. However, underground supply lines were not affected. Both agent orange and napalm caused injuries to thousands of innocent Vietnamese civilians.

The United States also used search and destroy tactics in an attempt to combat the Vietcong. Raids on villages would be based on information and would result in American forces killing or capturing Vietcong fighters and destroying the village. However, these raids were limited in effectiveness and often resulted in villages being destroyed and large numbers of innocent villagers being killed.

Exam tip

In your answer, focus on specific tactics of the American troops in Vietnam, using relevant terms such as "search and destroy" and "strategic hamlets".

Key fact

The draft was the name given to the lottery system where men were conscripted into the US Army. About one-third of those fighting in Vietnam were drafted and once called they had to serve for two years.

Why did the United States withdraw from Vietnam?

Reason	Explanation
Low morale	The use of guerrilla warfare affected the morale of the troops as they feared what might happen to them. Troops turned to illegal drugs and thousands of soldiers deserted. The average age of American troops was 19. After 1967 they were "drafted" (conscripted) into the army. Many had recently left school and just wanted to return home safely. They were often from poorer homes or immigrant backgrounds.
The Tet Offensive	Up to 1967 the war had been going well for the Americans. During the New Year holiday in January 1967, communist troops attacked major Vietnamese towns and cities, including the American Embassy in Saigon. The hoped-for revolution in South Vietnam did not materialise and the Vietcong were pushed back. The Tet Offensive was widely seen as a turning point for the United States, as it was realised that without increasing the number of combat troops, the war could not be won. Additionally, increased numbers of troops would bring even more casualties.
My Lai	In March 1968, an American troop patrol entered the village of My Lai. They were on a search-and-destroy mission, having been informed that members of the Vietcong were hiding there. No Vietcong were found, but nearly 400 civilians, many of whom were women and children, were massacred by the Americans. When details of the brutal massacre become known it shocked the American public, undermining support for the war. The horror of My Lai and the increasing view that the war was unwinnable led Johnson to decide not to run again for president.
Press and media	In the early years of the war, most American newspapers and news journalists were supportive of the war. The reports they produced were positive as they did not wish to undermine the American government's policy of containment. By 1967 many reports from Vietnam were via television programmes that often showed scenes of shocking violence from search-and-destroy raids. At the same time, television reporters were increasingly arguing that the war was unwinnable. One such reporter was CBS's Walter Cronkite. This changing attitude was not just influencing the American public but even President Johnson. American military leaders, including General Westmoreland, put forward the view that the media reduced support for the war effort in Vietnam.

Reason	Explanation
Protests against the war	Public opinion was changing. As more and more bodies of young servicemen were brought home in body bags the public began asking if the United States could win the war. To show disapproval, draft cards were burnt and President Johnson was taunted by students. American student anti-war protests reached their height towards the end of the 1960s. Participating students held the view that the war was morally wrong and they therefore did not wish to receive the draft. Often the protests involved the burning of the American flag and ended in violent clashes with the police. One such clash was at Kent State University where the US National Guard fired into a group of unarmed protestors. Four students were killed.
Human and economic cost	In 1967 *Life* magazine calculated that it was costing $400 000 for each Vietcong fighter killed. This meant cutbacks in the spending on social reforms in President Johnson's Great Reform programme. By 1968, 300 American soldiers were dying each week. Over 50 000 American troops eventually lost their lives.
Lack of support	There was declining support in South Vietnam. The winning of "hearts and minds" was seen as crucial to American success but the use of tactics that killed civilians lost the support of the Vietnamese people. At the same time, neighbouring countries of Vietnam showed sympathy to the Vietcong by allowing them to access arms and ammunition. The United States could not, for diplomatic reasons, enter these countries. Cambodia and Laos used the Ho Chi Minh trail to supply necessities to the Vietcong.

The end of war in Vietnam

It was left to President Nixon to find a way to withdraw from the Vietnam War. This was a difficult task. From 1965 the American government had argued that the war was just and vital. Nixon introduced a policy of "Vietnamisation": the United States would train and equip the South Vietnamese so that American troops could withdraw. In February 1973 a ceasefire was agreed.

South Vietnam soon fell to the communists, as did Cambodia and Laos. During 1975 communist troops took South Vietnam, including the capital, Saigon. In 1976 North and South Vietnam were reunited as a single communist country ruled by Ho Chi Minh. Relations between Vietnam and the United States remained hostile until 1993 when trade was resumed.

Fig. 5.8 *Nixon with advisers consulting on Vietnam*

Worked Example

Why did the Vietnam War become increasingly unpopular with the people in the United States? (6)

By 1968 the war was a stalemate. The United States could not defeat the Vietcong. The Tet Offensive showed that the Vietcong could not drive out the United States. However, the Tet Offensive and My Lai had horrified the American public as broadcasts showed wounded and dead soldiers and innocent civilians massacred. The American public began to see the war as unwinnable.

The war was also a huge drain on resources. The aim of President Johnson's Great Reform programme was huge social change, but with the vast sums spent on the war and the impact at home (such as policing anti-war protests) the war lost popularity with ordinary Americans.

Exam tip

The key to answering this question successfully is to address the term "increasingly unpopular" by identifying the factors that changed the public mood.

Review

1. Describe why the conflict in Korea developed. [4]

2. Describe the Bay of Pigs Invasion. [4]

3. Who were the Vietcong? [4]

4. Describe the My Lai incident. [4]

5. Why did the United States become involved in Vietnam? [6]

6. How successful was the United States in Vietnam in the period 1963–75? [10]

7. How successful was Kennedy's response to the Cuban Missile Crisis? [10]

For further information, review this section in the Student Book.

Raise your grade ↑

1. What was the domino theory? (4 marks)

The domino theory was an explanation of how the United States feared communism would spread from country to country during the Cold War. The fear was that as a country turned communist, it would infiltrate neighbouring states, then momentum for communism would develop.

This belief was a defining factor in American military action in the period—intervention in Korea and Vietnam was an attempt to stop the spread of communism.

The candidate offers a good explanation of the theory, and also applies it to American foreign policy to show how it led to military action in Vietnam and Korea. 4 marks awarded.

Plan your answer

- The question introduces a key term, so it is important that this is explained and the context of what it was referring to—in this case, communism—is made clear.

- In the answer, aim to make two good points that are well explained. The points should cover what the theory was and how it applied to American foreign policy.

- The United States was concerned that as one country became communist, another would too.

- There is no need to explain why American politicians felt threatened by communism; instead, focus on the explanation of the theory.

Mark scheme

1 mark for each relevant point, 1 additional mark for supporting detail; maximum 2 marks per point made.

2. Why did the United States become involved in Korea? (6 marks)

On 25 June 1950 the Korean War began when North Korea, supported by the Soviet Union and China, invaded South Korea, which was supported by the United States.

Korea had been separated at the end of the Second World War. North Korea became a communist regime under the leadership of Kim Il-Sung. South Korea became a democratic state under Syngman Rhee. The Korean War therefore meant conflict between the communist and the democratic sides.

The answer gives detail about what the Korean War was and states that each side had foreign support. However, there is no focus on reasons for the United States' involvement—there needs to be more explanation of why the United States became involved. 1 mark awarded.

Plan your answer

- The question references American involvement in the Korean War in the 1950s. For the answer, aim for two well-developed reasons why the United States felt the need to become involved.

- The United States supported South Korea in the conflict against the North. The South was democratic, while the North was communist.

- The US government viewed its involvement in the war as a way to prevent a communist takeover of the entire county.

- The United States' involvement was also prompted by the Soviet Union and China supporting North Korea.

Mark scheme

Level 1:	general answer lacking specific contextual knowledge (1 mark)
Level 2:	identifies AND/OR describes reasons (2–3 marks)
Level 3:	explains ONE reason (4–5 marks)
Level 4:	explains TWO reasons (6 marks)

3. How far was American public opinion the most important reason for the United States' withdrawal from Vietnam?

(10 marks)

It can be argued that public opinion was the most important reason for the withdrawal of the United States from Vietnam. The major turning point for American public opinion was the Tet Offensive in 1968. In January the Vietcong attacked towns and bases of South Vietnamese troops all over Vietnam. Thousands of troops died during the attack and it came as a complete shock to Americans, who thought that they had been close to winning the war. The US government and the public felt misled by the army leaders, from whom they had been receiving positive information about the war.

Events such as this, along with many others, such as the My Lai incident, were all exposed by media coverage. This and the change in public opinion about the war were the most significant reasons for the withdrawal of troops from Vietnam. The Vietnam War was the first to have full media coverage and people were able to see exactly how awful the war really was.

A shift in public opinion was seen with people burning their draft papers and refusing to agree to conscription. There were also other significant protests. In May 1970, protests on campus became out of control at Kent State University. Four students died and a few were injured as a result of gunfire from the National Guardsmen.

However, it was also the high cost of the war that put pressure on the government to withdraw troops from Vietnam. By the end of the war over $100 billion had been spent. This was money that could have been directed to address inequalities in American society but instead was being spent on the war.

The answer is strong in terms of its explanation of the importance of, and reasons for, public opinion about the Vietnam War. The student also offers a balanced view by presenting in the final paragraph the additional factor of the cost of the war. To improve the answer there needs to be more of a counter argument and more evaluation in the points made. 7 marks awarded.

Plan your answer

- A "How far?" question offers a chance to explore the factor in the question as well as considering other issues.

- In the answer, you should explore the factor and relevant issues then come to a conclusion.

- Public opinion was definitely important and this changed as the war went on.

- There is little doubt that by the late 1960s the reaction of the public to the war was becoming negative as protests rose.

- However, other issues need to be explored. The cost of war, the long duration of the conflict, and the fact that the war seemed unwinnable were all significant issues.

Mark scheme

Level 1:	general answer lacking specific contextual knowledge (1 mark)
Level 2:	identifies AND/OR describes reasons (2–3 marks)
Level 3:	gives a one-sided explanation (4–5 marks) or one explanation of both sides (4–6 marks)
Level 4:	explains both sides (7–9 marks)
Level 5:	explains with evaluation (10 marks)

6

How far was the USSR able to exert its influence over the eastern bloc states from the end of World War Two until 1989?

You need to know

- The reasoning behind opposition to Soviet rule in Hungary in 1956 and how it was dealt with
- Why there was opposition to Soviet control in Czechoslovakia in 1968 and how the Soviet Union reacted
- How events in Hungary in 1956 and Czechoslovakia in 1968 compare
- The reasoning behind the construction of the Berlin Wall in 1961
- How Poland's Solidarity movement helped limit Soviet influence across eastern Europe
- The role of Gorbachev in the decline of Soviet influence in eastern Europe

Background: Soviet control over eastern Europe, 1945–53

The end of the Second World War had brought Soviet control over the countries of eastern Europe. To some, this generated hope based on the significant industrial growth achieved by the Soviet Union prior to the war. However, the reality of Soviet control was very different: the right to democratic government and free speech was lost; newspapers were censored; government critics were put in prison; travel to countries in t he west was prohibited.

Eastern bloc factories produced the goods demanded by the Soviet Union rather than goods the ordinary people in eastern European countries wanted. There were shortages of basics including coal, milk, and meat. Clothing was very expensive and consumer goods such as electric kettles and radios were unavailable. Wages were even lower than in the Soviet Union.

When Stalin died in 1953 to be replaced by Khrushchev, Khrushchev talked of peaceful co-existence with the west and wanting to improve living standards for the people of eastern Europe. He indicated to countries in eastern Europe that they would be allowed greater independence to control their own affairs. Khrushchev even went as far as denouncing Stalin. A programme of de-Stalinisation was to follow. The people of eastern Europe saw this changing attitude as a positive step towards greater freedom. How, though, would Khrushchev respond to any challenge?

Fig. 6.1 *Eastern Europe after the end of the Second World War*

Challenging Soviet rule: explaining the revolts in Hungary 1956

Factor	Details
Politics	The country was run by the Hungarian Communist Party despite it only achieving 17 per cent of the vote.
	Political leaders were unpopular—the hard-line communist leader Rákosi lacked support and his replacement Gerö was just as unacceptable. The more acceptable Imre Nagy then took over to form a new government.
Conditions	Following the war, Hungary was poor and needed rebuilding, yet much of its industrial production was sent to the Soviet Union. Food produced was often sent to the Soviet Union, causing shortages and the standard of living to fall in Hungary.
Soviet control	The Hungarians suffered from repression and strict control. Soviet control had brought censorship, secret police, and restrictions on education.
	Religion was banned for being subversive.
	The Hungarians resented the presence of thousands of Soviet troops and officials in their country, especially as they had to pay for the troops.

Actions planned by Nagy's government

When Nagy took over he introduced a plan to change life in Hungary.

- Free elections would be held.

- Law courts would become impartial.

- Farm land would be restored to private ownership.

- There would be a reduction in the Soviet influence on the daily way of life in Hungary, including the total withdrawal of the Soviet army. (Some troops had already withdrawn.)

- Most dramatically, Nagy stated he intended to withdraw Hungary from the Warsaw Pact.

Why did the Hungarians think they would be successful?

- Khrushchev had stated that he was in favour of reduced control over the satellite countries following Stalin's death.

- When there had been an uprising of workers in Poland in June 1956, the Soviets had given in to some of their demands.

- The Hungarians thought they would have support from the United Nations and also the new US President Eisenhower, who had made supportive comments in speeches.

How did the Soviet Union react to this opposition?

At first, Khrushchev appeared to be prepared to accept some reforms, but he was not prepared to accept Hungary leaving the Warsaw Pact. On 28 October 1956 Khrushchev agreed to the demands of Nagy to remove Soviet troops from Hungary.

However, on 4 November, thousands of Soviet troops and 1000 tanks moved into Budapest, the capital. Bitter street fighting followed as the Hungarians did not surrender. Approximately 3000 Hungarians died, along with around 8000 Russians. Another 200000 fled the country. Nagy was imprisoned and later executed.

> **Key fact**
>
> Imre Nagy was a Hungarian politician who, although he was a communist leader with close ties to the Soviet Union, advocated greater liberalism and reform, with more independence for the Hungarian people away from Soviet control. Following the Hungarian Revolution of 1956, Nagy was arrested, tried in secret, and executed.

Why did some people oppose Soviet control in Czechoslovakia in 1968?

There were two main reasons for opposition to Soviet control in Czechoslovakia.

- Communism was restrictive. Censorship, lack of freedom of speech, and the activities of the secret police were aspects of daily life hated by the people.

- During the 1960s the Czechoslovakian economy struggled and the standard of living fell.

The Prague Spring

Alexander Dubček introduced the idea of the Prague Spring of 1968. This became known as "socialism with a human face". Dubček's proposals for change included:

- the abolition of censorship, allowing the press to print what they wanted

- freedom of speech, allowing criticism of the government in industry, the creation of workers' councils, and increased rights for trade unions

- freedom of movement for all people.

Wary of what had happened in Hungary, Dubček made a clear statement that Czechoslovakia did not wish to leave the Warsaw Pact or end its alliance with the Soviet Union.

Dubček, however, planned to cooperate with Romania and Yugoslavia, two countries with less close ties to the Soviet Union. This increased Soviet concerns.

How did the Soviet Union react to this opposition?

Reaction to Dubček

In 1968 Brezhnev had taken over as leader of the Soviet Union. He was just as determined as his predecessors to maintain Soviet control of eastern Europe.

Czechoslovakia was an important country within the Warsaw Pact because of the strength of its industry. Brezhnev knew that if Czechoslovakia gained more freedom, other eastern European countries would want the same. He took action to stop reform in Czechoslovakia.

- Brezhnev instructed Dubček to stop his reforms.

- Pressure was put on Brezhnev by the East German Leader, Ulbricht.

- Troops from countries within the Warsaw Pact carried out training exercises on the Czech border.

On 20 August 1968, Soviet tanks moved into Czechoslovakia. While some fighting occurred, there was nothing comparable to what had happened in Hungary. Generally, the Czechs refused to cooperate. Dubček was removed from power and taken to Moscow.

The Brezhnev Doctrine

This was introduced in order to stop such events happening again in other countries. It stated that all Warsaw Pact countries should work together to prevent any attempt by a country to leave the treaty. Military force could be used by the Soviet Union if any attempt to leave the Warsaw Pact was made by a member country.

Key fact

Alexander Dubček was a politician who served as the leader of Czechoslovakia from January 1968 to April 1969. He attempted to reform the Communist government during the Prague Spring but was forced to resign following the Warsaw Pact invasion in August 1968.

Key fact

The Warsaw Pact was the name given to the treaty between Albania, Bulgaria, Czechoslovakia, East Germany, Hungary, Poland, Romania, and the Soviet Union, which was signed in Poland in 1955. It called on the member states to come to the defence of any member attacked by an outside force and it set up a unified military command under Marshal Ivan S Konev of the Soviet Union.

Recap

Nagy believed that there was a genuine chance of reforms being made and more freedoms granted to Hungary. By withdrawing from the Warsaw Pact, he demonstrated that he wanted greater control for his own people over Hungary.

Recap

Czechoslovakia's attempt at reform was less revolutionary than in Hungary, and was met with a softer response from the Soviets. However, they refused to allow reforms and Dubček was unsuccessful.

Comparing the revolts in Hungary in 1956 and Czechoslovakia in 1968

	How were events similar?	How were events different?
Causes	Both countries had a long-term resentment of Soviet rule.	Hungary was affected by issues in other countries: the rebellion in Poland inspired the Hungarians to act. Czechoslovakia was affected by issues at home: economic depression and a desire for political change.
Aims of the rebels	Both sets of rebels wanted to give their people more rights and lessen the control of the Communist state.	In Hungary the political changes included withdrawing from the Warsaw Pact and Soviet influence. Czechoslovakia did not want to go that far.
Actions of the people	Both rebellions involved groups of people protesting.	In Czechoslovakia, the people's actions were largely started by their leader. It was his changes that encouraged them to protest. In Hungary, it was the people who acted first.
Why the Soviet Union intervened	The Soviet Union was very suspicious and fearful that any form of rebellion or change would spread and lead to a split in its control in other countries.	The political nature of Czechoslovakia was particularly dangerous for the Soviets; they had faced people-led rebellions before, like that in Hungary, but the Prague Spring was started by people who were meant to be under Soviet control.
How each state responded to Soviet intervention	Both leaders were removed from office. In both states there was mass emigration.	In Hungary the people armed themselves and fought when the Soviets attacked. In Czechoslovakia, following orders from the government, the people did not fight back. In Czechoslovakia there were several protests after the Russian invasion, including suicides.
Reaction of the wider world	Reactions to both were wholly negative to the Soviet use of force. The situation in Hungary was discussed at the United Nations with Czechoslovakia, the Soviet actions were condemned by different countries, including the United States.	With the Czechoslovakian invasion, some members of the communist Warsaw Pact expressed shock at Soviet actions. The Romanian leader complained about Russian intervention.

Worked Example

"There were more similarities than differences between the revolts in Hungary and Czechoslovakia." To what extent do you agree with this statement? Explain your answer. (10)

It can be argued that there were clear similarities between the two uprisings. They had a similar cause in that both in Hungary and Czechoslovakia there had been a long-standing resentment of Soviet rule since the Second World War. People had grown tired of the repressive nature of the Soviet-backed governments that had been put in place. In addition, both wanted to lessen Soviet influence in their countries, as well as giving the people personal freedoms and a greater sense of democracy.

Recap

There are significant differences between the rebellions in Czechoslovakia and Hungary. However, this might be due to the timing. The harsh response to the events in Hungary might explain not only why the Czech rebellion was less radical in its demands but also why the Soviets reacted differently.

Another similarity is the way that both revolts were dealt with. Russian troops were moved into Hungary and Czechoslovakia to take back control and the countries' leaders were forcibly removed.

However, there were clear differences between the two revolts. When the Soviet Union arrived in Hungary the people armed themselves and attempted to fight back, but in Czechoslovakia, following orders from the government, the people did not retaliate. While some protested in different ways, including through suicide, there were no clashes with troops. The revolts were also different regarding what the protesters wanted. The Hungarians wanted to be free of Soviet influence. The Czechs did not share this aim and made that clear.

Exam tip

In the answer, avoid simply agreeing with the question and only providing similarities between the two revolts. It is important to offer a balanced answer—so make sure you also consider the differences between the revolts.

Why was the Berlin Wall constructed in 1961?

What was the Berlin Wall?

At the end of the Second World War, the city of Berlin was split into four zones. A wall was constructed to seal East Berlin from the west. The wall was constructed on 13 August 1961. Originally, the wall was constructed of barbed wire but over time it became a permanent concrete structure. All crossing points were sealed except one, which became known as Checkpoint Charlie.

Berlin was now divided by a wall 87 miles long. The wall was to prevent the movement of people from east to west. Already nearly 2.6 million people had left East Germany for the west. Anyone trying to defect to the west was shot.

Why were people leaving East Berlin?

- The quality of life was much better in the west. West Germany had been able to use Marshall Aid to rebuild following the devastation of war.

- In West Berlin, shops were full of a variety of goods and freedom was greater, as was wealth. The attraction of capitalism was significant compared to the harsh regime of East Germany under hard-line communist leader Ulbricht.

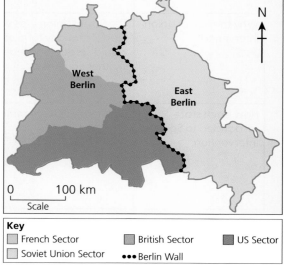

Key

☐ French Sector		☐ British Sector	☐ US Sector
☐ Soviet Union Sector	●●● Berlin Wall		

Fig. 6.2 *The Berlin Wall, 1961*

What was the impact of this movement on East Germany?

The communists feared a "brain drain" as skilled workers, including engineers, physicians, teachers, and lawyers were all leaving in high numbers.

Negative propaganda was created. In the context of the Cold War, the number of people leaving a communist country created a feeling of unpopularity for communism. It became good propaganda for the west—the west was attractive while the east had to erect a wall to keep people in.

What were the immediate consequences of the building of the Berlin Wall?

There were two immediate consequences:

- the flow of people from east to west stopped

- Berlin became a focus for the Cold War.

The west's reaction to the Berlin Wall was to be publicly horrified and demand that free transport to and around West Berlin continued. However, US President Kennedy stated that there would be no military action to remove the wall or any barriers between East and West Berlin.

Recap

- Berlin had been divided into four zones after the war.

- The wall was put up to stop people leaving—they could only cross from east to west and vice versa via the tightly controlled checkpoints.

- As the quality of life was better in the west, people were leaving the east in vast numbers.

Worked Example

Describe why the Berlin Wall was built. (6)

The wall was built in 1961 due to an increasing number of people migrating from the east to the west. The crushing of the Hungarian revolt in 1956 showed eastern Europeans that it was impossible to rebel against communist rule. It appeared that the only way to escape from communist rule was to leave their roots and move to the west. But the hatred of communist rule was not the only reason people moved: the pro-communists left due to poor living conditions.

Among the thousands of people fleeing to the west were many of the Soviet Union's most skilled workers and highly qualified managers. The Soviet government couldn't afford their loss. Khrushchev thought that thousands of people fleeing communist rule for a better life under capitalism undermined communism in East Germany and in general.

Apply

Draw a spider diagram showing the factors that led to the building of the Berlin Wall.

Exam tip

The Berlin Wall was built by the Soviet Union to address the large numbers of people moving to the west. Give more specific detail in the answer though—offer reasons why people were leaving and what the impact was.

How did Poland's Solidarity movement help limit Soviet influence across eastern Europe?

The rise of Solidarity

From the end of the Second World War, Soviet control of Poland increased in unpopularity. Over the years there had been numerous protests about wages and food prices in an attempt to improve the standard of living, but nothing challenging the rule of the Soviet Union.

	1979	The Polish economy reached crisis point. Food prices were rising and wages remained low.
The government was forced into increasing the price of goods, including food, while at the same time blocking any pay increases. People were facing poverty and responded by going on strike. The strikes spread quickly across the country.	**July 1980**	
	14 August 1980	The workers at the Lenin Shipyard in Gdansk (Danzig) went on strike. Dismayed with the conditions they were facing, they produced a list of 21 demands as well as demanding the right to form a trade union. The strike was led by Lech Walesa.
The right to form a union free from government control was accepted and by mid-September Solidarity was formed.	**End of August 1980**	

Fig. 6.3 *Timeline of events leading to the rise of Solidarity*

Why did the communist Polish government agree to meet the demands of Solidarity?

- **Fear of a general strike:** The government was afraid because a general strike would devastate Poland's economy. The government thought there might be a general strike as originally the Solidarity membership came mainly from important areas of shipbuilding and heavy industry.

- **Methods:** Walesa was careful not to provoke the Soviet Union, working to reinforce the view that Solidarity was not an alternative to the Communist Party. Violence was avoided. The strikers used methods such as distributing newspapers to spread their message of the need for reform.

- **Popularity:** The movement was thought of as trustworthy and represented around 80 per cent of workers from across Polish life. Walesa was seen as a folk hero by many.

- **Support of the Catholic Church:** In Poland the government was unable to crush the Church because of the strong faith of the people.

Why was action taken against Solidarity in December 1981?

General Jaruzelski became Prime Minister of Poland in February 1981. He and Walesa tried to work together but their relationship was tense. It finally failed in December. Jaruzelski claimed he had evidence that the Solidarity leaders were planning a coup, imposed martial law and Solidarity was outlawed. Walesa and most of the Solidarity leaders were put in prison.

How important was Solidarity?

In 1985 Mikhail Gorbachev became leader of the Soviet Union. His reforms included the release of political prisoners connected with Solidarity. However, his reforms did not improve Poland's economic situation.

Although Jaruzelski was technically still in power, Solidarity held the real power. It was only a matter of time before communism collapsed in Poland. By 1988 strikes had swept through Poland as food costs rose by 40 per cent. Walesa negotiated with the Polish government to find a solution.

In April 1989 Solidarity was again legalised, fielding candidates in the upcoming elections. Solidarity won every seat it contested and the first non-communist government of the post-war era was formed, with Walesa as President. Solidarity had demonstrated to the rest of the eastern bloc that communist control could be resisted.

Key fact

Foreign support for Solidarity: The movement had gained support in the west through positive media coverage and the charisma of Walesa. Attempting to crush the movement would reflect badly on the Soviet Union.

Key fact

Pope John Paul II's influence in the Solidarity movement should not be forgotten. Pope John Paul II was Polish, and spoke several times in the late 1970s and 1980s in support of the Polish people. He was seen to be a public face who gave the Polish people hope of change.

Apply

Write a fact file that gives the main reasons why Solidarity was important.

Worked Example

Why did the Solidarity movement succeed while other similar movements failed? (6)

The Solidarity movement was able to succeed because its followers were well organised and it attracted mass support. The timing of the revolt was also a factor.

In 1980 and 1981, 10 million people from across Polish society, including students, workers, and intellectuals, joined Solidarity. This represented over 80 per cent of Poland's workforce. No other popular movement had gained such support, and this can be seen as a reason for its success. Solidarity also succeeded in appealing to a wide range of people by championing national, not local issues—securing the support of many people and affecting the major industries.

Exam tip

One of the key reasons the Solidarity movement was able to succeed was timing. When writing your answer, consider the point that the context of what was happening in the Soviet Union gave Solidarity a far greater chance of success than the movement would otherwise have had.

Solidarity supporters were also well organised. The trade union's newspaper, *Solidarnosc*, was printed on the shipyard printing press. It enabled members to spread their message. The committee and spokesmen also ensured that a consistent message was clearly heard.

Finally, Solidarity succeeded because of timing. The initial Solidarity uprising in 1980 didn't succeed in the long term. While it did achieve some success and widespread support, it wasn't until 1989 that it was able to establish control over Poland and bring about all of the change it wanted. This came at the right time, as by 1989 Gorbachev had allowed eastern Europe greater freedom, meaning there was more freedom and opportunity for movements such as Solidarity. Before then, as events in Prague and Hungary had shown, the Soviet Union was too repressive.

What was the role of Gorbachev in the decline of Soviet influence in eastern Europe?

What was the state of the Soviet Union in 1985 when Gorbachev became leader?

- The controlling of other countries was outdated. The Soviet Union could no longer afford the cost of maintaining a military presence in European satellite states.

- The economy was very weak as too much money was being spent on the arms race and an unwinnable war in Afghanistan. The economy was still run in the same way as at the time of Stalin. Factories produced cheap, poor-quality goods. Food was in short supply.

- The standard of living was low compared to that in the west.

- There was much corruption in the government.

- Soviet rule was unpopular across eastern Europe—as dissatisfaction grew it became harder to keep control.

The role of Gorbachev

Gorbachev introduced two key policies.

One was glasnost (openness)—the freedom of expression with more freedom for the media, allowing news of government corruption and the criticism of government officials. Citizens became aware of some of Russia's past, with details about Stalin's brutal excesses being revealed.

The other was perestroika (restructuring). This aimed to make the Soviet economy more modern and efficient. It included:

- encouraging private ownership of Soviet industry and agriculture

- reducing state control over imports and exports

- allowing trade with non-eastern bloc countries

- allowing foreign investments in Russian businesses

- an increase in the production of, and trade in, consumer goods.

Crucially, Gorbachev realised that eastern Europe must be allowed to choose its own destiny. He made it clear he would not stand in the way of attempts at democracy in Warsaw Pact countries, and unlike in the past, troops would not be used to keep countries tied to the Soviet Union. He abandoned the Brezhnev Doctrine, making moves to establish a more friendly relationship with the west. Arms reduction treaties were signed with the United States.

Key fact

Mikhail Gorbachev was the eighth and last leader of the Soviet Union. He believed that the Soviet Union was in urgent need of modernisation and that the people of eastern Europe should be allowed self-determination.

Recap

Compared to other Soviet leaders, such as Brezhnev, Gorbachev held a reformist attitude. The two policies of glasnost and perestroika were central to this.

Apply

List the main things Gorbachev did that changed eastern Europe. Explain the results of each action.

The table below summarises the role of other factors.

Factor	Explanation
The war in Afghanistan	The war badly overstretched the Soviet economy and demoralised the military. Soviet actions were condemned by other countries who applied pressure for the Soviets to withdraw. The cost was significant, as was the loss of 10 000 Soviet soldiers. Even more important was the impact of the war on the Muslim world.
The role of the United States	US President Reagan sought to end the Cold War. The Soviet Union found it could not compete with the United States in the arms race and so had to use diplomacy to secure peace. Additionally, its outdated industry was causing environmental problems, such as the explosion at the Chernobyl nuclear power plant in 1986. Reagan and Gorbachev signed treaties to limit nuclear weapons.
The role of other countries	Between the spring of 1989 and the spring of 1991 every communist or former communist eastern European country held democratic parliamentary elections. Many people in eastern Europe were suffering from poverty. They were affected by food shortages, crime, and alcoholism. Gorbachev was unable to shield the public from the fact that eastern bloc countries were much poorer than the majority of people in the capitalist west.

Review

1. Describe the Hungarian revolution of 1956. [4]

2. Why did Berlin remain a focus of Cold War tensions during 1960–62? [6]

3. Why was Solidarity a threat to Soviet control? [6]

4. Why did the Polish government agree to Solidarity's demands in 1980? [6]

5. How significant was the part played by Solidarity in the loss of Soviet control in eastern Europe? [10]

6. How do the events in Hungary in 1956 and in Czechoslovakia in 1968 compare? [10]

7. How did Gorbachev change eastern Europe? [10]

8. How did the Soviet Union react to opposition to their rule in Hungary and Czechoslovakia? [10]

For further information, review this section in the Student Book.

Raise your grade ↑

1. What was the Prague Spring? (4 marks)

The Prague Spring was an attempt by the people to gain some control over their own lives and reform the communist system. That meant keeping the socialist model of government but creating a fairer system to ensure greater freedoms for the people and fewer restrictions imposed by Soviet control. This lasted for four months until it was crushed by the Soviet Red Army.

This is a good answer that defines what the protestors wanted to achieve, as well as providing some detail over the ultimate outcome. There is a lack of detail though—the student should state when the revolt took place, in which country, or who led it. 2 marks awarded.

Plan your answer

- The answer should include two explained points that refer to the question.
- Contextual knowledge is important—add details to explain a little about the uprising.
- The Prague Spring took place in 1968 in Czechoslovakia and the answer should place the uprising in this context.
- Alexander Dubc̆ek introduced the idea of the Prague Spring in an attempt to push for "socialism with a human face".
- It is important to note that the uprising wasn't against the Czech government, it was in response to the control imposed over the country by the Soviet Union.

Mark scheme

> 1 mark for each relevant point, 1 additional mark for supporting detail; maximum 2 marks per point made.

2. Why was the Soviet Union worried about events in Czechoslovakia in 1968? (6 marks)

Soviet leaders were worried about events in Czechoslovakia in 1968 as they seemed similar to the uprising in Hungary, which had resulted in the need for Soviet action and the deaths of thousands of anti-communist protestors. Any similar event would mean more loss of life and would add to the view that the Soviet Union was very oppressive.

Leaders in Moscow were also worried that if Czechoslovakia pushed for reform, other eastern European countries would do the same. There might be widespread rebellion against Moscow's leadership of the eastern bloc, weakening Moscow's power and influence over these states.

This is a good example of how it is possible to obtain full marks without writing a long answer. The student makes two well-developed points, focused on the fear of the spread of reformist ideas and also the need to avoid a similar event to that which occurred during the Prague Spring. 6 marks awarded.

Plan your answer

- In the answer aim to explain two reasons why the Soviet Union was worried, giving enough supporting detail for a full explanation.
- The Soviet Union was very suspicious and fearful that any uprising would spread and lead to a split in its control in other countries.
- The support that the attempted reforms had was widespread and potentially difficult to stop.
- Events in Hungary, where the Soviet Union had suppressed another uprising, had made the Soviet Union look oppressive and it was keen to avoid another similar issue.

Mark scheme

Level 1:	general answer lacking specific contextual knowledge (1 mark)
Level 2:	identifies AND/OR describes reasons (2–3 marks)
Level 3:	explains ONE reason (4–5 marks)
Level 4:	explains TWO reasons (6 marks)

3. How far was Gorbachev personally responsible for the collapse of Soviet influence over eastern Europe? (10 marks)

Gorbachev was responsible for the collapse of the Soviet empire to some extent. In 1985 when he came to power, he realised that the Soviet economy was devastated and facing many problems, with communism making the situation much worse. Gorbachev realised that reforms were needed to stabilise the economy. He also realised that the controlling of other countries was outdated. The Soviet Union could no longer afford the cost of maintaining a military presence in other states, particularly those who wanted reform.

Gorbachev introduced two key policies—glasnost and perestroika. Glasnost meant that freedom of expression was allowed, with more freedom for the media, allowing reports of government corruption and the criticism of government officials. Perestroika reformed the economy, encouraging private ownership of Soviet industry and agriculture, reducing state control over imports and exports, and leading to an increase in the production of and trade in consumer goods. Gorbachev was also responsible because he implemented an end to the Brezhnev Doctrine in the satellite states and Russia. This broke the bond of union and ended the enforcement of communism.

The student clearly understands the role of Gorbachev in the collapse of Soviet control and makes good points about glasnost, perestroika, and the end of the Brezhnev Doctrine. However, the answer is too one-sided. It needs to explore the wider issues that didn't involve Gorbachev. The role of the United States, the war in Afghanistan, and populist movements such as Solidarity are all factors. 5 marks awarded.

Plan your answer

- In the answer, consider the role of Gorbachev and his actions in bringing change in eastern Europe. As well as this, compare Gorbachev's involvement to other factors that led to reform in eastern Europe.

- Gorbachev's rule in the Soviet Union led to dramatic change and saw the end of Soviet influence across many countries in Europe.

- His openness to reform, and key policies such as glasnost and perestroika, meant that the tight restrictions of communism were lifted and the economy took on more capitalist elements.

- Crucially, Gorbachev believed that eastern Europe should be allowed to choose its own destiny and had no wish to keep countries that were dissatisfied as part of the Soviet Union.

- However, other factors are important. US President Reagan was also key in pushing for an end to the Cold War, and external events such as the war in Afghanistan further strained the Soviet Union's resources and ability to keep control in eastern Europe.

Mark scheme

Level 1:	general answer lacking specific contextual knowledge (1 mark)
Level 2:	identifies AND/OR describes reasons (2–3 marks)
Level 3:	gives a one-sided explanation (4–5 marks) or one explanation of both sides (4–6 marks)
Level 4:	explains both sides (7–9 marks)
Level 5:	explains with evaluation (10 marks)

You need to know

- Why there was stalemate on the Western Front
- The significance of the Battles of Mons, Marne, and Ypres, and the race to the sea
- What trench warfare was like
- The importance of new developments such as tanks, machine guns, aircraft, and gas
- The role of soliders from the British Empire on the Western Front
- The significance of the Battles of Verdun and the Somme
- Whether it was a "world war"
- The significance of the war at sea and the Battle of Jutland
- Why the Gallipoli campaign of 1915 failed
- Why Russia left the war in 1918
- The role of Japan, India, and South Africa, and the Arab revolt
- The impact of war on the home front
- Why the German offensive in 1918 was unsuccessful
- The end of the war, including events in Germany
- Why Germany asked for an armistice in 1918
- Why the armistice was signed

Background: Events immediately before the First World War

On 28 July 1914, Austria declared war on Serbia. Two days later, despite warnings from Germany, Russia began the mobilisation of its armed forces. On 1 August, Germany declared war on Russia and then, on 3 August, on France. The following day the Schlieffen Plan was put into operation and Germany invaded Belgium. This action brought Britain into conflict with Germany. The First World War had started.

Why was the war not over by December 1914?

How was the Schlieffen Plan intended to work?

The Schlieffen Plan was originally designed to prevent Germany having to fight a prolonged war on two fronts. By dealing with the French threat in the west within six weeks, Germany would then be able to turn east to fight Russia. The German General Staff believed it would take Russia ten weeks to mobilise its forces. Moving the army through neutral Belgium, Germany planned to avoid the heavily defended Franco-German frontier and did not expect to encounter much resistance from the Belgians.

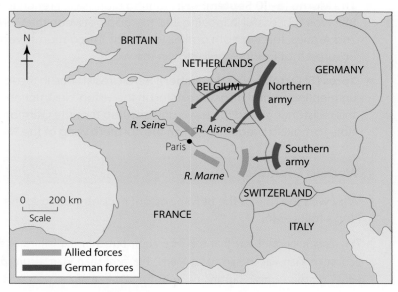

Fig. 7.1 *The Schlieffen Plan*

Worked Example

What did Germany hope to achieve through its use of the Schlieffen Plan? (4)

The plan aimed to defeat France without the need to occupy the whole country: the plan assumed that the capture of Paris would lead to the surrender of France.

Germany also hoped to avoid fighting a war on two fronts, against France in the west and Russia in the east. This was because France and Russia were part of a rival alliance against Germany when the plan was written in 1905. The plan enabled Germany to defeat France first, before turning east to fight Russia who, it was believed, would take a lot longer to mobilise troops.

Exam tip

To answer this question, you need to give two examples of what Germany hoped to achieve, supported by relevant factual detail.

Recap

The success of the Schlieffen Plan depended upon several important assumptions proving to be correct.

In practice, the plan did not proceed as von Schlieffen had envisaged.

- In 1906, von Schlieffen's successor as Chief of Staff, von Moltke, revised the plan to avoid going through the Netherlands.

- Von Moltke also weakened the German right flank to strengthen Germany's border with France.

- The many assumptions von Schlieffen had made about the operation of the plan did not come true.

Apply

List the important assumptions that were made about the successful operation of the Schlieffen Plan, but did not come true.

How successful was the British Expeditionary Force (BEF)?

Dismissed by Kaiser Wilhelm II as "General French's contemptible little army", the **British Expeditionary Force (BEF)** played a vital role in holding up the German advance in 1914. The BEF played a significant role in the following battles.

- **Mons (23 August):** Outnumbered almost 2:1 by the German 1st Army, the BEF held out for over six hours before being forced to retreat. Although the BEF was not able to halt the German advance, its rear-guard action crucially delayed German progress towards Paris by a day, giving more time for the French to organise their defences.

- **Le Cateau (26 August):** The retreat from Mons continued at Le Cateau where the BEF put up a brave defence of its position. However, once again overwhelmed, the BEF suffered 7000 casualties and was forced to retreat towards the French position on the Marne.

- **The Marne (6–10 September):** Fighting alongside French troops, the BEF was successful in moving into the gap between the German 1st and 2nd Armies, forcing both armies to retreat. This action saved Paris and ensured that France could stay in the war.

- **Ypres (19 October–30 November):** Heroic resistance in the face of unrelenting frontal attacks resulted in the virtual destruction of the BEF, but this resistance saved the town and ensured that the Germans were not able to make a breakthrough on the northern wing of the Western Front.

Key term

The British Expeditionary Force (BEF)—the British Army sent to fight in the Low Countries alongside France against Germany prior to the First Battle of Ypres on 22 November 1914. Unlike the conscripted forces of Germany and France, the BEF consisted of volunteer troops, who were renowned for their shooting skills.

Worked Example

Why was the role of the BEF important in contributing to the Schlieffen Plan's failure? (6)

The most important way that the BEF contributed to the failure of the Schlieffen Plan was in its role at Mons. The Schlieffen Plan assumed that Britain would remain neutral, but the delay to the advance of German troops through

Exam tip

To answer this causal question you need to provide two fully explained reasons. Remember to provide precise examples to support the points you make.

Belgium was compounded by the intervention of the British. The quality of the BEF's shooting inflicted heavy casualties on the Germans and delayed their advance by at least a day.

The BEF also contributed to the plan's failure by fighting alongside the French at the Marne in early September. The German advance had started to slow by the time its troops reached the Marne, and the French and British action at the Marne brought an end to the Schlieffen Plan and forced the Germans to retreat.

Why did both sides introduce trenches?

By the middle of September 1914 both sides had started to dig shallow trenches as defensive positions. By the end of the year, a complex network of trenches had emerged, stretching from the Belgian coast to the Swiss frontier. The inability of either side to achieve a breakthrough or outflank the enemy meant that both armies were forced to dig trenches to protect their soldiers from enemy machine gun and artillery fire.

Worked Example

"The failure of the Schlieffen Plan was the main reason why both sides introduced trenches on the Western Front." How far do you agree with this statement? Explain your answer. (10)

On the one hand, this statement is correct. After the Battle of the Marne, von Falkenhayn ordered his troops to dig trenches in order to provide protection from enemy artillery, but also to ensure that his forces did not lose the land that they had gained in France and Belgium since the start of the war. He had assumed that the war would be a war of movement and the Schlieffen Plan would be successful. However, the Belgian defence, along with British and French involvement, brought the German advance to a standstill by the end of September 1914.

The failure of the Schlieffen Plan was also a significant reason for the introduction of trenches as it meant that the war was now unlikely to be a short one and both sides needed to prepare strong enough defensive positions to resist an attack from their enemy and from which to launch attacks themselves.

The failure of either side to outflank the other in the **race to the sea** after the Schlieffen Plan had failed was also important in the introduction of trenches. The British defence of Ypres in November 1914 prevented the Germans gaining access to the French Channel ports, but meant that they were faced by the Germans on three sides at Ypres. Digging trenches therefore provided some protection from the enemy. Both sides were now facing each other from the Belgian coast down to the Swiss frontier without the opportunity to achieve a breakthrough in the winter of 1914.

However, both sides also introduced trenches because of developments in weapon technology. The development of machine gun technology—a typical machine gun could fire 11 rounds per second—meant that soldiers needed to dig trenches in order to protect themselves after an attack had broken down.

Overall, the failure of the Schlieffen Plan was the most important reason why both sides introduced trenches because if the plan had succeeded then France would likely have fallen and the war would have been a short one.

Key term

Race to the sea—the attempt by both sides to capture the Channel ports and outflank each other from the middle of September until the middle of October 1914.

Exam tip

The answer should provide a balanced response, ideally providing two arguments for each side and a conclusion evaluating how far you agree with the statement.

Fig. 7.2 *Soldiers in a First World War trench*

The emergence of deadlock on the Western Front

Trench warfare

The nature of a soldier's routine would depend upon which part of the Western Front he found himself on and the level of fighting at any given time. Typically, he would follow a cycle of time on the front line, followed by time in close support trenches, then in reserve, followed by a short break.

The daily routine would invariably begin with the "stand to" when soldiers were woken by an officer, quickly followed by the "**morning hate**". After breakfast, there would be kit inspections and daily chores, with time for sleep and personal duties, such as writing letters home, allowed once the chores were done. As dusk approached, the trench systems teemed with activity with trench repairs, patrols into no man's land, supply missions to the rear, and relief of front line units taking place at night.

Soldiers faced many hazards in the trenches.

- **Artillery:** Shelling and mortar fire became increasingly important as methods for smashing enemy trenches after the end of the war of movement. Artillery fire caused most of the casualties, and it has been estimated that approximately 10 million tons of shells were fired during the course of the war.

- **Snipers:** Raising one's head above the parapet for even a second could mean death, such was the quality of snipers on both sides. Many snipers kept tallies of how many men they had killed, particularly how many officers.

- **Raids:** Trench raids were tactics intended to gain intelligence on the enemy's position and to capture or kill enemy prisoners.

> **Key term**
>
> **Morning hate**—all sides in the First World War would attempt to prevent a surprise dawn raid by firing rifles and throwing grenades in the direction of the enemy; this was frequently repeated at dusk.

- **Rats:** Apart from the enemy, rats were the biggest source of fear for soldiers in the trenches. Feeding off remains of food and even human corpses, they could be as big as cats and carried infectious diseases.

- **Lice:** These bred rapidly and were often found in the seams of soldiers' clothing. Even when soldiers washed, lice were very hard to shift.

- **Trench fever:** This was an especially unpleasant and contagious disease. The main symptoms were high fever, headaches, aching muscles, and sores. Treatment often involved 12 weeks away from the trenches. By 1918 it was established that having body lice was the main cause of trench fever.

- **Trench foot:** A fungal infection that could lead to gangrene, this was caused by cold and wet conditions. Severe cases could result in amputation.

How important were new developments such as tanks, machine guns, aircraft, and gas?

Machine guns: By 1914 machine-gun technology allowed gunners to fire around 500 rounds per minute and up to 2700 metres in range which, coupled with the use of **enfilade** tactics, allowed defenders to create virtually impenetrable "force fields" of fire. Specialist gunners contributed to attacks across no man's land by concentrating fire over their own men's heads.

Gas: The first gas attack was launched on the Eastern Front in January 1915. Within four months, both sides were using this new method of warfare on the Western Front. Different types of gas were used, the first being an early form of tear gas, followed by chlorine, phosgene, and **mustard gas**.

Aircraft: Aircraft played several important roles during the conflict, evolving from a reconnaissance function in the early stages to operating as fighter and bomber aircraft as the war developed.

Tanks: First used by the British at Flers in September 1916, tanks were initially slow, mechanically unpredictable, and unsuited to trench warfare. When allied to better tactics they could be highly effective weapons, but they still did not prove to be the war-winning weapon Britain and France had hoped for.

> ### Key terms
>
> **Enfilade fire**—First World War tactic of firing across the longest line of soldiers to create a "beaten zone" of fire which would entrap enemy troops as they attempted to progress forward.
>
> **Mustard gas**—chemical weapon used by the Germans for the first time at Ypres in 1917, its sulphuric compound created blisters, burning the eyes, skin, and lungs.

Empire and the Western Front

The role of soldiers from the British Empire on the Western Front during the First World War was significant and played a crucial part in the overall Allied effort. The British Empire, at that time, was a vast imperial power, and its contributions to the war were not limited to just the British Isles. Troops from the British Empire, including those from Britain, Canada, Australia, New Zealand, India, and other colonies, constituted a substantial portion of the Allied forces on the Western Front. The sheer number of soldiers from the empire played a vital role in sustaining the front lines and engaging in large-scale battles.

The Battle of the Somme is one of the most notable examples of the British Empire's involvement. Troops from the United Kingdom, Canada, Australia, and other dominions participated in this massive offensive. The battle aimed to relieve pressure on the French forces at Verdun, but also became emblematic of the trench warfare and hardships faced on the Western Front.

The contributions of British Empire forces were also strategically important in holding key sectors of the Western Front. For example, the Canadian Corps gained a reputation for its effectiveness and bravery in various battles, such as Vimy Ridge in 1917. Furthermore, troops from India made up half of the attacking forces at the Battle of Neuve Chappelle in 1915.

Worked Example

What problems did many soldiers face when living in trenches on the Western Front? (4)

Serious injury or death were constant threats on the front line. Snipers, shelling, and mortars, as well as the dangers posed by enemy raiding parties, all contributed to the risks faced by soldiers in trenches.

Living conditions were also poor and created further problems for soldiers. The numerous rats, which could eat rations as well as spread disease, along with the risk of trench foot caused by prolonged exposure to damp conditions, and the risk of catching trench fever from lice, made life a misery for men in the trenches.

Exam tip

You should not attempt to include a long list of problems in the answer to this short, descriptive question. Instead, focus on two main problems and include relevant supporting details.

Verdun and the Somme?

By early 1916 German and British commanders were keen to achieve a breakthrough that would bring the war to a swift end.

Verdun (February–December 1916)

At the end of 1915 German Chief of General Staff Erich von Falkenhayn proposed a new strategy for ending the war: eliminate France from the war, which would lead Britain to seek peace, deprived of its ally on the Western Front. He therefore settled on a prolonged attritional attack on the historic town of Verdun, which he believed France would attempt to defend at all costs. In the process, France would sustain unbearable losses, leading to its withdrawal from the war.

The Verdun Offensive lasted from February to December 1916 and was the longest offensive of the entire war. Each side suffered approximately 350 000 casualties during the battle, which ultimately failed to remove France from the war.

Recap

The failure of the Verdun campaign was attributable to several factors, not least the determination of the French despite huge casualties.

The Somme (July–November 1916)

The Allies were also developing their own plans to win the war at the end of 1915. Britain agreed to take greater responsibility for the fighting on the Western Front, and Field Marshal Haig agreed a plan with the French to launch a joint offensive on the Somme in the summer of 1916. Haig's plan was to batter the German lines across a 20-mile front with a week-long artillery barrage, creating holes in the lines. His infantry and cavalry could then rush through the damaged lines and fan out into open country.

Haig's plan appeared, in the short term, to have failed spectacularly: 20 000 British soldiers died on the first day, 1 July, with nearly 70 000 dying during the entire offensive. Although some troops made gains on the first day, by mid-November the front line had only shifted 10 kilometres.

Some historians, however, view the Somme Offensive in a different light and suggest that it was vital in helping relieve the pressure on Verdun. They point out that the Germans suffered such heavy casualties on the Somme that they realised they would not be able to win the war on the Western Front. They therefore decided to retreat to a shorter, easier-to-defend line (the Hindenburg Line) in February 1917, and switched their offensive strategy away from the Western Front and towards a campaign of **unrestricted submarine warfare**.

Key term

Unrestricted submarine warfare—a German naval strategy in the First World War which declared the waters around Great Britain to be a war zone; all shipping in that zone could be targeted, without warning.

Worked Example

Why did the Somme Offensive fail to achieve its objectives? (6)

The main reason why the Somme Offensive failed to achieve its objectives was that the preparations for the attack were not good enough. Although there was a week-long bombardment immediately prior to the men going over the top, a quarter of the shells did not explode. Those that did explode failed to destroy the German barbed wire as they had been expected to. This meant that the German defences were not as badly damaged as Haig had hoped they would be.

The week-long bombardment gave the enemy advance notice that an attack was imminent, and as soon as it stopped the German soldiers were able to get to their machine guns before the British and French started to move. This contributed to another key reason why the attack failed: the sheer loss of men throughout the campaign. On the first day Britain suffered nearly 20 000 fatalities, and lost nearly 70 000 men in total during the Somme Offensive.

Exam tip

It might be tempting to respond to this question by disputing the assumption behind it—that the Somme Offensive was a failure—but that would be a mistake. Remember to focus on what the question is asking, and give two explained reasons why the Somme Offensive failed.

How important were other fronts?

East African Campaign: Indian troops, primarily from British India, played a crucial role in the East African Campaign against German forces. Indian Expeditionary Forces participated in operations in German East Africa, providing essential manpower for the Allies. They engaged in battles against German colonial forces led by General Paul von Lettow-Vorbeck. Indian soldiers demonstrated resilience and adaptability in the challenging terrain of East Africa.

South West Africa: South African forces played a significant role in the campaign to capture German South West Africa (now Namibia) from German colonial forces. The campaign, which began in 1914, resulted in the occupation of the German territory by South African forces under General Louis Botha.

The Arab Revolt: Arab forces, led by figures like Sharif Hussein bin Ali and his sons, rebelled against the Ottoman Empire, which was aligned with the Central Powers. The Arabs sought independence and were promised support by the Allied powers, particularly the British, in exchange for their assistance against the Ottoman Empire. The revolt had strategic importance, diverting Ottoman forces and contributing to the weakening of their military.

The role of Japan in the Allied victory

Japan was one of the Allied powers during the war, and it mainly focused on naval activities in the Pacific and on protecting its interests in East Asia. In line with its treaty obligations with Britain, Japan declared war on Germany in 1914. Japanese forces quickly moved to seize German-controlled territories in East Asia and the Pacific. This included the capture of German possessions in China and the Pacific Islands.

One of the most significant contributions was the Japanese capture of the German-controlled port of Tsingtao (Qingdao) in Shandong Province, China, in November 1914. This action eliminated a key German naval base and allowed Japan to extend its influence in the region. The Imperial Japanese Navy played a crucial role in securing sea lanes in the Pacific and Indian Oceans. Japanese warships were involved in patrolling and protecting Allied shipping routes, which contributed to the overall success of the Allied naval efforts.

Japan contributed naval vessels to the British Royal Navy and the French Navy. Japanese warships, especially destroyers, operated in the Mediterranean and the Indian Ocean to counter the threat posed by German and Austro-Hungarian submarines.

The war at sea

In the years 1914–16 the primary naval objective of Britain and Germany was to gain control of the North Sea. This culminated in the Battle of Jutland, 31 May–1 June 1916. The extent to which Jutland proved to be a British victory is a hotly debated topic.

The case for a British victory	The case for a British defeat
The German High Seas Fleet never risked a major naval battle again.	More British ships (14) than German ships (11) were sunk.
Britain kept control of the North Sea.	There were more British casualties (6784) than German casualties (3058).
Britain was able to maintain its blockade of the German coast.	

Apply

Write a list of bullet points to answer this question: To what extent was the Battle of Jutland a success for Germany?

Arguably, the main naval contribution to the Allied victory was through the British blockade of the German coast. This had a devastating effect on imports, creating unsustainable pressure on Germany's ability to feed its population or provide sufficient raw materials to service its war needs.

Germany attempted to carry out its own blockade of the British coast through the use of submarines; in particular, with its campaigns of unrestricted submarine warfare in 1915 and 1917. To cope with the significant threat this posed to its own ability to feed its population, Britain used a variety of tactics to tackle the U-boat threat.

- **Q ships:** Heavily armed, converted merchant ships were deployed.

- **Convoy system:** Battleships escorted packs of merchant ships across the Atlantic, providing protection and the ability to sink U-boats.

- **Mines:** Thousands of anti-submarine mines were placed across the North Sea.

- **Sonar:** Sound waves helped to detect submarines under the water.

The Dardanelles adventure, 1915

With stalemate established on the Western Front, First Lord of the Admiralty Winston Churchill devised an ambitious plan to win the war by defeating Turkey and coming to the aid of Britain's ally, Russia. The campaign resulted in over 140 000 Allied casualties and a humiliating withdrawal from the Turkish peninsula. Several explanations for the campaign's failure have been put forward.

- **The plan was flawed from the start:** Churchill, Kitchener, and Hamilton have all been criticised for their roles in devising a beach-landing plan and having poor understanding of the terrain and Turkish defences.

- **Conditions at Gallipoli:** Because most of the Turkish defences were on hills overlooking Allied positions, the chances of progress were slim. In addition, extreme heat, flies, and dysentery hindered the campaign.

- **The trench system:** With little progress moving off the beaches and towards the Turkish lines, a complicated network of trenches quickly emerged, creating the type of stalemate the Allied forces were trying to break out of on the Western Front.

- **Turkish defences:** At the start of the war, Liman von Sanders helped construct Turkish defences. After the failure of the British naval assault in March 1915 he reinforced the defences along the Gallipoli coast, using natural defences along with existing fortifications.

Why did Russia leave the war in 1918?

On the Eastern Front, Russia's war started better than expected, with a rapid mobilisation and advance into eastern Germany. However, following defeats at Tannenberg and the Masurian Lakes in the first two months of the war, the Russians were steadily pushed back, and continued to suffer defeats against the German army throughout 1915.

Although the Russians experienced some successes against the Austrians, for example in the Brusilov Offensive in summer 1916, the devastating impact of war contributed to the downfall of Tsar Nicholas II in February 1917, and ultimately to the rise to power of the Bolsheviks in October 1917. In March 1918 Russia negotiated the Treaty of Brest-Litovsk with Germany, which resulted in Russia withdrawing from the war.

These are the main reasons why Russia had to withdraw from the war:

- Russian forces were not strong enough to defeat the German military. They were badly led by the Tsar and his senior officers.

- Ordinary Russian soldiers lacked motivation. They were fighting in a war as a result of treaty obligations. This unwillingness led to several mutinies and mass desertions.

- Political events in Russia resulted in a new government led by the Bolsheviks, who had no intention of continuing the war against Germany.

- Russian forces lacked essential supplies, including food and weapons.

> ### Key fact
>
> The Bolshevik Party consisted of communists led by Lenin. After the fall of the Tsar, Lenin returned from exile and committed the Bolsheviks to opposing the ruling Provisional Government and refusing continued participation in the war.

> ### Worked Example
>
> How important was the role of Nicholas II in contributing to Russia's defeat in the First World War? (40)
>
> Arguments that Nicholas II was important in contributing to Russia's defeat in the First World War include:
>
> - the poor commanders he had appointed to lead the Russian army when the war started
> - his move to Commander-in-Chief in August 1915
> - his rejection of support from the Duma.
>
> Arguments that other reasons were more important in contributing to Russia's defeat in the war include:
>
> - lack of equipment in 1914–15, especially rifles and shells
> - deteriorating support for the war from the Russian people
> - the Bolshevik seizure of power.

> ### Exam tip
>
> This is an example of a Paper 4 question: in one hour you are expected to answer one question. To score highly you must provide a focused, balanced, and well-argued response.
>
> This worked example suggests arguments that could be used to answer this question—but note that, in addition, a conclusion is required. The conclusion needs to make a clear judgement, evaluating the relative importance of the main reasons given.

War on the home front

Civil liberties: The outbreak of war brought many restrictions to the lives of civilians. The British government introduced the Defence of the Realm Act (DORA). The United States also passed major legislation to ensure that the war effort was not threatened. Measures passed included making it illegal to release classified information or to interfere with the recruitment of troops.

Conscription: Each of the major combatants introduced conscription, although Britain relied on a volunteer army until 1916. Some men refused to be conscripted and were known as conscientious objectors.

Food shortages: Most combatant nations suffered from food shortages. Common causes were a loss of farm workers to the military and blockades. Britain was vulnerable to blockade, with the German campaign of unrestricted submarine warfare having a devastating effect on the import of essential food.

Germany's civilians suffered similarly as a result of the Royal Navy blockade. Food shortages in Russia were mainly caused by the poor quality of the railway network and the backward agricultural system.

France was less affected by food shortages as it was able to feed its population from agricultural land unaffected by the war. The United States was also self-sufficient and able to provide essential supplies for its allies.

Rationing of food was introduced in both Britain and Germany.

Employment of women: Britain created the Women's Land Army in 1915. Another area where opportunities for women increased was within the industrial workforce, often in munitions factories. In Britain women accounted for 37 per cent of the workforce by 1918.

Civilian deaths: It is thought around 940 000 civilians lost their lives as a result of military action. Almost 6 million died from disease, malnutrition, and accidents.

> **Key fact**
>
> "Ersatz goods" were introduced by Germany to help to deal with food shortages caused by the Royal Navy blockade. Ersatz goods were substitute goods; for example, acorns and beechnuts were used as a coffee substitute.

> **Worked Example**
>
> How important was the role of women in assisting the war effort in Britain during the First World War? (40)
>
> Arguments that the role of women was important in assisting the war effort in Britain are as follows:
>
> - The Suffrage movement, including the WSPU, abandoned the campaign for the vote and devoted themselves to winning the war.
> - The Women's Land Army was essential in helping with food production.
> - Women played a role in the recruitment campaign.
>
> Arguments that the role of women was not that important in assisting the war effort in Britain include the following:
>
> - Rationing (voluntary and compulsory) was the important factor in ensuring that demands for food were met.
> - The increase of the role of women was simply part of a wider sense of patriotism that was present.

> **Exam tip**
>
> This is another Paper 4 question. As with the previous example, a range of possible arguments that could be used to answer the question are provided.

The end of the war

The United States enters the war

The United States entered the war in April 1917 as a result of Germany resuming its campaign of unrestricted submarine warfare and because of the publication of a telegram that was intercepted by the British. This telegram was sent by the German Foreign Minister to the German Ambassador to Mexico and offered United States territory to Mexico in return for joining the war on Germany's side.

Initially, the United States was not prepared for war and American troops were slow to arrive. When they did arrive, the first ones were short of uniforms and equipment.

> **Recap**
>
> In Britain, rationing was introduced gradually.
>
> - Voluntary rationing was introduced in February 1917.
> - Compulsory rationing was introduced in stages between December 1917 and February 1918.
> - Ration books were introduced in July 1918 for butter, margarine, lard, meat, and sugar.

Destroyers and merchant ships were sent to increase anti-submarine capabilities. Additional support aided the destruction of mines in the North Sea.

American forces reached France in small numbers. By March 1918 there were 300 000 American soldiers in France; by July, a further 800 000 were in position. These soldiers provided valuable support in combating the German offensives of June and July.

The arrival of the Americans provided a tremendous morale boost following the disasters of 1917 when the effects of the German unrestricted submarine campaign, the Battle of Passchendaele, and Russia's withdrawal from the war threatened victory.

Worked Example

What was the Zimmerman Telegram? (4)

The Zimmerman Telegram was a message the German Foreign Minister sent to the German Ambassador in Washington instructing him to offer Mexico the states of Arizona, New Mexico, and Texas if the Mexicans agreed to enter the war against the United States.

The message was intercepted by the British in January 1917, who presented and decoded it for the Americans. When it was published in newspapers, and the German minister admitted sending it, the American public was horrified. Already furious at the resumption of unrestricted submarine warfare, Americans increased calls for the United States to enter the war against Germany, which it did in April 1917.

Exam tip

There will be 1 mark awarded for each relevant point, with additional marks for supporting details. To achieve 4 marks you need to make two relevant points and explain each of them.

Fig. 7.3 *German soldiers training before Operation Michael*

The Ludendorff Offensive, March 1918

In January 1918 Germany's war prospects were not good. German troops were still fighting on the Eastern Front, the submarine campaign had failed to achieve its target, and recruits for the army were drying up. Furthermore, the United States was expected to send large numbers of fighting men to the Western Front.

On 21 March 1918 Germany launched **Operation Michael**, conceived by General Ludendorff. The offensive was initially a success: German forces, including many transferred from the Eastern Front, broke through the Allied lines and advanced 56 kilometres in the first three weeks. The German army was now 8 kilometres from Paris.

This German push was stopped by an Allied counter-offensive, but at great cost. Britain suffered 178 000 casualties and France 77 000. German casualties numbered over 1 million during the offensives of 1918.

German troops of 1918 were not as good as those of 1914. Their discipline was poor and they were badly fed and supplied. Crucially, they did not have reserves to call upon. The numerical advantage of the well-equipped Allies was beginning to make an impact and between May and August the Germans made no further progress.

The failure of Ludendorff's plan can be firmly placed within the reasons for its initial success. By breaking out from the heavily fortified Hindenburg Line, the Germans changed the war from one of attrition into one of movement.

This transformation played into the hands of the Allies who had more tanks, men, and aircraft than Germany. On 8 August, the Allies launched a counter-attack along the Western Front and by late September, they had reached the Hindenburg Line. September saw the Germans in full retreat.

A serious influenza epidemic within the German army left only two of its 13 divisions fit for action, and by the end of September it had become a question of when, rather than if, Germany would surrender.

Key term

Operation Michael—a German offensive launched in 1918 to push troops into France; also referred to as the Ludendorff Offensive or Spring Offensive.

Apply

Write a short fact file stating when and where the Hindenburg Line was created and what its purpose was.

The 1918 German Revolution

The war effort	Generals Hindenburg and Ludendorff began to interfere in domestic affairs under the pretext of directing the country's war effort. At the same time, the Reichstag started to question the war effort.
	The long-term cause of the German revolution was war weariness and by July 1917 the Reichstag was demanding peace.
New government	The first stage of the revolution in October 1918 occurred following the formation of a new government under the newly appointed Chancellor von Baden. He asked US President Wilson for an armistice. This was refused until Germany agreed to allow "true representatives of the German people" to negotiate.
	On 26 November the Kaiser introduced the October reforms that transferred power to the Reichstag.
Mutiny	The second stage was triggered by the mutiny of sailors at the naval bases of Kiel and Wilhelmshaven.
Riots	Riots broke out across Germany and the Kaiser abdicated, fleeing to the Netherlands. Friedrich Ebert was appointed as the new Chancellor.

Why was the armistice signed?

- **To avoid a Russian-style revolution:** Revolutions were threatened across Germany and Ebert feared a Bolshevik (communist) revolution.

- **Conditions in Germany:** The blockade had brought terrible shortages of food, causing ill health.

- **To take advantage of Wilson's Fourteen Points.**

- **Fear of invasion:** On 28 September, Ludendorff and Hindenburg agreed that Germany had no choice but to surrender. Failure to do so would result in the destruction of the army and the invasion of Germany.

- **Morale:** By early November the morale of German forces was extremely low and the troops were in a state of permanent retreat.

- **The Central Powers were defeated:** Bulgaria called for an armistice following defeat at Monastir-Doiron. Turkey agreed a peace deal on 30 October and four days later Austria did the same.

Worked Example

Why did revolution break out in Germany in October and November 1918? (6)

The German revolution in October and November 1918 was caused firstly by war weariness. In July 1917 the Reichstag had passed a peace resolution calling for a peaceful end to the war, which was ignored by both the German government and the Allies. However, at the end of October 1918, sailors at Wilhelmshaven and Kiel mutinied in protest at plans to take the German fleet out to sea again. These protests spread across Germany as sailors' councils, or **soviets**, were set up.

The hardship caused by the war was also a key long-term cause of the revolution. The food shortages worsened by the Allied naval blockade resulted in average daily rations of 1000 calories in early 1917, while ersatz goods replaced many staples. For example, in the winter of 1917, the turnip replaced the potato as a staple in the German diet. In addition, the onset of influenza in 1918 caused over 400 000 fatalities among Germans who lacked the nutrition to survive the onslaught of the disease.

Exam tip

The key to success with this type of question is to provide two fully explained reasons. Remember to answer what is being asked of you: do not think that this is a question about the defeat of Germany in the war.

Key term

Soviet—a council made up of workers.

Review

1. Describe the role played by Belgium in the failure of the Schlieffen Plan. [4]

2. What new methods of technology were used to break the stalemate on the Western Front? [4]

3. What did Germany hope to achieve through the 1918 Spring Offensive? [4]

4. Describe the main features of the Treaty of Brest-Litovsk. [4]

5. Describe the main features of the 1914 Defence of the Realm Act. [4]

6. Why did the United States enter the war in 1917? [6]

7. Why did Russia withdraw from the war in 1918? [6]

8. Why was conscription introduced in Britain in 1916? [6]

9. Why did Britain introduce rationing in 1918? [6]

10. "The failure of the Gallipoli campaign was mostly due to poor leadership." How far do you agree with this statement? Explain your answer. [10]

11. "The weakness of Germany's allies was the decisive factor contributing to its decision to seek an armistice in 1918." How far do you agree with this statement? Explain your answer. [10]

12. How important in the defeat of the Central Powers was the entry of the United States into the war in 1917? [40]

For further information, review this section in the Student Book.

Raise your grade ↑

1. Why did the Schlieffen Plan fail to achieve its objectives? (6 marks)

The Schlieffen Plan failed to achieve its objectives for three main reasons.

First, Britain intervened in the war, which Germany did not expect.

Second, the French held the Germans up at the Marne, slowing the German timetable for success in the west.

Third, the Russians mobilised much quicker than German war planners had believed possible when the Schlieffen Plan was drawn up in 1905.

Three relevant reasons are provided in this answer. To develop the response, the student should instead offer two reasons that are much better developed and explained. 4 marks awarded.

Plan your answer

- The answer to a 6-mark causation question needs to include two well-supported reasons.

- There are several reasons why the Schlieffen Plan failed, but the answer could focus on two general areas of German mistakes in implementing the plan, such as weakening its right wing and opposition actions that contributed to its defeat, such as the intervention of the BEF at Mons.

Mark scheme

Level 1:	general answer lacking specific contextual knowledge (1 mark)
Level 2:	identifies AND/OR describes reasons (2–3 marks)
Level 3:	explains ONE reason (4–5 marks)
Level 4:	explains TWO reasons (6 marks)

2. "Haig deserves his reputation as butcher of the Somme." How far do you agree with this statement? Explain your answer. (10 marks)

General Haig was a very controversial officer in the First World War, and has been described as the butcher of the Somme because of the large number of soldiers who died in France between 1 July and mid-November. The Somme Offensive was intended to smash a hole in the French lines, leading to a cavalry and infantry charge through the German rear. It was also intended to relieve pressure on Verdun, which had been besieged by Germany since February.

The offensive was a complete failure, with Allied forces only managing to capture approximately 10 kilometres of land. It is estimated that 70 000 British soldiers lost their lives during the campaign, meaning that Haig does deserve his reputation as butcher of the Somme.

This question requires a candidate to analyse and evaluate, not to describe events. Unfortunately, this response is largely descriptive and does not attempt any meaningful

analysis. Instead, it should have presented an argument that Haig does deserve this reputation, perhaps referring to the number of casualties sustained in the face of continuing lack of success, but looking at the other side of the argument as well, pointing to the achievements of the Somme campaign. Finally, some kind of evaluative judgement is required. 3 marks awarded.

Plan your answer

- This question needs a balanced response: first, a range of arguments to support the statement, then a counter argument.

- Arguments to support the statement could include the number of casualties suffered during the Somme Offensive, Haig's tactics, and the length of the campaign.

- The counter argument could defend Haig's reputation and challenge the statement with points such as the Somme was ultimately a British victory and Haig was anxious to protect his untested new army.

- Remember to finish with a conclusion that gives a final judgement on the statement.

Mark scheme

Level 1:	general answer lacking specific contextual knowledge (1 mark)
Level 2:	identifies AND/OR describes reasons (2–3 marks)
Level 3:	gives a one-sided explanation or one explanation of both sides (4–6 marks)
Level 4:	explains both sides (7–9 marks)
Level 5:	explains with evaluation (10 marks)

3. How important was the role of technology in the defeat of Germany by 1918? **(40 marks)**

Technology did not play an important role in the defeat of Germany. Instead, the fact Germany had to fight a two-front war after the failure of the Schlieffen Plan was the most important reason why Germany lost the war. Fighting on two fronts meant that Germany always had to divide its forces between the west and the east, while also having to send troops onto the southern part of the Eastern Front to prop up Austria in the conflict with Russia. This was especially important in 1916 when von Falkenhayn was attempting to destroy the French at Verdun but was forced to send troops not only to defend the Somme once the Allied campaign had begun there, but also to Galicia to prevent Austria completely collapsing as a result of the Brusilov Offensive.

Another factor that contributed to the defeat of Germany was the British naval blockade, which had caused severe suffering in Germany by the end of 1918. One effect was that money became virtually worthless and Germans had to resort to bartering. As a result, the government found it difficult to pay suppliers for the war effort and many ordinary Germans found it difficult to buy essential items. Working-class Germans felt that wealthier Germans were able to survive because of the black market and food riots took place from 1916. The shortages caused by the blockade were blamed on the government and became a major cause of the revolution in October 1918, which led to the agreement to the armistice.

Technology did play a part, but only in an indirect fashion. For example, the development of Q ships and sonar helped defeat the U-boat threat in 1917, ensuring that Britain could continue in the war. Tanks were not effective until allied with appropriate tactics in 1918 when they were used with infantry to blaze a trail through enemy lines.

In conclusion, German defeat became virtually inevitable after the failure of the Schlieffen Plan in autumn 1914 as the war would now be fought on two fronts and the side with the greatest capacity of men and materials would be most likely to win.

This example of a Paper 4 question would require a lengthy response (the paper requires one question to be answered in an hour) featuring a strong analytical approach: each paragraph should explicitly answer the question, providing a clear reason for the defeat of Germany. The student should have started by explaining the role of technology, before introducing alternative explanations for Germany's defeat in 1918, so as to produce a balanced answer. Reasons should be fully explained and illustrated by relevant supporting details, with the answer culminating in a substantiated judgement and conclusion. A mark is not given here as this is only a small sample of the full answer.

Plan your answer

- As this is a 40-mark question, you are expected to display depth and range of knowledge and avoid producing something superficial and limited in scope.

- The best responses will provide a range of well-supported arguments, leading to a sustained conclusion.

- This question requires you to focus on the role of technology in the defeat of Germany, so you would have to relate the role of technology to wider factors that contributed to Germany's defeat. These could include the role of tanks in the combined approach used on the Western Front in the summer of 1918, or the development of sonar or Q ships to enable Allied shipping to survive and defeat the U-boat campaigns.

- You should also provide a counter argument that technology did not contribute much to the defeat of Germany, perhaps explaining the limitations of technology: the issues with tanks 1916–18 would be one good example to use.

- Other factors in the defeat of Germany should then be provided, with a final conclusion where you weigh up the relative importance of technology in Germany's defeat.

Mark scheme

Level 1 (1–8 marks)	• Demonstrates little relevant contextual knowledge.
	• Demonstrates limited ability to select and organise information.
	• Describes a few key features, reasons, results, and changes of societies, events, people, and situations relevant to the question.
	• Answer shows little understanding of the question.
Level 2 (9–16 marks)	• Demonstrates some, but limited, contextual knowledge.
	• Selects and organises some relevant information. This is only deployed relevantly on a few occasions.
	• Identifies and describes key features, reasons, results, and changes of the societies, events, people, and situations relevant to the question, but with little awareness of the broad context.
	• Attempts conclusions but these are asserted, undeveloped, and unsupported.
	• Presents a recognisable essay structure, but the question is only partially addressed.
Level 3 (17–24 marks)	• Demonstrates and selects relevant contextual knowledge and deploys it appropriately to support parts of the answer.
	• Selects and organises mostly relevant information, much of it deployed appropriately with a structured approach, either chronological or thematic.
	• Demonstrates some understanding of the key features, reasons, results, and changes of the societies, events, people, and situations relevant to the question with some awareness of the broad context.
	• Produces structured descriptions and explanations.
	• Points support conclusions although they are not always well substantiated.

Level 4 (25–32 marks)	• Deploys mostly relevant and accurate contextual knowledge to support parts of the answer.
	• Selects a range of relevant information which is generally well organised and deployed appropriately.
	• Demonstrates a reasonable understanding of the significance of the key features, reasons, results, and changes of societies, events, people, and situations relevant to the question with awareness of the broad context. Has some understanding of the interrelationships of the issues in the question.
	• Can produce developed, reasoned, and supported conclusions.
Level 5 (33–40 marks)	• Selects and deploys a range of relevant and accurate contextual knowledge to effectively support the answer.
	• Selects, organises, and deploys effectively and relevantly a wide range of information to support conclusions.
	• Demonstrates a good understanding of the key features, reasons, results, and changes of societies, events, people, and situations relevant to the question. Demonstrates an awareness of the importance of the broad context and of the interrelationships of the issues of the question.
	• Produces well-developed, well-reasoned, and well-supported conclusions.

8 Germany: From the end of World War One to the end of World War Two

You need to know

- To what extent the Weimar Republic was doomed from the start
- The impact of the Treaty of Versailles on the Weimar Republic, including domestic unrest
- To what extent the Republic recovered after 1923 under Stresemann
- The impact of the Great Depression on Germany and how it led to Hiter's rise to power
- Why Hitler was able to become Chancellor by 1933
- Why Hitler was able to dominate Germany by 1934
- How Hitler consolidated his power in 1933–34
- How effectively the Nazis controlled Germany, 1933–45
- What it was like to live in Nazi Germany
- How the Second World War changed life in Nazi Germany

Background: The formation of the Weimar Republic

The First World War was brought to an end by the signing of the armistice on 11 November 1918. Shortly before the signing, Kaiser Wilhelm II of Germany abdicated and a democratic government, the Weimar Republic, was set up. By removing the Kaiser, Germany hoped for a more lenient peace settlement. This didn't happen and the Weimar Republic was to last 14 years before Hitler's accession to power and the establishment of the Nazi dictatorship until 1945.

To what extent was the Weimar Republic doomed from the start?

What state was Germany in at the end of the First World War?

Ebert's priority when he became President in 1918 was to tackle the challenges faced by the new government. These included the following.

> **Key fact**
>
> The Weimar Republic and Ebert: Germany was declared a republic on the day the Kaiser abdicated. Ebert, leader of the Social Democrat Party (SDP), became the first President. His first task was to restore law and order but he faced a number of challenges.

> **Apply**
>
> Draw a timeline from 1918 to 1923 that shows the events that were Ebert's main challenges as President.

Anger at the Treaty of Versailles	The new government became immediately unpopular by signing the Treaty of Versailles in 1919. The government's members became known as the "November Criminals". Most Germans were furious that the government had accepted the terms of the Treaty of Versailles. They thought their treatment was too harsh, especially as most did not believe that Germany had lost the war.
The threat from the extreme left	The communists in Germany, known as Spartacists, wanted a revolution similar to the one that occurred in Russia in 1917. In January 1919, the left-wing activists led by Rosa Luxemburg and Karl Liebknecht seized power in Berlin. They were crushed by the Freikorps, who were ex-soldiers and bitter enemies of the communists.
The threat from the extreme right	In March 1920 Wolfgang Kapp, an extreme nationalist, together with some Freikorps units, seized power in Berlin. This was known as the Kapp Putsch. The nationalists wanted a strong government. The army refused to intervene. Kapp was not supported by the Berlin workers, who went on strike, refusing to cooperate. After four days Kapp and his supporters fled Berlin.
	In 1923 another right-wing attempt to seize power was led by Adolf Hitler and his growing NSDAP party. The Munich Putsch attempted to seize power and install a right-wing government. It was unsuccessful and put down by loyal troops. Hitler was arrested and imprisoned for two years.

A new constitution

As a republic, Germany needed a new constitution and its new governments were to be more democratically elected than ever before. The new system created a few issues for the Weimar Republic.

- Through proportional representation some extremist parties were represented in the Reichstag, giving them a voice and publicity.

- Proportional representation prevented overall control by one party—coalition governments were made up from several political parties.

- Article 48 gave the President so much power that he had the opportunity to act undemocratically.

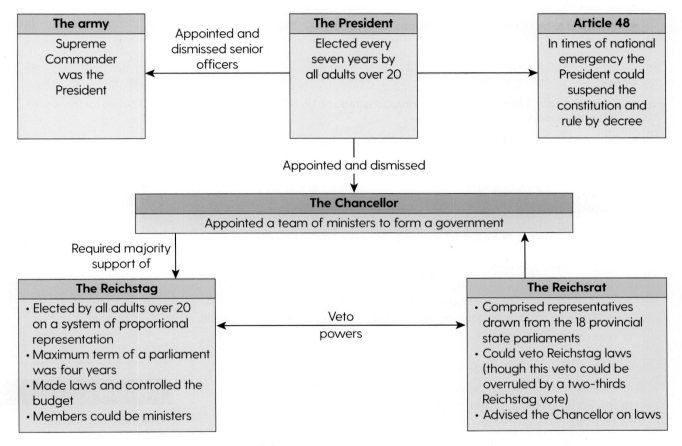

Fig. 8.1 *The constitutional organisation of the new government*

Recap

- Germany had expected a lenient settlement after it had changed the leadership of the country and tried to become more democratic.

- Germany would face serious difficulty in rebuilding economically. Not only did the Treaty of Versailles restrict Germany's ability to raise revenue through the loss of territory, but also reparations were set so high that a significant amount of money would be spent repaying the debt to the Allies.

- The psychological impact was also significant—the army and the people felt that they had been let down by those who had signed the treaty.

How did the Treaty of Versailles affect the Weimar Republic?

The table below summarises the terms of the treaty.

Land	Army
• Surrender of all German colonies to the League of Nations • Return of Alsace-Lorraine to France • Poland given a "corridor" to the sea, cutting East Prussia off from the rest of Germany • Other territories lost to Poland, Denmark, and Lithuania • Germany forbidden to unite with Austria • Rhineland to be occupied by Allied troops for 15 years	• German armed forces restricted to 100 000 • Conscription prohibited • German naval forces limited to 15 000 men, six battleships, six cruisers, and 12 destroyers • Poison gas, armed aircraft, tanks, and armoured cars prohibited • Rhineland demilitarised
Money	**Blame**
• Germany to pay 226 billion marks in reparations, reduced in 1921 to 134 billion marks • France awarded the Saar coal-producing region until a plebiscite in 1934	• Article 231 assigned blame for the war to Germany and its allies

Worked Example

Why was the Weimar Republic in danger of collapse in 1919–23? (6)

A range of challenges in 1919–23 severely tested the new Republic. The German people bitterly resented the Treaty of Versailles' terms of reparations, war guilt, and loss of territory. There were challenges from right-wing groups, such as the Kapp Putsch (1920) and the Munich Putsch (1923)—both were serious attempts to remove the government.

The treaty also caused major economic issues. Germany had lost territory, and struggled to pay reparations fixed at 226 billion marks. This led to the **Ruhr** crisis of 1923: French troops occupied the German region to take raw materials when Germany defaulted on payments. There was hyper-inflation in Germany, and great economic instability, endangering the new Republic.

Exam tip

The answer needs to include two well-explained points about why the Republic seemed at risk. You could choose issues relating to the Treaty of Versailles or to the constitution.

Key term

The Ruhr—the heavily industrialised area of western Germany named after the river that flows through the region. It was a huge centre for the coal, iron, and steel industry.

The Germans had believed the Treaty of Versailles was to be based on Wilson's Fourteen Points. They were furious at its harsh terms and it was regarded as a "diktat"–a dictated peace. The Germans were not allowed to attend the Conference to discuss the terms. Several aspects caused particular resentment.

- Germany had to accept the blame for starting the war (the War Guilt Clause). The Germans thought this was unfair as they believed the start of the war was due to the actions of a range of countries, not just Germany.

- The reparations figure was about 2 per cent of Germany's annual output. Germany feared it would be unable to repay this money and rebuild the country. The loss of territory, including the industrial areas of the Saar and Upper Silesia, made it more difficult to pay the reparations.

- Limiting the army to 100 000 men increased unemployment in a country already suffering serious economic problems.

Stage 1: The first instalment of reparations was paid by Germany in 1921.

Stage 2: In 1922 Germany couldn't pay the amount due and asked for more time. The British agreed, the French did not.

Stage 3: The French, together with the Belgians, occupied the Ruhr to seize coal and iron as reparations. In January 1923, the occupation of the centre of German industry began.

Stage 4: German workers used "passive resistance"; that is, German workers would not work in the mines or accept orders from the occupiers. The result was that there would be nothing to take away.

Stage 5: The French reacted harshly, killing over 100 workers and expelling over 100 000 old-age pensioners. The halt in production caused the collapse of the German currency.

Stage 6: The government's response was to print money. This caused prices to rise out of control and resulted in hyperinflation. The German currency was virtually worthless. People's savings became valueless and old-age pensioners suffered as they were on fixed incomes. Prices rose faster than incomes. Prices in the shops were increasing almost every hour. People could not afford food and heating. The Weimar government was in danger of collapse.

Stage 7: In August 1923, Gustav Stresemann became Chancellor. He introduced a rescue plan that:

- ended passive resistance in the Ruhr
- stopped the printing of money in November 1923 and stabilised the currency by introducing the temporary Rentenmark
- resumed reparation payments to the Allies
- resumed production in the Ruhr.

Fig. 8.2 *Stages of the crisis in the Ruhr*

To what extent were 1924–29 the golden years of the Weimar Republic?

The next six years were characterised by economic recovery and some have called them the "golden years" of the Republic. There were certainly some positives, as outlined below.

Area	Positive developments	Remaining issues
The economy	• Stresemann introduced a temporary currency, the Rentenmark, and the Ruhr industries restarted production. In 1924 this temporary currency was replaced by the permanent Reichmark. • In 1924 Stresemann agreed the Dawes Plan with the United States. This linked Germany's reparations payments to economic performance. In addition, American loans of 800 million gold marks helped to kick-start the German economy. German industry benefited from this investment: inflation and unemployment fell, industry expanded, and exports increased. By 1928 German industrial production was greater than pre-war levels.	• Some groups, including shopkeepers, farmers, and small businessmen still struggled. • Unemployment still remained too high. • The economic recovery was based on American loans, which needed to be repaid.

	• The Young Plan of 1929, which reduced reparations, further helped Germany's economic recovery.	
Foreign policy	• Germany signed a wider European agreement called the Locarno Treaties of 1925. Germany agreed to accept the terms of the Treaty of Versailles. The Locarno Treaties placed Germany on an equal level with signatories, providing guarantees for the frontiers of Germany, France, and Belgium. • France left the Ruhr by 1925. • In 1926 Germany was admitted to the League of Nations as a responsible member of the international community.	• Some felt that by accepting the Treaty of Versailles and not seeking to change the terms, Stresemann was further betraying Germany.
Cultural aspects	• The 1920s was a decade of cultural revival in Germany, especially Berlin. • The new democratic republic was committed to civil liberties. It lifted censorship, encouraged artists, writers, film and theatre directors, and designers. The rejection of traditional approaches resulted in the favouring of expressionism. • At a popular level, night clubs, dance halls, cafés, and restaurants increased, allowing opportunities for cabaret artists, singers, and dance bands.	• Many of these developments were regarded with shock and disgust by the right wing of German politics. Artistic development was seen as a sign of decadence, corruption, and moral decay.

The Golden Age of the Weimar Republic was not to last though. The Great Depression that followed the Wall Street Crash had a devastating effect on Germany.

Renewed economic crisis

- Following the Wall Street Crash of October 1929 the American economy went into recession and many of the loans offered to Germany since 1924 were recalled.

- The German economy suffered a double blow. The Germans had to cope with a world depression and the consequent reduction in export orders, but had to repay substantial amounts of money to the United States. Unemployment rose to alarming levels. By 1932 the German unemployment figure stood at 6 million—one-third of the workforce.

Political instability

- Support for the moderate parties that made up the coalitions of the Weimar governments began to decline.

- As the German people searched for alternatives and saw governments fail, support for the two extreme parties, the Nazis and the communists, rose from 13 per cent in 1928 to 52 per cent in 1932.

Why was Hitler able to control Germany by 1934?

What were the Nazi Party objectives in the 1920s?

Key points from the Nazi Party objectives published in 1920 included:

- the union of all Germans in a Greater Germany

- the destruction of the Treaties of Versailles and St Germain (which would then allow the union of Germany and Austria)

Recap

- The Weimar Republic recovered in the years 1924–28 and solved many of the problems of the immediate post-war period.

- The work of Stresemann was crucial to this.

- The improvements were temporary though, and depended largely on foreign investment, particularly from the United States.

- The years 1924–28 can only be considered the golden years of the Republic if you compare them to the years before and after.

- German citizenship exclusive to those of German blood (excluding Jews)
- no more immigration of non-Germans
- a strong central government in Germany
- generous provision for old-age pensioners.

The German Workers' Party (DAP, the forerunner of the Nazi Party) was established by Anton Drexler in January 1919. It was an extremist national party. At the end of the war Hitler had stayed in the army working for the intelligence services. Sent to spy on the DAP, Hitler was impressed by its political views and joined the party. Soon he was taking responsibility for publicity, propaganda, and public speaking.

In 1920 the party published its 25-Point Programme and renamed itself the National Socialist German Workers' Party (known as Nazis). The programme showed strong nationalist and **anti-Semitic** features. The swastika was used as the party badge.

In July 1921 Hitler replaced Drexler as leader. In August 1921 he founded the SA (Storm Troopers), who were noted for their violence against any opposition.

> **Key term**
>
> **Anti-Semitism**—hostility to, prejudice, or discrimination against Jews, Judaism, and Jewishness.

The Munich Putsch, 1923

Hitler wanted to achieve the violent overthrow of the unpopular Weimar Republic and replace it with a Nazi government. He viewed the current government as weak due to the Ruhr Crisis and its handling of hyperinflation. Supported by wartime leader General Ludendorff, he attempted to seize power.

- **8 November:** Storm Troopers forced their way into a political meeting in a Munich beer hall. They planned to take over Munich and march into Berlin. Kahr, the Prime Minister of Bavaria, was forced at gunpoint to give support to the revolution.

- **9 November:** Kahr went back on his promise. Hitler marched through the streets of Munich to gain support. Armed police opened fire, killing 16 Nazis.

- **26 February:** Hitler was placed on trial for treason. He used his trial as a propaganda exercise, generating publicity for his views and media attention. He was leniently sentenced to five years in prison and served only nine months. Ludendorff was acquitted.

Was the Munich Putsch a failure for Hitler?

Yes	No
The army remained loyal to the Weimar government. Hitler and Ludendorff were arrested and charged with high treason.	The trial gave Hitler the opportunity to gain publicity for his ideas.
The loyalty of Bavarian politicians had been underestimated.	Hitler used his time in prison to write *Mein Kampf* (*My Struggle*).
Hitler miscalculated the mood of the German people. They did not rise to support him.	The trial showed that Hitler had sympathisers within the judiciary.
Hitler was branded a criminal and imprisoned.	Hitler only served nine months and this was in great comfort at Landsberg Castle.
The Nazi Party was banned.	

> **Key fact**
>
> *Mein Kampf* is an autobiographical book by Adolf Hitler. It outlines his political ideology and future plans for Germany. It heavily emphasises the superiority of the German (Aryan) race, especially in comparison with Jews and Slavs; the dangers of communism; the need for *Lebensraum* or living space; and ambition for Germany to become the dominant state in Europe.

By the end of the 1920s, the Nazis were a minority party. In the general election of May 1928 they won 12 seats in the Reichstag, polling 2.6 per cent of the votes.

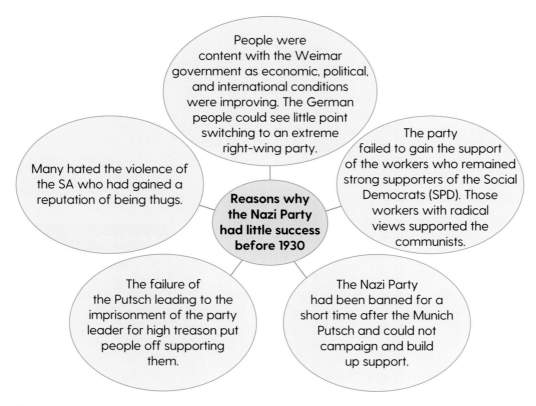

Fig. 8.3 *Reasons why the Nazi Party had little success before 1930*

How was Hitler elected as Chancellor by 1933?

In October 1929 Stresemann died. The economy he had built up was fragile, being dependent on American loans. In the same month, disaster struck as the Wall Street Crash occurred.

As unemployment increased, many Germans felt let down by the Weimar Republic and turned to extremist parties. Support for the Nazis and communists increased. In the 1930 elections the communists (KPD) gained 77 seats, the

Nazis 107. There are several reasons why Hitler was elected Chancellor in 1933.

The impact of the Great Depression	The Wall Street Crash in the United States started the Great Depression. As a result, many American banks recalled their loans. German businesses began to close. Millions became unemployed. By 1930 unemployment had reached 4 million. It was at 6 million by 1932.
The appeal of the Nazis	Hitler and the Nazis promised to get people back to work and to provide food. They gained support from all areas of German society, including powerful industrialists. They also offered a strong response to the rising communists and a promise to return Germany to its pre-war standing and power.
The fear of communism	In the 1930 elections the communists (KPD) gained 77 seats. There was fear of a communist revolution. This worried many industrialists and farmers. They turned to the Nazis, who opposed the communists. The SA and SS gave an impression of discipline and order.
Political unrest	Germany was thrown into economic chaos and no government could solve the problems. President Hindenburg ruled by decree. There were five governments in the period 1929–32, each in power for only a few months. As mainstream politicians failed to address the problems Germany faced, people began to look to alternatives such as the Nazis, who offered radical solutions.
Long-term issues	The reliance on money from the United States came about as a result of the treaties signed in the 1920s. For some this showed the long-term damage of the Treaty of Versailles and resentment grew once more. The Nazis offered a return to traditional values, away from the cultural experimentation of the 1920s and back to uniting behind one leader.

Goebbels introduced new campaigning methods to increase the Nazi share of the vote, including the following.

- The Nazis relied on generalised slogans rather than detailed policies.
- They repeatedly accused the Jews, the communists, and the Weimar politicians of causing the nation's difficulties.
- Posters and pamphlets were widely distributed and displayed.
- Large rallies were held.
- The Nazis provided soup kitchens and hostels for the unemployed.
- Hitler was a powerful speaker. He travelled by plane to rallies all over Germany.
- Film, radio, and records brought the Nazi message to everybody.

Recap

The Nazi appeal was broad and offered something to many disgruntled voters. At a time when other politicians looked uncertain and weak, the Nazis appeared to be a party of action—promising jobs, a more nationalistic foreign policy, and strength against communism.

Exam tip

General tip: in questions on how the Nazis gained popularity, it is important to note the skilled tactics they used.

	March 1932	Presidential election 1932: Hitler opposed the elderly President Hindenburg and campaigned under a promise to build a better Germany and overturn Versailles. This was not enough to get him the support he needed and despite going to a second vote, Hitler was unsuccessful.
Elections for the Reichstag: The NSDAP won 230 seats and was the largest party in the Reichstag, although it lacked an overall majority. The election campaign had been a violent one with street battles between Nazis and communists. Nearly 100 people were killed.	**July 1932**	
	November 1932	Elections for the Reichstag. A government formed under von Papen lacked support and was forced to call another election. The support for the Nazis dropped to 192 seats but theirs remained the largest party.
Elections for the Reichstag. Another government, this time led by von Schleicher, found it impossible to govern. In the resulting election the Nazis won 288 seats and theirs was by far the biggest party, although it still lacked a majority.	**March 1933**	

Key fact

President Hindenburg was a former war hero who had commanded the German military during the second half of the First World War. He became president in 1925. He was old-fashioned in his views and strongly supported the right wing.

Fig. 8.4 *Timeline of the elections of 1932–33*

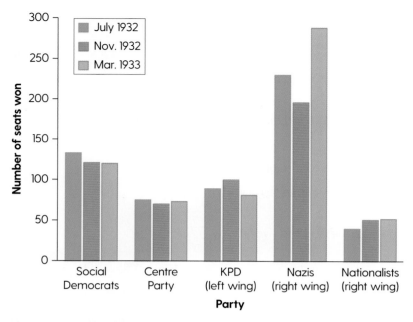

Fig. 8.5 *Results of the elections of 1932–33*

How did Hitler become Chancellor in January 1933?

Faced with the continued rise of the NSDAP and the popularity of Hitler, von Papen managed to persuade Hindenburg to agree a political deal. Hitler would become Chancellor with von Papen as Vice Chancellor. With only a few Nazis in the Cabinet, von Papen was confident that Hitler could be controlled. On 30 January 1933 Hitler was named Chancellor.

How did Hitler establish his control 1933–34?

Why Hitler was not a dictator	Events that occurred	Consequences
Other parties could oppose him	**The Reichstag Fire, 27 February 1933** On the evening of 27 February 1933 the Reichstag building burnt down. A Dutch communist, van der Lubbe, was arrested and charged with starting the fire. Hitler claimed it was proof of a communist plot against the state. Hitler took the opportunity to whip up public fear against the supposed communist threat. There were many theories as to how the fire started, including that the Nazis might have started it themselves.	President Hindenburg was persuaded by Hitler to issue an emergency decree. The decree gave Hitler wide-ranging powers, including the power to deal with the "state of emergency" that had arisen following the Reichstag Fire. The decree curbed freedom of speech and the right of assembly. It gave the police an excuse to arrest communists. In Prussia over 4000 were arrested in the days immediately after the fire. Hitler was now out of control.
He did not have total political control	**The Enabling Act, 23 March 1933** Hitler still did not have enough elected support to have complete control of Germany. He wanted to pass any laws he chose without the use of the Reichstag, but to change the constitution in this way he required two-thirds of the votes of the Reichstag members. To gain this level of votes he expelled the 81 communist members from the Reichstag and ordered the SA to continue their intimidation of the opposition. Only the Social Democrats dared oppose the measure. The Act was passed by 441 votes to 94.	Hitler was now dictator of all Germany. He could now pass laws for four years without consulting the Reichstag. He was able to ban all other political parties. Germany was now a one-party state. In May 1933 the trade unions were abolished, their leaders arrested, and funds confiscated. Strike action was made illegal. All workers had to belong to the German Labour Front. The civil service was purged of all Jews. The democratic Weimar Republic had been destroyed.

Why Hitler was not a dictator	Events that occurred	Consequences
Elements of his party were a threat to him	**The Night of the Long Knives, 30 June 1934** Hitler was worried about the growing independence of Ernst Röhm, the leader of the SA. He decided to take action at the end of June. There were rumours that Röhm was in favour of merging the army with the SA under his leadership, and Röhm was open in his view that he favoured a "second revolution" and more extreme nationalistic policies. Hitler felt he needed to reassure the army and show the SA leaders who was in control. On the night of 30 June 1934 Röhm and other SA leaders were arrested and shot. During the next two weeks several hundred senior SA men, other rivals, and potential enemies, including von Schleicher, were also murdered by the SS.	The army could no longer be in any doubt that Hitler favoured its members in preference to the SA. The SA was brought firmly under the control of Hitler's leadership.
President Hindenburg could remove him	**Death of Hindenburg, 2 August 1934** When President Hindenburg died on 2 August 1934, Hitler proclaimed himself Chancellor and Reich Führer.	As such, he was Head of State and Commander-in-Chief of the Army. Every soldier was required to swear an oath of personal loyalty to Adolf Hitler. Hitler's dictatorship was now a matter of fact as well as a matter of law. Hitler had achieved total power.

Recap

- In a period of 18 months Hitler established himself as a dictator.
- The Enabling Act gave him total political power over the Reichstag and other parties.
- The Night of the Long Knives meant that potential threats in his own party were eliminated.
- The death of Hindenburg meant that Hitler could combine the role of President with the role of Chancellor. The position of Führer was established.

How did the Nazis control Germany, 1933–45?

The SS: Led by Heinrich Himmler, the SS had extensive powers to arrest, detain without charge, interrogate, search, and confiscate property. They were responsible for running the concentration camps and implementing Nazi racial policies, including the Final Solution.

The Gestapo: The German secret police, the Gestapo, were feared by the ordinary citizens as they had sweeping powers. They spied on Germans by tapping telephones, intercepting mail, and accessing information through a network of informers, which made it unsafe for anyone to express anti-Nazi views.

Control through terror

The courts and judges: Judges had to take an oath of loyalty to Hitler. Jewish judges and lawyers were sacked. Capital offences were increased to make, for example, telling anti-Nazi jokes and listening to a foreign radio station punishable by the death sentence.

Concentration camps: Enemies of the Nazis were sent to the camps as well as gypsies, beggars, and tramps. Discipline was harsh and there were many deaths from beatings and torture. During the Final Solution, these camps were used for the extermination of the Jewish population. The first camp was opened at Dachau, Germany in 1933.

Fig. 8.6 *Control through terror*

Worked Example

Who were the Gestapo? (4)

The Gestapo acted as Nazi Germany's secret police force. Under the control of Himmler, the head of the SS, the Gestapo were responsible for the monitoring of German people and their activities. Using informants and observation, they targeted those considered a threat to Nazi Germany. The Gestapo acted outside of the normal judicial process and had their own courts, with the power to send people to concentration camps or to be killed. During the war the Gestapo targeted resistance movements who sought to oppose the German war effort.

Exam tip

To answer this question, think about what the Gestapo did as well as who its members were. Aim to write two well-developed points.

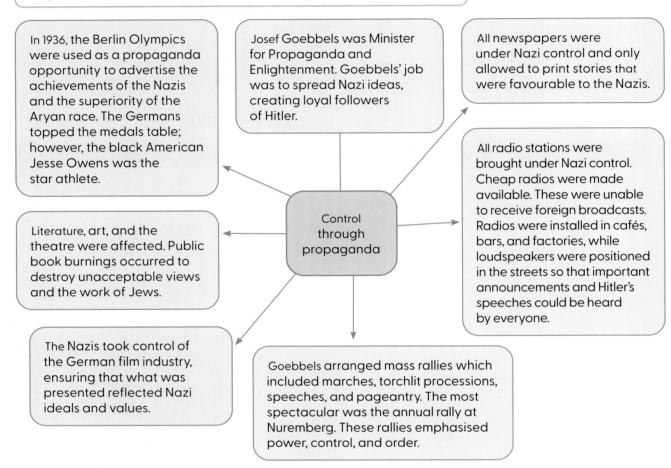

Fig. 8.7 *Control through propaganda*

What was life like for ordinary Germans under Nazi rule?

The Nazi regime affected the lives of young people through formal education and the youth movement. This combination would ensure future generations of loyal Nazis and prepare them for their future role in society.

Schools

- Schools in Germany were controlled by the Nazi Ministry of Education.
- Teachers had to take an oath of loyalty to Hitler and join the Nazi Teachers' League.
- Jewish teachers were sacked.
- All schools were to give the same message.

- The curriculum was changed to ensure that Nazi ideas and racial beliefs were reflected in the teaching of subjects such as biology, history, and mathematics.

- Religious education was removed from the curriculum.

- Emphasis was placed on sport and physical education.

- Girls were taught "home-making" skills.

Youth movements

- The Hitler Youth was available outside of school. It was founded as a voluntary organisation in 1926. The Hitler Youth Law of 1936 made attendance virtually compulsory. Other youth groups were banned.

- There were separate sections for boys (Hitler Youth) and girls (German League of Maidens) and for different age groups.

- Children were indoctrinated with Nazi ideas, including extreme prejudice against Jews and the idea that the peace settlement was an injustice.

- Boys were given basic military training and discipline including drill, campcraft, map reading, and looking after a rifle. Running, hiking, and tracking enhanced physical fitness.

- Girls were prepared for motherhood, learning domestic skills such as cooking, sewing, and managing the household budget.

What was it like to be a young person under the Nazi regime?

Not all young Germans enjoyed the opportunities offered by the Hitler Youth. Some expressed themselves through the Swing movement and the Edelweiss Pirates. These groups believed in freedom of expression and values that often conflicted with those of the Nazis.

Worked Example

"Nazi policies towards young people were effective in controlling them." How far do you agree with this statement? Explain your answer. (10)

It can be argued that the Nazi state was successful in its policies towards young people. The youth movements set up, with the Hitler Youth for boys and the League of German Maidens for girls, proved successful in that by 1939 they had over 7 million members. They were used to prepare boys and girls for their roles in life and offered opportunities to participate in camps, hikes, and parades, for example. The Nazis' policies in schools were also effective at controlling young people. Tight control over the curriculum and teaching within schools meant that the education system reflected what the Nazis wanted their young people to learn.

However, it can be argued that the policies directed towards young people were not effective as the Nazi state failed to achieve total obedience. Opposition groups from young people emerged, such as the White Rose Group and the Edelweiss Pirates. These groups refused to conform with the Nazi state, and instead promoted activities that directly opposed Nazi ideals, such as smoking and listening to jazz music. As the war developed, these groups distributed leaflets encouraging others to challenge the Nazi state.

Overall, the Nazis achieved largely what they wanted in terms of young people—those growing up in the regime were mainly obedient and prepared for later life. As the regime developed though, so did disengagement as the young fought against the need to conform and found ways to express themselves.

Exam tip

This question needs a balanced answer that considers the two sides of the question. Think about how the Nazis were effective in controlling young people and the successes of organisations such as the Hitler Youth, before evaluating them with evidence about alternative organisations, for example, the White Rose Group.

What was it like for women under the Nazi regime?

The Nazis believed in traditional Aryan family values including women's role as wives and mothers—partly because this gave stability but more importantly to raise the birth rate. Nazi ideals were encouraged through specific measures.

- In 1933 marriage loans were introduced for Ayran couples. Couples could receive up to 1000 Reichsmarks if the woman gave up her work. Goods rather than cash were given to stimulate the economy. For each child the couple had, 25 per cent was taken off the loan amount.

- Enrolment for women at university was severely restricted.

- Divorce was made easier so that women could remarry and have more children.

- Women were forced out of work. They were expected to remain at home to look after their husband and children. After 1937 there was a reversal in this policy as women were needed to work in the armaments factories.

What was the impact of these policies?

- The birth rate had increased by 1939.

- Marriages increased from 516 000 marriages in 1932 to 772 000 in 1939.

- The number of women working increased between 1933 and 1939. The number of women working in agriculture increased from 4.6 million to 4.9 million; in industry the figure increased from 2.7 million to 3.3 million.

- The number of women studying at university drastically fell.

Did ordinary Germans benefit from Nazi rule?

When Hitler came to power, unemployment was at almost 6 million. By 1938 there was almost no unemployment. The Nazis introduced public works schemes: building autobahns, schools, hospitals, and houses. Rearmament created jobs, as did the introduction of conscription to the armed forces. Increased opportunities came from an attempt at introducing self-sufficiency to reduce the need for imports of raw materials and food. The key change for workers was the creation of the Nazi Labour Front after trade unions were abolished—membership was optional but without it workers struggled to find a job. The Nazis also introduced other measures for workers.

- The Strength Through Joy programme gave workers cheap theatre and cinema tickets.

- The Beauty of Labour movement improved working conditions by introducing washing facilities and low-cost canteens.

- The Reich Labour Service was set up to tackle unemployment. All 18–25-year-olds had to serve for six months. They provided cheap labour for state projects.

- Workers were offered cut-price cruises on the latest luxury liners.

- Workers saved in a state scheme to buy a Volkswagen Beetle, although no worker ever received a car.

However, all this came at a cost. Wages were low while working hours increased. The availability of consumer goods was also limited and worsened as the war began.

Fig. 8.8 *Strength Through Joy poster, "Go skiiing", 1930s*

Why did the Nazis target certain groups in German society?

In Hitler's view, the German people constituted the Aryan race. They were the master race, superior in terms of intelligence, physique, and work ethic. To preserve the purity of the Aryan race, it was essential to maintain its separateness. Hitler also believed that Germany was overburdened with "undesirables" (people he did not want in German society). He regarded these people as a drain on the resources of the state. Hitler's views had been evident in his book, *Mein Kampf*, in the 1920s, but now in power, he introduced legislation to persecute the half a million Jews living in Germany.

Anti-Semitism

	March 1933	Jews were banned from the professions and government employment.
Aryan and non-Aryan children were forbidden from playing together.	**April 1933**	
	September 1933	Race Studies became a part of the school examination syllabus.
The Nuremberg Laws removed German citizenship from Jews and forbade marriage between Jews and non-Jews.	**September 1935**	
	January 1936	Jews had all electrical equipment, bicycles, typewriters, and records confiscated.
The Nazis organised Kristallnacht (Night of Broken Glass) as a reprisal for the shooting of a German diplomat by a Jew. Nazi mobs attacked and burnt Jewish shops, homes, businesses, and synagogues. Over 100 Jews were murdered.	**November 1938**	
	February 1939	Jews had all jewellery, gold, and silver confiscated.
Jews could be evicted from their homes without a reason being given.	**April 1939**	

Fig. 8.9 *Timeline of anti-Semitic measures*

Persecution of other groups

The Nazis persecuted many other groups they thought to be inferior.

Gypsies violated the Nazis' racial and efficiency requirements and were sent to concentration camps. Other undesirable groups suffered the same fate.

Following the Sterilisation Law of 1933, mentally ill people were compulsorily sterilised. In 1939 such people were killed in euthanasia programmes.

Who opposed the Nazi regime?

Group	Actions taken
Religious opposition	At first the Catholic Church agreed not to interfere with Nazi policies (Concordat of 1933), in return for protection of the rights of the Catholic Church in Germany. However, Hitler broke the agreement and the Nazis were denounced as anti-Christian by the Pope.
	Many churchmen spoke out against the Nazis, including Pastor Niemöller, who spent eight years in a concentration camp for forming a rival church to the Nazi Reich Church.
	Bishop Galen spoke out strongly against euthanasia, forced sterilisation, and concentration camps. He was kept under house arrest until the end of the war.
Opposition among the young	Although many young people joined the Hitler Youth, there were some who rejected this influence. Members of the Swing movement were condemned by the Nazis because they were interested in British and American popular music and dance, including banned jazz music. They also accepted Jews into their groups.
	The Edelweiss Pirates mocked the Nazis through song, attacked members of the Hitler Youth, distributed broadsheets, and scrawled graffiti on walls. During the war they spread anti-Nazi propaganda and, in 1944, took part in an attack on the Gestapo during which an officer was killed. Twelve Pirates were publicly hanged in November 1944.
	The White Rose Group formed by university students in Munich was another group of young opponents. The leaders, Hans and Sophie Scholl, were executed in 1943 for anti-Nazi activities.
Military opposition	In 1944 a group of senior army officers planned to assassinate Hitler. They placed a bomb in a suitcase under a table at a meeting Hitler attended. The bomb went off, but Hitler was unharmed. The July Bomb Plot had failed and it led to 5000 executions.

How did the Second World War change life in Nazi Germany?

- Food rationing began in September 1939. Clothes rationing followed in November 1939.

- Propaganda encouraged support of the war effort. The Gestapo watched for people who did not give their support.

- The gamble of invading the Soviet Union in 1941 resulted in civilians facing cutbacks, shortages, and longer working hours. Labour shortages saw increasing numbers of women in the factories.

- From 1942 Albert Speer began to direct the war economy, focusing on the armaments industry.

- In 1944 Germany directed all its resources in a "total war".

- The cinemas remained open and were the only entertainment on offer. They showed propaganda films.

- There were massive bombing raids on German cities, undermining morale. One of the most significant was the bombing of Dresden.

- By the end of the war, 3 million civilians had died. The survivors experienced food shortages.

Key fact

Why was there not more opposition? The harsh punishments suffered by those who opposed the regime, coupled with the fear of the Gestapo and SS, meant that most Germans conformed with the Nazi state. The effective measures taken by the Nazis to establish control meant that there was very little opportunity to organise meaningful opposition.

The Final Solution

- As the German army captured huge areas of eastern Europe, millions of Jews came under Nazi control. The SS shot around 800 000 Jews.

- At the Wansee Conference in January 1942 it was decided to eliminate all European Jews. Captured Jews were taken to remote death camps in Poland, which were equipped with gas chambers and crematoria.

The Nazis killed around 6 million Jews through gassing, shooting, working them to death, and starvation. They tried to cover up their murderous acts.

Review

1. What problems did Germany face immediately following the end of the war in 1918?   [4]

2. What was the Reichstag Fire?   [4]

3. Describe the occupation of the Ruhr in 1923.   [4]

4. Describe the Munich Putsch of 1923.   [4]

5. Why were the people of Germany unhappy with the Treaty of Versailles?   [6]

6. Why were the achievements of the Nazi Party limited before 1929?   [6]

7. Why did the Nazis attempt to control young people?   [6]

8. Why was the Enabling Act important?   [6]

9. Why did Hitler arrange the Night of the Long Knives?   [6]

10. Why was the death of Hindenburg important?   [6]

11. Why were there so many uprisings in Germany in the years 1919–22?   [6]

12. Why was there an economic crisis in 1923?   [6]

13. How important was the Reichstag Fire as a reason for Hitler being able to establish a dictatorship?   [10]

14. "Most people benefited from Nazi control of Germany." How far do you agree with this statement? Explain your answer.   [10]

For further information, review this section in the Student Book.

Raise your grade ↑

1. What was the Night of the Long Knives? (4 marks)

The Night of the Long Knives occurred in June 1934 and was an attempt by Hitler to brutally crush those he thought might be capable of plotting to replace him. The main targets were members of the SA, including their leader Ernst Röhm. Röhm and hundreds of others were killed over several nights of violence. Hitler had feared that the SA was increasingly out of control, and there seemed to be a disagreement about what policies Germany should be following. With the action taken, Hitler ensured that the threat posed by the SA was eliminated and his control of Germany was secure.

This is an excellent, thorough answer. It offers good explanation of the events, some detail of what occurred, and motives and outcomes for Hitler. 4 marks awarded.

Plan your answer

- In the answer aim to make two well-explained points about the event that consider actions, details, and motive.

- The question focuses on the events between 30 June and 2 July 1934 when Hitler targeted his political opponents and potential threats.

- Leading members of the SA, including the leader Ernst Röhm, were killed.

- Members of the SA, former political rivals such as von Schleicher, and others were also killed.

- Hitler's motives were to ensure that those who remained were loyal to him and the state, and that the threat posed by the SA was eliminated.

Mark scheme

1 mark for each relevant point, an additional mark for supporting detail; maximum 2 marks per point made.

2. Why has the period 1923–29 been described as the "golden years"? (6 marks)

The period in question is often referred to as the "golden years" of Weimar Germany as it was a time of relative improvement. The credit for this work goes in large part to Gustav Stresemann, who acted as Chancellor and Foreign Minister in this period. There is no doubt his work was important, as he helped rebuild Germany both with regard to the economy, which had suffered severely in the years of hyper-inflation that followed the Ruhr crisis, and also with its poor relations with other European countries after the war and the Treaty of Versailles.

The answer starts well and correctly identifies several reasons. However, there isn't enough explanation and the reasons need to be expanded in order to achieve higher marks. 3 marks awarded.

Plan your answer

- In the answer aim to make two well-explained reasons that focus on the improvements Germany made.

- The work of Stresemann in this period is the focus in the question.

- Germany made great improvements in the areas of politics, the economy, and also in terms of foreign policy.

- A more stable economy followed after agreement with the Dawes Plan and Young Plan regarding debt repayments and loans from the United States.

- In terms of foreign policy, Germany benefited from better relations with other European countries after the Locarno Treaties.

Mark scheme

Level 1:	general answer lacking specific contextual knowledge (1 mark)
Level 2:	identifies AND/OR describes reasons (2–3 marks)
Level 3:	explains ONE reason (4–5 marks)
Level 4:	explains TWO reasons (6 marks)

3. "The Night of the Long Knives was the most important step in Hitler's consolidation of power in the period 1933–34." How far do you agree with this statement? Explain your answer. **(10 marks)**

The murderous events of the Night of the Long Knives were clearly important in the consolidation of power in the period 1933–34 for Hitler, as they meant that the threat that political rivals posed to him was dealt with and Hitler had firmly established power over his party.

However, while the Night of the Long Knives was important, it came quite late in the period of consolidation and by this point Hitler had largely established a political dictatorship. The Enabling Act of 1933 was crucial in this, as it meant that Hitler could now pass laws for four years without consulting the Reichstag. Using this power he was able to ban all other political parties, abolish trade unions, and centralise Nazi power. This helped consolidate his power as he was able to ensure he had political dominance.

An even earlier event had also helped consolidate his power. The Reichstag fire of February 1933 helped eliminate the communist threat and ensure that communists were seen as a public enemy. When the Reichstag building burnt down, a Dutch communist, van der Lubbe, was arrested and charged with starting the fire. Hitler claimed it was proof of a communist plot and used it to create fear of the supposed communist threat. This allowed him to pass further laws restricting people's liberties.

The answer is very strong on the opposing factors and does well to explain political issues and also the importance of the Reichstag Fire. However, there could be more detail on the Night of the Long Knives, as it is the factor raised in the question. 7 marks awarded.

Plan your answer

- The answer needs to cover the importance of the Night of the Long Knives, but balanced against other factors that consolidated Hitler's power.

- Hitler's consolidation of power centred on ensuring that the threats to his position were eliminated.

- The Night of the Long Knives focused on the threat posed by members of the SA. This action ensured that they could no longer challenge him.

- However, there are other issues to consider—the Enabling Act gave Hitler political power which meant that a dictatorship was all but established. Furthermore, the death of Hindenburg meant that there was no longer a person with the authority to remove Hitler's power.

Mark scheme

Level 1:	general answer lacking specific contextual knowledge (1 mark)
Level 2:	identifies AND/OR describes reasons (2–3 marks)
Level 3:	gives a one-sided explanation (4–5 marks) or one explanation of both sides (4–6 marks)
Level 4:	explains both sides (7–9 marks)
Level 5:	explains with evaluation (10 marks)

You need to know

- The main features of Russia before the First World War
- Why there was a revolution in 1905
- What problems the First World War brought to Russia
- Why the Tsar was overthrown in 1917
- How effective the Provisional Government was
- Who the Bolsheviks were, why they could seize power in 1917, and the role of Lenin
- The impact of the Civil War
- The events of the struggle for power after Lenin's death and why it was Stalin who succeeded him
- How Stalin controlled Russia
- What Stalin's Five-Year Plans and collectivisation were
- What it was like to live under Stalin's rule

Background: Russia in the lead-up to the Second World War

The period from 1905 to 1941 in Russia was marked by significant political, social, and economic upheavals, culminating in the tumultuous events of the Russian Revolution and the subsequent establishment of the Soviet Union. In 1905, discontent among the Russian population erupted into the first Russian Revolution, leading to the establishment of a State Duma and limited constitutional reforms.

Fig. 9.1 *Joseph Stalin (1878–1953)*

However, political instability persisted, exacerbated by Russia's involvement in the First World War. The February Revolution of 1917 resulted in the abdication of Tsar Nicholas II and the rise of a Provisional Government. This interim government faced numerous challenges, including the Bolshevik seizure of power in the October Revolution, which laid the groundwork for the establishment of a socialist state. The ensuing Russian Civil War (1918–22) saw the Red Army, led by the Bolsheviks, emerge victorious, solidifying the foundation of the Soviet Union in 1922. Under leaders such as Vladimir Lenin and later Joseph Stalin, Russia experienced radical economic transformations, industrialisation, and **collectivisation**, but also political repression and mass purges. This chapter delves into the complex dynamics of Russia during this period, exploring the factors that shaped its trajectory from the early 20th century to the eve of the Second World War in 1941.

Russia up to 1914

The Tsarist regime faced numerous challenges in ruling Russia up to 1914. While there were periods of stability and economic growth, there were also significant difficulties that highlighted the shortcomings of the autocratic system.

- **Autocracy and lack of political reform:** The Tsarist regime maintained a strict autocratic form of government. There was little political representation or participation from the general population. The absence of political reforms and the refusal to establish a constitutional monarchy contributed to social unrest and discontent.

- **Economic challenges:** Russia's economy faced challenges due to outdated agrarian practices and slow industrialisation. Most of the population were peasants, and the lack of land reforms led to widespread rural poverty. The industrial sector struggled to keep up with western counterparts, leading to economic disparities and discontent among the urban working class.

- **Social inequality:** There was a stark divide between the privileged aristocracy and the impoverished masses. Most Russians lived in difficult conditions, while the nobility enjoyed vast estates and privileges.

- **National minorities and ethnic tensions:** The Russian Empire was characterised by its diverse population, comprising various ethnic groups. However, the Tsarist regime often pursued policies that marginalised and oppressed minority groups.

- **Ineffective leadership and decision-making:** Nicholas II's leadership style was often indecisive and he faced challenges in making crucial decisions. His reliance on unpopular advisers and Rasputin's influence further damaged the reputation of the monarchy.

- **Military failures:** The Russo–Japanese War (1904–1905) highlighted the weaknesses of the Russian military and exposed the inefficiencies of the government.

The role of the 1905 Revolution

The 1905 Revolution was a series of events that unfolded throughout the year, marked by a combination of social, political, and economic unrest.

> **Key term**
>
> **Collectivisation**—a policy pursued between 1928 and 1933 to consolidate individual land and labour into state farms.

> **Key fact**
>
> The role of Grigori Rasputin has always caused controversy. His association with the Romanovs, especially Tsarina Alexandra, fuelled scandal and rumours of corruption. Rasputin's perceived influence on political decisions, appointments, and his role in undermining public confidence became symbolic of the monarchy's moral decay. His controversial presence contributed to the discontent that, combined with broader issues like economic hardships and military failures, fuelled revolutionary sentiments.

Events   Response

Bloody Sunday, 22 January 1905
The revolution began with a peaceful workers' demonstration in St Petersburg, led by Father Georgy Gapon, demanding better working conditions, higher wages, and political reforms. The marchers approached the Winter Palace to present a petition to Tsar Nicholas II. However, the Imperial Guard opened fire on the crowd, resulting in numerous casualties. This event became known as Bloody Sunday and fuelled widespread outrage and anti-government sentiment.

Spontaneous strikes and uprisings: Bloody Sunday triggered a wave of strikes, protests, and uprisings across the country. Workers in various industries went on strike, demanding better conditions and political reforms.

Peasant uprisings occurred in rural areas, with peasants seizing land from landlords. There were also instances of mutinies within the armed forces.

Formation of the St Petersburg Soviet, October 1905
In response to the unrest, workers in St Petersburg established the St Petersburg Soviet (Council). The Soviet was a council of workers' deputies that played a significant role in coordinating and leading the revolutionary activities in the capital.

The October Manifesto, 17 October 1905
Faced with growing unrest and pressure, Tsar Nicholas II issued the October Manifesto in an attempt to quell the revolutionary fervour. The manifesto promised civil liberties, the establishment of a State Duma (parliament), and constitutional reforms. The manifesto aimed to divide and weaken the opposition by offering concessions to more moderate elements while maintaining the Tsar's authority.

The October Manifesto led to the establishment of the State Duma in 1906. It represented a limited constitutional monarchy, as the Tsar retained significant powers, including the ability to dissolve the Duma. The first Duma, elected in 1906, was dominated by moderate and conservative elements, as the electoral laws favoured landowners and the aristocracy.

Fig. 9.2 *Timeline of events in 1905*

Worked Example

What was Bloody Sunday? (4)

Bloody Sunday in Russia occurred on 22 January 1905, during the early stages of the Russian Revolution of 1905. Thousands of unarmed protesters, predominantly workers and their families, marched towards the Winter Palace in St Petersburg to present a petition to Tsar Nicholas II, requesting better working conditions, higher wages, and political reforms.

However, the peaceful demonstration turned violent when the Imperial Guard opened fire on the protesters, resulting in numerous deaths and injuries. Bloody Sunday in Russia marked a turning point in the revolution, causing public outrage and further fuelling revolutionary sentiment against the autocratic rule of the Tsar. It led to widespread strikes, protests, and the spread of revolutionary fervour across the Russian Empire. Additionally, it undermined the credibility of the Tsarist regime and ultimately contributed to the downfall of the Romanov dynasty in the Russian Revolution of 1917.

Exam tip

With a question like this, make sure you don't just say what happened at Bloody Sunday, but also address why it was a significant event in terms of impact.

Recap

While the revolutionary wave of 1905 subsided, the events of that year left a lasting impact on Russian society. The establishment of the State Duma did not fully address the underlying issues of political representation and social inequality.

Reforms after the 1905 Revolution

Peter Stolypin, who served as the Prime Minister of Russia from 1906 to 1911, implemented a series of reforms aimed at addressing various social, economic, and political challenges facing the Russian Empire. Stolypin's reforms were wide ranging and encompassed areas such as agriculture, the legal system, and political structure.

Area	Reforms
Land reforms	Stolypin sought to address the issue of land tenure and rural poverty by introducing the premise of Kulaks—a class of prosperous and conservative land-owning peasants. The government encouraged the consolidation of small, scattered peasant plots into larger and more efficient farms.
	Voluntary peasant resettlement: Stolypin's government encouraged peasants to voluntarily leave the commune (traditional village community) and move to new lands where they could establish independent farms.
	Stolypin abolished the traditional system of redemption payments that peasants had to make to the state for the land they received during the emancipation of the serfs in 1861.
Legal reforms	Stolypin aimed to strengthen the legal system and increase its efficiency. He introduced a series of judicial reforms, including the establishment of a more independent judiciary and the introduction of trial by jury in some cases.
Education reforms	Stolypin implemented reforms in the education system, aiming to improve literacy rates and modernise the curriculum. The government sought to provide a more practical and vocational education, particularly in rural areas.
Political reforms	Introduction of the State Duma: While the establishment of the State Duma was a result of the 1905 Revolution and the October Manifesto, Stolypin worked with the Duma to strengthen the authority of the central government. He dissolved the First Duma (1906) and changed the electoral laws to favour conservative elements in subsequent Dumas.
Counter-revolutionary measures	Stolypin's government took harsh measures to suppress revolutionary activities. This included the execution of political dissidents and the use of military force to maintain order.

The impact of the First World War

The outbreak of the First World War in 1914 put immense pressure on Russia's resources. The military and economic strain exacerbated existing problems and contributed to the eventual collapse of the Tsarist regime.

Recap

The revolutionary spirit and activism generated during 1905 contributed to the radicalisation of various political groups, setting the stage for the more successful and transformative revolutions of 1917

Worked Example

Why was the Tsar's decision to take personal command of the Russian army during the First World War important? (6)

The Tsar's decision to take personal command of the Russian army during the First World War held significant implications. Firstly, it symbolised a desperate attempt to bolster his image as a strong leader, aiming to rally support for the war effort. However, lacking military expertise, his interference often led to disastrous decisions, exacerbating the already dire situation on the Eastern Front. This demonstrated the Tsar's detachment from the realities of warfare and deepened resentment towards the autocratic regime among soldiers and civilians. Moreover, the decision weakened the central government as it sidelined the Tsar from the political centre in St Petersburg, leaving governance in the hands of incompetent ministers. This further eroded public confidence in the monarchy and contributed to growing discontent, ultimately playing a pivotal role in the events leading up to the Russian Revolution of 1917.

Exam tip

With a question like this, focus on the specific aspects mentioned, such as the importance of the Tsar's decision to take personal command of the Russian army during the First World War. Identify three main reasons why the Tsar's decision was important, ensuring each point is distinct and well developed. This could include factors such as symbolism, political ramifications, and military consequences. Keep your response concise and to the point, avoiding unnecessary elaboration or repetition.

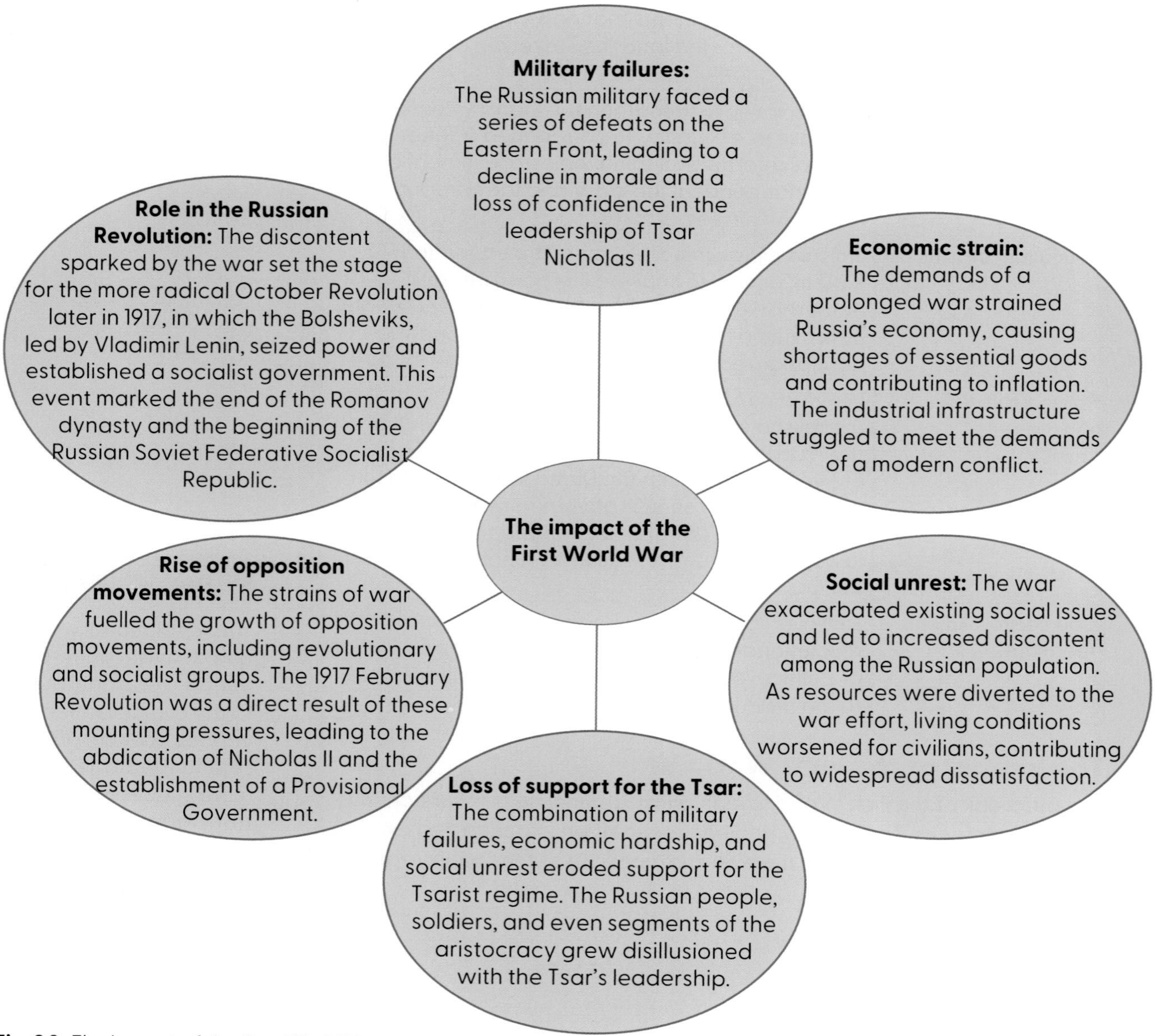

Military failures: The Russian military faced a series of defeats on the Eastern Front, leading to a decline in morale and a loss of confidence in the leadership of Tsar Nicholas II.

Role in the Russian Revolution: The discontent sparked by the war set the stage for the more radical October Revolution later in 1917, in which the Bolsheviks, led by Vladimir Lenin, seized power and established a socialist government. This event marked the end of the Romanov dynasty and the beginning of the Russian Soviet Federative Socialist Republic.

Economic strain: The demands of a prolonged war strained Russia's economy, causing shortages of essential goods and contributing to inflation. The industrial infrastructure struggled to meet the demands of a modern conflict.

The impact of the First World War

Rise of opposition movements: The strains of war fuelled the growth of opposition movements, including revolutionary and socialist groups. The 1917 February Revolution was a direct result of these mounting pressures, leading to the abdication of Nicholas II and the establishment of a Provisional Government.

Social unrest: The war exacerbated existing social issues and led to increased discontent among the Russian population. As resources were diverted to the war effort, living conditions worsened for civilians, contributing to widespread dissatisfaction.

Loss of support for the Tsar: The combination of military failures, economic hardship, and social unrest eroded support for the Tsarist regime. The Russian people, soldiers, and even segments of the aristocracy grew disillusioned with the Tsar's leadership.

Fig. 9.3 *The impact of the First World War on Russia*

The March Revolution

The March 1917 Revolution was, to a large extent, a spontaneous uprising. A combination of events, including International Women's Day protests, labour strikes, and discontent among soldiers, led to mass demonstrations that quickly escalated.

The Petrograd garrison, comprised of soldiers who were sympathetic to the revolutionary cause, played a key role. As unrest grew, many regiments of the garrison sided with the protesters and refused to suppress the demonstrations. Various political groups, including liberal and socialist factions, joined forces to demand political change. The moderate nature of these initial demands created a broad-based coalition against the autocracy.

All these factors created a situation where the Tsarist regime lost control, leading to the abdication of Nicholas II and the establishment of the Provisional Government.

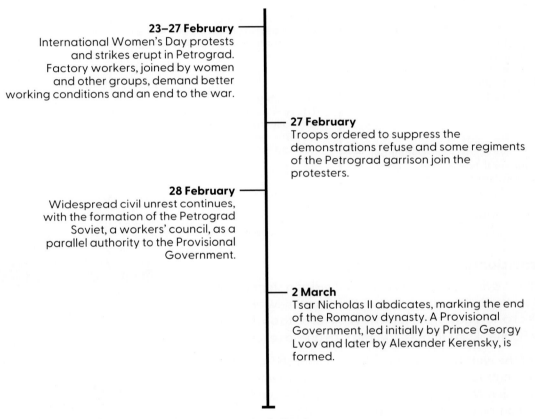

23–27 February
International Women's Day protests and strikes erupt in Petrograd. Factory workers, joined by women and other groups, demand better working conditions and an end to the war.

27 February
Troops ordered to suppress the demonstrations refuse and some regiments of the Petrograd garrison join the protesters.

28 February
Widespread civil unrest continues, with the formation of the Petrograd Soviet, a workers' council, as a parallel authority to the Provisional Government.

2 March
Tsar Nicholas II abdicates, marking the end of the Romanov dynasty. A Provisional Government, led initially by Prince Georgy Lvov and later by Alexander Kerensky, is formed.

Fig. 9.4 *Timeline of events leading to the Tsar's abdication*

The rule of the Provisional Government

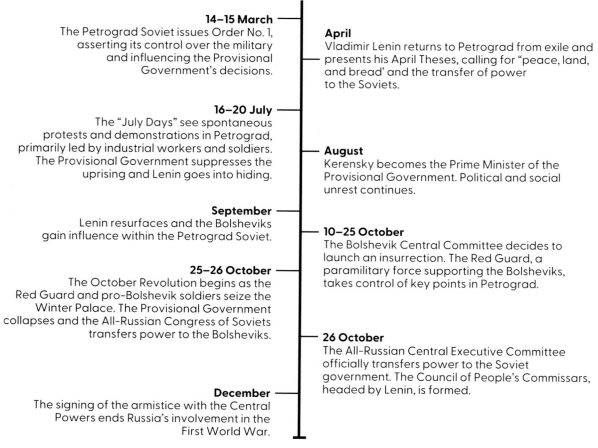

14–15 March
The Petrograd Soviet issues Order No. 1, asserting its control over the military and influencing the Provisional Government's decisions.

April
Vladimir Lenin returns to Petrograd from exile and presents his April Theses, calling for "peace, land, and bread' and the transfer of power to the Soviets.

16–20 July
The "July Days" see spontaneous protests and demonstrations in Petrograd, primarily led by industrial workers and soldiers. The Provisional Government suppresses the uprising and Lenin goes into hiding.

August
Kerensky becomes the Prime Minister of the Provisional Government. Political and social unrest continues.

September
Lenin resurfaces and the Bolsheviks gain influence within the Petrograd Soviet.

10–25 October
The Bolshevik Central Committee decides to launch an insurrection. The Red Guard, a paramilitary force supporting the Bolsheviks, takes control of key points in Petrograd.

25–26 October
The October Revolution begins as the Red Guard and pro-Bolshevik soldiers seize the Winter Palace. The Provisional Government collapses and the All-Russian Congress of Soviets transfers power to the Bolsheviks.

26 October
The All-Russian Central Executive Committee officially transfers power to the Soviet government. The Council of People's Commissars, headed by Lenin, is formed.

December
The signing of the armistice with the Central Powers ends Russia's involvement in the First World War.

Fig. 9.5 *Timeline of the Provisional Government's rule, 1917*

Why did the Provisional Government fail?

By its very nature, the Provisional Government was there as a stopgap, put in place after the Tsar had been removed to rule Russia until new elections could be held to elect a new government. However, it failed to do this and was overthrown by the Bolsheviks in October 1917. This was due to several factors.

- **Continuation of the war:** The Provisional Government chose to honour Russia's commitments to the Allies and continue its involvement in the war. This decision was deeply unpopular among the war-weary Russian population, who desired an end to the conflict.

- **Land reform delay:** The government's delay in implementing meaningful land reforms disappointed peasants who had hoped for the redistribution of land. The issue of land ownership was a critical demand of the Russian peasantry and the government's hesitation eroded support.

- **Failure to address economic issues:** Economic challenges, including food shortages and inflation, persisted under the Provisional Government. The government's inability to address these pressing economic issues contributed to social unrest and dissatisfaction.

- **Dual authority with the soviets:** The existence of the Petrograd Soviet as a parallel authority created a situation of dual power. The Provisional Government often had to compromise with the soviet, leading to indecisiveness and a lack of clear governance.

> **Recap**
>
> Two specific events were also key in the downfall of the Provisional Government: the July Days Uprising, and the Kornilov Affair. Both highlight the government's vulnerability. In the July Days Uprising, the attempt to suppress the spontaneous protests further weakened the Provisional Government's position. The Kornilov Affair exposed the government's internal weaknesses and dependence on unreliable military support.

- **Political instability and factionalism:** The Provisional Government was a coalition of various political factions, including liberals and socialists. Internal divisions and conflicts among these factions weakened the government's ability to make cohesive decisions.

How did Lenin seize and maintain power in 1917?

The Bolsheviks, led by Vladimir Lenin, were able to seize power in November 1917 through a combination of strategic planning, popular discontent, and decisive action.

- **The leadership of Lenin:** His clear and radical vision, as outlined in the *April Theses*, resonated with the desires of many Russians for an end to the war, land redistribution, and the transfer of power to the soviets.

- **Bolshevik control of the Petrograd Soviet:** Key Bolshevik leaders, such as Leon Trotsky, played significant roles in the soviets, which allowed them to coordinate and plan the insurrection effectively.

- **Military support:** The Bolsheviks had the support of the Red Guard, a paramilitary force composed of workers and soldiers who were sympathetic to the Bolshevik cause. The Red Guard played a crucial role in seizing key points in Petrograd during the insurrection.

- **Dual authority and the weakness of the Provisional Government:** The Provisional Government, weakened by its decision to continue the war and internal divisions, faced a situation of dual authority with the Petrograd Soviet. The indecisiveness and inability to address pressing issues created an opportunity for the Bolsheviks to present themselves as a decisive alternative.

- **Timing and strategic planning:** The timing of the insurrection coincided with the Second All-Russian Congress of Soviets, providing them with a platform to present their agenda and rally support.

- **The storming of the Winter Palace:** On the night of 25–26 October 1917, Bolshevik forces, including Red Guard units and sailors from the Kronstadt naval base, stormed the Winter Palace in Petrograd, which served as the seat of the Provisional Government. The operation, though less dramatic than later depictions suggest, symbolised the Bolshevik takeover. As Bolshevik forces took control of key points in Petrograd and the Winter Palace, the Provisional Government's authority crumbled. Many ministers were arrested and power was effectively transferred to the Bolsheviks.

- **Support from workers and soldiers:** The Bolsheviks garnered support from industrial workers and soldiers, who were disillusioned with the Provisional Government's failure to address their demands. The slogans of "Peace, Land, and Bread" resonated with the grievances of these key segments of the population.

The Civil War and War Communism

Following the Bolshevik seizure of power in the October Revolution of 1917, civil war quickly broke out. The Bolshevik Red Army, led by Vladimir Lenin and the Communist Party, were opposed by the White Army, composed of anti-Bolshevik factions with diverse ideologies all attempting to prevent the spread of Communism. Foreign powers, including Britain, France, the United States, and Japan, intervened to support the Whites.

War Communism

Introduced as an emergency measure to sustain the Red Army and the newly established soviet state in the face of internal and external threats, War Communism was the policy followed from 1918–21. The key aspects of the controversial policy included:

- **state control of industry:** the Bolsheviks implemented centralised control over industry, with the state taking over factories and production facilities

- **nationalisation of banks:** the government could allocate funds based on its priorities, focusing on the needs of the military and war-related industries

- **grain requisitioning:** to supply the Red Army and urban population, the Bolshevik government initiated a policy of grain requisitioning from peasants, often using force to ensure compliance

- **abolition of private trade:** private trade and businesses were largely abolished. Instead, the state controlled the distribution of goods and services, aiming to eliminate profiteering and speculation

- **introduction of rationing:** rationing systems were established to ensure a more equitable distribution of food and essential goods

- **suppression of opposition:** the policy was enforced through harsh measures, including the Red Terror, which involved mass arrests and executions of perceived counter-revolutionaries and opponents of the Bolshevik government.

> **Recap**
>
> War Communism was driven by the urgent need to secure the survival of the Bolshevik government during the Russian Civil War. While it achieved certain short-term goals, such as sustaining the Red Army and ensuring centralised control, it had severe consequences for those who lived under it.

How did the Bolsheviks win the Civil War?

Strengths of the Bolsheviks	Weaknesses of the Whites
The role of Trotsky: The Red Army, under the leadership of Leon Trotsky, demonstrated a high degree of discipline and unity of command. Trotsky's organisational skills and strategic acumen played a crucial role in coordinating military operations.	**Foreign intervention:** The intervention by foreign powers, including Britain, France, the United States, and Japan, to support the White Army was counterproductive. It fuelled nationalist sentiments and the presence of foreign troops on Russian soil united many factions against the common external threat.
Control of industrial centres: The Bolsheviks maintained control over key industrial centres, including Moscow and Petrograd, which provided them with the industrial capacity to produce weapons and supplies crucial for the war effort.	**White faction disunity:** The White Army was internally divided along ideological, political, and regional lines, hindering effective coordination and cooperation.
Geographic advantage: The Red Army had a strategic advantage in terms of geography. The central location of Moscow allowed the Bolsheviks to maintain better communication and transportation networks, facilitating the movement of troops and resources.	**War weariness of White forces:** The protracted nature of the Civil War, coupled with internal divisions and external pressures, led to war weariness among the White forces. Many elements within the White Army lacked the same level of commitment and motivation that characterised the Red Army.
Effective use of propaganda: The Bolsheviks skilfully employed propaganda to boost morale, maintain loyalty, and shape public perception. They framed the conflict as a defence of the socialist revolution against counter-revolutionary forces, creating a powerful narrative that resonated with their supporters.	

The New Economic Policy

In March 1921, in the naval base of Kronstadt, near Petrograd, an uprising occurred. It was fuelled by dissatisfaction with Bolshevik policies, including economic hardships under War Communism, political repression, and military discontent. The sailors and workers in Kronstadt, who had initially supported the Bolsheviks, became disillusioned with the direction of the government. The rebels demanded greater political freedoms, the end of one-party rule, and the return to the principles of the October Revolution. The Bolshevik government, led by Lenin and Trotsky, responded with force. While the Kronstadt Uprising did not achieve its immediate goals, it marked a turning point in Soviet policies, leading to a shift away from War Communism and the initiation of the
New Economic Policy (NEP).

The NEP was an economic reform introduced by the Bolshevik government in 1921. It marked a shift away from the strict War Communism policies that had caused economic hardship and social unrest and allowed for a limited return to market-oriented mechanisms, permitting small-scale private enterprise and commerce. Farmers were allowed to sell surplus produce in a free market and small businesses could operate independently.

Did it work?

- Some individuals and businesses prospered, leading to the emergence of a class of relatively prosperous peasants (Kulaks) and entrepreneurs, creating social tensions.

- The NEP faced opposition within the Communist Party, with some members, including Joseph Stalin, advocating for a more rapid transition to full socialism. This internal dissent eventually contributed to the shift away from the NEP.

- The success of the NEP was partially dependent on favourable world prices for Soviet exports, particularly grain. Fluctuations in global economic conditions could impact the success of the policy.

- Some critics argued that the NEP compromised socialist principles by allowing elements of capitalism to re-emerge. It sparked debates within the Communist Party about the long-term direction of Soviet economic policies.

- Ultimately, the NEP was discontinued in the late 1920s with the rise of Joseph Stalin, who pursued a more centralised and planned approach to economic development known as the First Five-Year Plan.

Recap

The NEP can be seen as a pragmatic response to the immediate challenges faced by the Soviet government, providing breathing space for economic recovery, but it was not a permanent or universally acclaimed solution.

Worked Example

Which was more important for the Bolsheviks, War Communism or the NEP? Explain your answer. (10)

The Bolsheviks implemented two key economic policies following the Russian Revolution: War Communism and the New Economic Policy (NEP). Both policies played significant roles in shaping the future of Soviet Russia, but their importance for the Bolsheviks differed in terms of their economic impact, political implications, and long-term consequences.

War Communism, introduced during the Russian Civil War, was characterised by state control over industry, nationalisation of banks and key industries, and requisitioning of agricultural surplus. This policy was crucial for the Bolsheviks as it allowed them to mobilise resources for the Red Army and ensure the survival of the Bolshevik regime during a period of intense internal and external conflict. However, War Communism also resulted in widespread famine, economic chaos, and social unrest, undermining popular support for the Bolsheviks and fuelling opposition from within the party itself.

In contrast, the New Economic Policy (NEP), introduced by Lenin in 1921, represented a partial retreat from War Communism and the reintroduction of limited capitalist elements such as private enterprise, markets, and profit incentives. The NEP was important for the Bolsheviks as it helped stabilise the economy, improve living standards, and consolidate Bolshevik power by appeasing peasants and small business owners who had been alienated by War Communism. By allowing for greater economic flexibility and individual initiative, the NEP contributed to a period of relative prosperity and social stability in the early 1920s.

In comparing the importance of War Communism and the NEP for the Bolsheviks, it is evident that while War Communism was crucial for the Bolsheviks' survival during a period of crisis and conflict, the NEP played a more significant role in laying the foundations for Soviet economic development and consolidating Bolshevik power in the long run. The NEP's pragmatic approach to economic policy helped stabilise the country after the tumultuous years of War Communism and allowed the Bolsheviks to maintain control while gradually transitioning towards socialism. Therefore, while both policies were important for the Bolsheviks, the NEP ultimately proved to be more consequential in shaping the course of Soviet history.

The rise of Stalin

Lenin had been a key founder of the Russian Revolution and the establishment of the Soviet state. As his health deteriorated due to a series of strokes, concerns about the future leadership of the Soviet Union intensified. Lenin's death in 1924 initiated a complex struggle for power among the leading figures of the Communist Party.

Stalin vs Trotsky

Joseph Stalin, the General Secretary of the Communist Party, gradually consolidated power in the years following Lenin's death. He skilfully used his position to appoint allies to key positions and build a power base within the party apparatus.

Leon Trotsky, a prominent Bolshevik leader and military commander, initially struggled to assert his influence. Trotsky's ideas of "permanent revolution" clashed with Stalin's policy of "socialism in one country".

The United Opposition and defeat of Trotsky

In 1926, Trotsky, Zinoviev, and Kamenev formed the United Opposition to challenge Stalin's leadership. They opposed Stalin's policies and advocated for greater democracy within the party. By 1927, Stalin had successfully marginalised Trotsky and his allies. Trotsky was expelled from the Communist Party and exiled from the Soviet Union in 1929.

The rule of Stalin

Rule by terror: The Purges

The Purges, also known as the Great Purge or the Great Terror, were a series of political repression campaigns in the Soviet Union orchestrated by Joseph Stalin during the 1930s. These campaigns targeted perceived enemies of the state, including political rivals, intellectuals, military officers, party members, and ordinary citizens. The Purges were characterised by widespread arrests, show trials, executions, and imprisonment in labour camps. Notable figures, including Leon Trotsky, Grigory Zinoviev, Lev Kamenev, and Nikolai Bukharin, were among those purged.

Exam tip

To effectively answer a 10-mark question like this one, it's important to provide a balanced analysis that considers both War Communism and the New Economic Policy (NEP) in depth.

Define War Communism and then discuss the importance of War Communism for the Bolsheviks, emphasising its role in addressing immediate wartime challenges, such as mobilising resources for the Red Army, and ensuring the survival of the Bolshevik regime.

Now define the NEP and then discuss the importance of the NEP for the Bolsheviks, highlighting its role in stabilising the economy, improving living standards, and consolidating Bolshevik power by appeasing peasants and small business owners.

Evaluate which policy was more important overall, taking into account the context of the time period, the specific challenges faced by the Bolshevik government, and the extent to which each policy contributed to the Bolsheviks' survival and consolidation of power.

Key features of the Purges included:

- **Show trials:** Prominent figures, including former high-ranking party officials and military leaders, were subjected to highly publicised show trials. These trials were often characterised by fabricated charges, forced confessions, and coerced testimonies. The accused were typically charged with treason, espionage, and conspiracy against the state.

- **Targeting of party members:** The Purges targeted members of the Communist Party, including those who had been loyal Bolsheviks during the early years of the Soviet Union.

- **Mass arrests:** The NKVD (People's Commissariat for Internal Affairs), the Soviet secret police, conducted mass arrests, rounding up individuals based on perceived political unreliability or association with alleged counter-revolutionary activities.

- **Exile and imprisonment:** Many individuals were exiled to remote regions of the Soviet Union or sent to labour camps (Gulags) as a form of punishment. Conditions in these camps were often harsh and the survival rate was low.

- **Purging the military:** The Red Army was significantly affected by the Purges. High-ranking military officers were accused of plotting against the state and many were executed. The military Purges weakened the Soviet Union's military capabilities in the lead-up to the Second World War.

- **Cultural purges:** The Purges extended to the cultural and intellectual spheres. Writers, artists, and intellectuals were targeted for their perceived deviation from socialist realism or alleged connections to foreign influences.

- **Impact on society:** The Purges created an atmosphere of fear and mistrust within Soviet society. People became reluctant to express dissent or criticise the government for fear of being labelled as enemies of the state.

The exact number of casualties during the Purges is difficult to ascertain, but estimates range from hundreds of thousands to millions of people who were executed, imprisoned, or exiled. The Purges had profound and lasting effects on the Soviet Union, shaping the political landscape and influencing the course of Soviet history for years to come.

Worked Example

What were the Purges? (4)

The Purges refer to a series of systematic campaigns of political repression and persecution carried out by Stalin's regime in the Soviet Union during the late 1930s. These Purges targeted perceived political opponents, including high-ranking officials within the Communist Party, military leaders, intellectuals, and ordinary citizens suspected of disloyalty or dissent.

The Purges involved mass arrests, show trials, executions, and imprisonment in labour camps (Gulags). Many of those accused were tortured or coerced into confessing to crimes they did not commit. The Purges resulted in the removal of potential rivals to Stalin's leadership and the consolidation of his power within the Soviet Union.

Exam tip

There are two aspects to a really good answer here. Explain what the Purges were, both in who was targeted and also by what methods.

Recap

The primary objectives of the Purges were to eliminate potential opposition, consolidate Stalin's power, and instil fear and obedience within the population.

Stalin and the role of propaganda

Propaganda also played a crucial role in Joseph Stalin's consolidation and maintenance of power in the Soviet Union. Stalin understood the power of shaping public perception and utilised propaganda to promote his cult of personality, control information, and maintain political loyalty.

Cult of personality: Stalin's image was elevated to almost god-like status through propaganda. His portraits adorned public spaces and his speeches were published widely. The cult of personality portrayed Stalin as the wise and infallible leader, the "Father of Nations", and the rightful successor to Vladimir Lenin. Stalin's image was skilfully crafted to convey strength, wisdom, and benevolence. Portraits and posters depicted him as a stern, fatherly figure, often with a pipe in hand. Such imagery aimed to create a connection between Stalin and the people, reinforcing the idea that he was guiding the nation with a paternalistic concern.

Public events and rituals: Mass events, parades, and public rituals were organised to reinforce the cult of personality. May Day celebrations, anniversaries of the October Revolution, and other events became opportunities to showcase Stalin as the central figure in Soviet achievements.

Heroic narratives: Propaganda often presented Stalin as the hero of the Soviet Union, guiding the nation through challenging times. His role in the Russian Civil War, victory over Nazi Germany during the Second World War, and efforts to industrialise the country were emphasised in a heroic narrative.

Censorship and control of media: The state exercised strict control over the media, ensuring that only approved narratives were disseminated. Newspapers, radio, and other forms of media were used to convey propaganda messages, while dissenting voices were silenced through censorship.

Rewriting history: Historical narratives were revised to align with Stalin's vision. Textbooks, literature, and art were altered to portray Stalin as a central figure in the Bolshevik Revolution and a key architect of Soviet success. Lenin and Stalin were depicted as inseparable in their revolutionary endeavours.

Political campaigns and slogans: Propaganda campaigns were orchestrated to coincide with political initiatives. Slogans, such as "Stalin is the Genius of the Revolution" and "Stalin's Plan is the Plan of the People", were widely shared to reinforce the leader's role and agenda.

Fig. 9.6 *Stalin's use of propaganda*

Was Stalin in total control of Russia by 1941?

Yes	No
Political purges and elimination of opposition	Dissent and opposition
Establishment of a cult of personality	Economic challenges
Control of the party apparatus	Legacy of the Purges
Secret police and surveillance	Challenges of the Second World War
Authoritarian economic policies	
Control of the military	

Apply

For the points in the table, expand and explain the reasoning to argue both sides of the argument.

Did Stalin's economic policies work?

Stalin introduced the Five-Year Plans during the late 1920s to rapidly transform the predominantly agrarian society into an industrialised powerhouse. Motivated by national security concerns, political uncertainty in Europe, and the ideological goal of achieving socialism within the country's borders, the plans aimed to modernise the economy, prioritise heavy industry, and bolster defence capabilities.

The strategy also involved the collectivisation of agriculture to generate surplus food and raw materials for the growing industrial centres. Emphasising centralised control, the plans were part of Stalin's broader vision of a planned socialist economy, seeking to overcome the perceived economic backwardness of the Soviet Union.

The Five-Year Plans

The Five-Year Plans were intended to rapidly industrialise the country and achieve specific production targets within five-year periods.

Plan	First Five-Year Plan (1928–32)	Second Five-Year Plan (1933–37)	Third Five-Year Plan (1938–41)
Objectives	The primary focus was on the development of heavy industry, including sectors such as coal, iron, steel, and machinery. The plan aimed to build a strong industrial base to support military preparedness and defend against potential external threats.	Building on the successes and lessons of the first plan, the second plan continued the emphasis on heavy industry, but also included targets to produce consumer goods, machinery, and chemicals.	The plan aimed to further diversify the economy by expanding sectors such as aviation, automotive, and synthetic rubber. Military preparedness remained a priority, especially given the looming threat of war.
Key features	Rapid collectivisation of agriculture, establishment of industrial centres, construction of infrastructure such as the Moscow Metro, and the creation of the Gulag system for forced labour.	Expansion of heavy industry, growth in the production of consumer goods, development of the electrical power industry, and construction of the Moscow–Volga Canal.	Increased production targets for aviation and automotive industries, development of synthetic rubber production, and preparation for the possibility of war.

After the war, the Soviet Union continued with subsequent Five-Year Plans.

Collectivisation

The policy of collectivisation aimed to reorganise agriculture by consolidating individual farms into collective or state-controlled farms. Stalin believed that collectivisation would increase agricultural productivity and efficiency by replacing small, individually owned farms with larger, mechanised collective farms. Collectivisation allowed for greater state control over agricultural production, distribution, and food supply. It also served to eliminate the influence of prosperous farmers or Kulaks, who were considered potential opponents of the socialist system.

First phase: Voluntary collectivisation (1928–29)

Initially, the government encouraged peasants to voluntarily join collective farms (kolkhozy) or state farms (sovkhozy). Peasants were promised benefits such as shared machinery, access to modern technology, and the opportunity to participate in a socialist transformation of agriculture.

Many peasants resisted collectivisation due to concerns about losing their private property and independence. The voluntary approach had limited success because a significant number of peasants were hesitant to give up their individual farms.

> **Exam tip**
>
> It's important to note that the plans had to be adjusted due to external factors, including the global economic downturn and the impending threat of war in the late 1930s. The outbreak of war in 1939 disrupted the third plan, leading to a shift in economic priorities towards supporting the war effort.

Second phase: Forced collectivisation (1929–33)

Faced with widespread resistance, Stalin shifted to a more coercive approach. The government initiated mass campaigns to force peasants into collectives, often employing violence, intimidation, and propaganda.

The policy included the persecution and deportation of wealthier peasants, known as Kulaks, who were viewed as class enemies. Many were sent to labour camps or exiled and their property was confiscated.

Forced collectivisation led to social upheaval, disruption of traditional farming practices, and widespread hardship. Millions of peasants resisted the policy, resulting in violent clashes and a significant loss of life.

The impact of collectivisation

- The rapid and forceful implementation of collectivisation disrupted agricultural production. The breakdown of traditional farming methods, coupled with resistance from peasants, led to a decline in productivity.

- The policy of collectivisation, particularly in Ukraine, contributed to a devastating famine in 1932–33. Grain requisitions and the confiscation of food by the state led to widespread starvation and millions of Ukrainians perished in what is known as the Holodomor.

- The policy strengthened state control over agriculture and facilitated the implementation of central planning in the Soviet economy. The government could regulate production, set quotas, and allocate resources more effectively.

> **Recap**
>
> The policy of collectivisation was a central component of Stalin's efforts to transform the Soviet economy and society. While it aimed to achieve economic and political objectives, the coercive methods used and the social disruption caused significant human costs and long-term consequences.

> **Worked Example**
>
> Why was collectivisation opposed by many peasants? (6)
>
> Collectivisation encountered significant opposition from many peasants for various reasons. First, peasants valued their autonomy and independence as individual farmers. Traditionally, they owned their land and means of production, which provided them with a sense of self-sufficiency and control over their livelihoods. Collectivisation, however, involved the state confiscating private land and livestock, effectively stripping peasants of their property rights and forcing them into collective farming arrangements. This loss of control over their land and resources was deeply resented by many peasants, who viewed it as a direct infringement on their autonomy and way of life.
>
> Second, collectivisation often subjected peasants to harsh working conditions and low wages on collective farms (kolkhozy). Many peasants found the prospect of forced labour unappealing compared to the relative freedom and potential for individual profit offered by private farming. The state's imposition of collective labour arrangements further fuelled resentment and resistance among peasants, who saw it as exploitative and unjust.
>
> Collectivisation also disrupted long-standing cultural and social ties within rural communities. Peasants often had deep-rooted attachments to their land, which held cultural and familial significance. The forced consolidation of farms into collective units undermined these communal bonds and traditional ways of life. Peasants resented the disruption of their social networks and the imposition of unfamiliar collective structures by the state.

> **Exam tip**
>
> For this question, you need to identify two reasons why peasants opposed the collectivisation of agriculture. Make sure you explain them too.

What was the impact on the Soviet people?

The changes brought about by policies such as industrialisation, collectivisation, and the Five-Year Plans had profound effects on the Soviet people.

Apply

Match the area of change in the table with the correct description. One of the descriptions doesn't have a heading to go with it. What would you label it as?

Area of change	Description
1. Urbanisation	**a.** The demand for labour in industrial centres resulted in a shift in traditional gender roles. Women increasingly entered the workforce, taking on roles in factories, construction, and other industrial sectors. This shift marked a departure from more traditional expectations for women in Soviet society.
2. Employment opportunities	**b.** The fear of retribution fostered a culture of informing on friends, family, and colleagues, as individuals sought to protect themselves from potential accusations. The state encouraged citizens to report on perceived anti-Soviet activities.
3. Culture	**c.** The forced collectivisation of agriculture disrupted traditional rural life and communal farming practices. The elimination of individual farms and the persecution of wealthier peasants (Kulaks) resulted in social upheaval and a loss of cultural and familial ties.
4. Agriculture	**d.** The period was marked by cultural repression, where artistic and intellectual freedom was curtailed. Literature, art, and cinema were expected to adhere to socialist realism, glorifying the achievements of the state and its leaders.
5. Political repression and fear	**e.** The political climate of the time, marked by Stalin's Great Purge, created an atmosphere of fear and suspicion. Accusations of disloyalty or association with perceived enemies of the state could lead to imprisonment, exile, or execution. The Purges affected individuals across various sectors, including party members, intellectuals, military officers, and ordinary citizens.
6. Human costs of industrialisation	**f.** The expansion of heavy industry and infrastructure projects created employment opportunities in sectors such as mining, manufacturing, and construction. However, the demand for labour often meant harsh working conditions, long hours, and low wages.
7. Shift in women's roles	**g.** The rapid industrialisation and construction projects of the Five-Year Plans were achieved at significant human costs. Workers faced gruelling conditions, inadequate safety measures, and a lack of workers' rights. Accidents and fatalities were common.
	h. The push for industrialisation led to rapid urbanisation as people migrated from rural areas to cities in search of employment in newly established industrial centres. This shift altered traditional agrarian lifestyles and created a new urban working class.

Review

1. What was a collective farm? [4]
2. Describe the influence of Rasputin on the Tsar. [4]
3. What was the NEP? [4]
4. Why did the Reds win the Civil War? [6]
5. What are the Purges? [6]
6. Why did Tsar Nicholas II issue the October Manifesto in 1905? [6]
7. "The Bolsheviks won the Civil War because of their own strengths rather than the weaknesses of the Whites." How far do you agree with this statement? Explain your answer. [10]
8. To what extent did Stalin succeed in transforming Russia? [10]
9. "The ends justify the means." To what extent is this statement true of Stalin's Russia? [10]
10. Assess the factors that contributed to the outbreak of the Russian Revolution in 1905 and its significance in the lead-up to the 1917 revolutions. [10]

For further information, review this section in the Student Book.

Raise your grade ↑

1. What was the October Manifesto? (4 marks)

The October Manifesto was issued by the Tsar in October 1905 to win support from liberal reformers who opposed his regime. It contained many features that liberal reformers might support, such as the creation of a Duma and the holding of parliamentary elections. It also included many rights and freedoms that people had been protesting for throughout 1905. These included freedom of speech, religion, and movement. Although Tsar Nicholas opposed the introduction of these reforms, the October Manifesto was successful in ending the 1905 Revolution.

The student has done well and provided a detailed description of the Manifesto, explaining the reasons for it as well as identifying relevant features of the plan. 4 marks awarded.

Plan your answer

- To answer this 4-mark question you need to provide two specific features of the October Manifesto. Make sure you explain the features and not just identify them.
- The Manifesto was introduced by the Tsar in 1905 in response to the uprising in the same year.
- It offered a chance for an elected assembly.
- It also offered further reforms to keep the people happy.

Mark scheme

1 mark for each relevant point, 1 additional mark for supporting detail. Maximum of 2 marks per point made.

2. Why did Stalin, not Trotsky, succeed Lenin? (6 marks)

Stalin, not Trotsky, succeeded Lenin for several key reasons. Stalin held key positions within the Communist Party's bureaucracy, such as General Secretary. This allowed him to appoint loyal supporters to important positions and consolidate power gradually. Trotsky's failings also meant it was Stalin who was appointed successor. Trotsky was a prominent figure but had alienated some within the party due to his uncompromising stance during the Civil War. Stalin skilfully exploited these divisions and formed alliances with other leaders, such as Zinoviev and Kamenev, to side-line Trotsky.

In terms of policy, Stalin's idea of "socialism in one country" resonated with many party members, as it prioritised strengthening the Soviet Union internally. Trotsky's vision of "permanent revolution" seemed more radical and less practical.

The student has done well to identify a range of reasons and offered a detailed explanation of the first reason. However, the second factor, a policy difference, has been identified but not fully explained. This answer would be awarded 5 marks.

Plan your answer

- To answer this 6-mark question you need to give reasons why Stalin won the leadership race against Trotsky.

- Stalin was able to position himself to be the chosen successor.

- He was more visible than Trotsky, who seemed aloof and isolated in comparison.

- There were key policy differences between the two, with Stalin wanting to consolidate the revolution within Russia, whereas Trotsky favoured looking to spread communism's influence abroad.

Mark scheme

Level 1:	general answer lacking specific contextual knowledge (1 mark)
Level 2:	identifies AND/OR describes reasons (2–3 marks)
Level 3:	explains ONE reason (4–5 marks)
Level 4:	explains TWO reasons (6 marks)

3. "Nicholas II fell from power in 1917 due to a failure to learn from the mistakes of 1905." How true is this statement? (10 marks)

While it is true that Nicholas II's failure to fully implement political reforms after the events of 1905 contributed to his downfall in 1917, it is essential to recognise that a multitude of other factors, such as the impact of the First World War, played an arguably more significant role in the fall of the Russian Tsar. Therefore, attributing his downfall solely to the mistakes of 1905 is an oversimplification of the historical context.

One key factor contributing to the downfall of the Tsar was the series of military failures and substantial losses suffered by Russia during the First World War. The Russian army was ill-equipped, poorly led, and faced logistical challenges on the Eastern Front. The war effort strained the country's resources, leading to widespread shortages, food scarcity, and economic hardships for the civilian population. As the war dragged on, the discontent among soldiers and civilians grew, fuelled by the perception that the Tsar was responsible for the military failures and the resulting suffering. The inability to achieve military success eroded the Tsar's legitimacy and authority, fostering resentment and paving the way for the rise of revolutionary sentiments.

The immense social and economic strains imposed by the demands of the First World War exacerbated existing issues within Russian society. The war effort led to the mobilisation of millions of men from the agricultural sector, resulting in a shortage of labour and a decline in agricultural productivity. This, coupled with the disruption of transportation networks, contributed to food shortages and soaring prices. The economic hardships intensified social unrest and deepened class divisions. The industrial sector also faced challenges as resources were diverted to the war, leading to inflation and deteriorating living conditions for urban workers. The strain on the economy and the resulting discontent among both the urban and rural population created a fertile ground for revolutionary movements to gain traction. The war thus acted as a catalyst for social and economic discontent, ultimately fuelling the revolutionary fervour that led to the overthrow of the Tsarist regime during the Russian Revolution of 1917.

The student has done well here in terms of focus on the impact of the First World War. There is depth of knowledge, clear focus, and solid reasoning. However, the student fails to present a balanced argument. They should answer the other side of the question, where there is an evaluation of whether

the Tsar failed to correct broader issues that had existed since 1905. There is also a lack of a conclusion. As this answer only addresses one side of the argument it would only score 5 marks.

Plan your answer

- 1905 created huge issues for the Tsar to solve. While the October Manifesto brought some change, it wasn't long-lasting and the Tsar was reluctant to make further improvements.

- As well as the issue of 1905, though, the First World War created more problems which the Tsar was unable to solve. This needs to be evaluated as a contributing factor to the Tsar's downfall.

- With a question such as this, there needs to be an element of judgement; make sure you include a conclusion once you have argued both sides.

Level 1:	general answer lacking specific contextual knowledge (1 mark)
Level 2:	identifies AND/OR describes reasons (2–3 marks)
Level 3:	gives a one-sided explanation (4–5 marks) or one explanation of both sides (4–6 marks)
Level 4:	explains both sides (7–9 marks)
Level 5:	explains with evaluation (10 marks)

10 The United States, 1919–41

You need to know

- How far the American economy improved in the 1920s
- How far American society changed in the 1920s
- How intolerance was a feature of American society
- What Prohibition was and its role in American society
- The role of women during the 1920s
- The events and consequences of the Wall Street Crash
- What Hoover did to try to combat the Great Depression
- Why Roosevelt won the election of 1932
- How Roosevelt acted in his First Hundred Days
- What the New Deal was and an evaluation of its impact
- How far the New Deal changed after 1933
- Why the New Deal faced opposition
- Why unemployment wasn't solved despite the New Deal

Background: The build-up to the 1920s boom

Industry in the United States, based on huge natural resources of coal, timber, iron, and oil, as well as farming, had grown steadily since the mid-19th century. Although only involved in fighting towards the end of the First World War, American businesses made money supplying arms and equipment as well as loaning money.

The 1920s became the boom years in the United States. However, not everyone shared in the boom with many, notably black, Americans continuing to suffer poverty.

How far did the American economy improve in the 1920s?

Factors on which the economic boom was based	
Invention and innovation	Advances in chemicals and synthetics brought rayon, Bakelite (a form of plastic), and cellophane into common use.
	Electricity meant consumer goods, including radios, washing machines, vacuum cleaners, and refrigerators, became widely available.
Republican policies	The Republican governments of the 1920s followed financial policies favourable to industry. The approach taken was known as laissez-faire, where the government favoured non-intervention.
	Taxation was kept low and high import tariffs were introduced.
Mass production	Assembly-line production was used by Henry Ford in the manufacture of cars. This method of production was copied for other goods and led to a fall in their prices.
The car industry	The car industry was central to economic success in the United States. With the cost of a car reducing in price, one in five Americans owned one by 1929.
	The car industry boosted a wide range of associated industries, including producers of glass, rubber, steel, and leather. The number of roads increased, as did roadside filling stations, hotels, and restaurants.
Mass marketing	Advertising for radio and the cinema was developed, while giant billboards displayed posters alongside highways.
	New merchandise was advertised in magazines, newspapers, and mail-order catalogues.

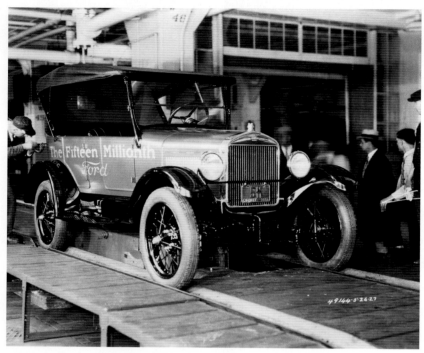

Fig. 10.1 *Model T Ford car coming off the production line*

Why was there a boom?

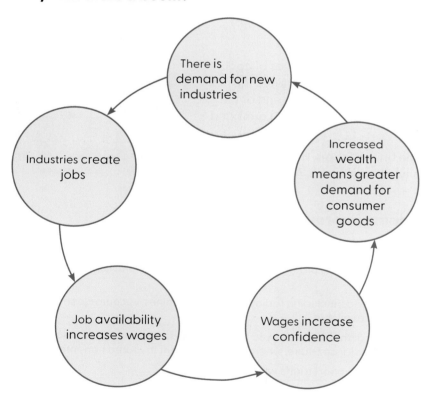

Fig. 10.2 *Factors leading to a boom*

Recap

Production-line manufacturing meant reduced prices and quicker production of goods. Cars, household items, and radios were mass produced at a cheap price.

Low taxation and a laissez-faire approach from the government were also prevalent.

As jobs became more available, wages rose—and so did personal spending.

Did all industries benefit from growth?

Industry grew	Agriculture did not share in the prosperity
The 1920s were a golden age for the construction industry. New businesses required offices and showrooms and they had to be connected by new roads. Many public buildings, including schools, were constructed, as were skyscrapers.	During the First World War, agriculture had boomed with exports to Europe. These exports were no longer needed once the war had ended.
Steel production, which was an established industry, gained significant new business from the construction sector. The steel industry was also boosted by car manufacture, as were the industries producing glass, rubber, and leather.	One of the problems was overproduction. The United States could not eat all the food that was produced; neither could the surplus be exported. As a result, prices fell.
	American agriculture was facing competition from Canada and Argentina.
While there was an increased demand for clothes, there was less demand for cotton and woollen textiles. The demand was for clothes manufactured using synthetic materials such as rayon.	Many European countries would not take American farm products because the United States had placed high tariffs on imports.
The coal industry suffered from the increased use of cleaner and more efficient oil, gas, and electricity alternatives.	Crops were also lost to pests. For example, in cotton-growing areas many crops were devastated by the boll weevil during the 1920s.

Which Americans didn't benefit from the boom?

- **Families:** By 1929, around 60 per cent of families lived below the poverty line.
- **Black Americans:** With the agricultural slump many moved north to work in the lowest paid sectors such as domestic service. They were segregated into slum areas such as Harlem in New York.
- **Native Americans:** They mainly lived in reservations where agricultural land was poor quality. Those who remained in the reservations suffered from poverty, poor education, and ill health.
- **immigrants:** Often only the lowest paid jobs were available to immigrants. Many suffered religious discrimination and lacked education.

Worked Example

How far did all Americans benefit from the boom? (4)

It can be seen that for some Americans the boom in the 1920s wasn't really a boom. Minority groups suffered.

Black Americans still suffered from segregation and from living in slum areas. The roles they took in society were often the lowest paid, such as jobs in domestic service.

Native Americans suffered, as many still lived in reservations and suffered from poverty, poor education, and ill health. The land they had was poor in quality, making it difficult to grow crops.

How far did American society change in the 1920s?

Is it fair to call it the Roaring Twenties?

Following the end of the First World War, Americans benefited from increased prosperity. Some spent their new wealth on entertainment.

For some young women, life was much freer. For example, this was the decade of less-restrictive clothing than previously: skirts and dresses were shorter and made from lightweight material. Other aspects of a freer life for some young women were wearing make-up, going out without a chaperone, going to night clubs, and dancing to jazz music.

Recap

Industry grew: for example, the 1920s were a golden age for the building industry, with dazzling new skyscrapers and many public buildings constructed during this period. The car industry also prospered.

Agriculture suffered: farmers struggled, crops were lost to pests, and overproduction with no foreign market to sell to resulted in great financial hardship for farmers.

Exam tip

While many Americans benefited greatly from the boom, certain groups didn't. To answer this question, choose two groups who suffered rather than benefiting and explain briefly why they suffered.

The car gave Americans the freedom of movement to visit clubs, cinemas, and restaurants.

For the majority of the population, however, the Roaring Twenties were more an image than a reality.

Entertainment opportunities	
Cinema	Cinema provided an opportunity to escape from the mundane parts of everyday life. Cinema audiences more than doubled, reaching 95 million in 1929.
	Many new stars were created by Hollywood, including Charlie Chaplin, Mary Pickford, and Rudolph Valentino. "Talkies" arrived in 1927 with the release of the film *The Jazz Singer* starring Al Jolson.
	Some Americans expressed concern that movies corrupted public morals.
Jazz	Jazz music originated in the African American community of the south.
	Jazz was linked to dance music and led to the formation of many night clubs. One well-known jazz performer was Duke Ellington. Jazz also appealed to young white people who found it exciting, dynamic, and modern. A new dance, the Charleston, became popular.
Radio	Radio broadcast light musical entertainment to a mass audience, producing the age of the great dance bands.
	As variety theatres declined, radio provided a fresh start for many artists.
Sport	Sport became a form of mass entertainment. For example, huge crowds attended baseball games.

How widespread was intolerance in American society?

- Many established Americans wanted to maintain traditions and were fearful of those who threatened the American way of life.

- Many perceived a threat coming from new immigrants: communists, anarchists, black people, Jews, and Catholics.

- It was the ambition of many Americans to maintain the supremacy of the white, Anglo-Saxon, Protestant community (WASPs).

Cause	Details	Examples of behaviour
The Red Scare	This was caused by the large number of immigrants arriving from southern and eastern Europe. It was thought that they would attempt to spread communist and anarchist ideas following the Bolshevik Revolution in Russia in 1917.	Suspected agitators were arrested and deported. A series of bomb blasts in 1919 offered evidence of a supposed conspiracy against the state. The case of Italian immigrants Vanzetti and Sacco, who were executed for murder despite evidence being flawed, illustrates the widespread fear of immigrants from southern and eastern Europe.
Religious intolerance	Fundamentalist Christians in rural areas of the south believed in a literal interpretation of the Bible rather than accepting Darwin's theory of evolution.	The fundamentalists succeeded in outlawing the teaching of evolution in six states. In Tennessee, biology teacher John Scopes deliberately broke the law by teaching evolution. The so-called "monkey trial" of 1925 was a national sensation. Scopes was found guilty.
The Jim Crow laws	In the south, black people suffered from segregation under the Jim Crow laws. Most lived in poverty and permanent fear of lynch mobs.	Laws covered everything from marriages to hospital treatment and included the education of children: "[The County Board of Education] shall provide schools of two kinds"; (Texas law)
Immigration policy	This law restricted the entry of certain national groups to the United States.	This affected immigrants from southern and eastern Europe. Immigrants from China and Japan were completely barred. The law resulted in 85 per cent of immigrants to the United States coming from northern Europe.

Cause	Details	Examples of behaviour
The Ku Klux Klan	The Ku Klux Klan (also known as simply "the Klan") was the most extreme example of intolerance and racism during the 1920s.	The Klan claimed to have a membership of 5 million in 1925. Membership included high-ranking politicians and government officials. The Klan's hatred went wider than their hatred of black people. The most extreme forms of persecution included beating, mutilation, and lynching.

What was Prohibition?

The 18th Amendment to the American Constitution was passed through Congress in 1919. This prohibited the manufacture, transport, and sale of alcohol.

Why was Prohibition introduced?

- It was claimed that alcohol caused social problems such as poverty, crime, violence, and ill health. The Anti-Saloon League and the Women's Temperance Union were strong campaigners for abolition, suggesting the United States would become a better place.

- The Protestant Church supported the cause, believing that alcohol brought a decline in moral standards and damaged family life in the big cities.

- Some believed that grain used for alcohol could be better used for making bread.

- Some politicians saw it as an opportunity to gain votes.

- Some industrialists, including Nelson Rockefeller, argued that Prohibition would be good for the economy as it would reduce workers' absenteeism and increase efficiency.

Why was Prohibition repealed?

- Consumption of alcohol actually increased as illegal bars, called "speakeasies", became common. It is believed that by 1929, New York had 32 000 illegal drinking bars.

- Some people tried to make their own alcohol. This was called "moonshine". Drinking moonshine could cause death.

- It was impossible to prevent alcohol being smuggled into the United States. Many of those involved in this illegal trade made large amounts of money. "Bootleg" rum was smuggled from the West Indies and whisky from Canada.

- Prohibition boosted crime. Organised gangs controlled the manufacture and sale of alcohol. There was much feuding between the gangs, leading to incidents such as the Valentine's Day Massacre of 1929, when rival gang members were murdered by Al Capone's gang.

- State officials, judges, senior police officers, and jury members were often given bribes to overlook evidence of consumption of alcohol or to make a lenient judgement.

> **Apply**
>
> Write a fact file about three types of intolerance in American society in the 1920s and 1930s.

Why did Prohibition end?

Practicality	The policy proved unworkable. It was clear by the early 1930s that Prohibition had failed.
Context	At the time of the Depression it seemed illogical to spend public money trying to enforce the law. This money would be better used in creating jobs for the unemployed.
Cost	Money could be made from imposing taxes and duties on alcohol.

When Roosevelt came to power he supported the proposal to repeal Prohibition. This was done under the 18th Amendment. Prohibition ended in December 1933.

Worked Example

Why was Prohibition repealed? (6)

Prohibition was ended as it seemed to have been a failed policy. Despite attempts to stop the sale of alcohol, consumption of alcohol actually increased as illegal bars, called "speakeasies", became common. It has been claimed that New York had 32 000 illegal drinking bars by 1929. Some people even tried to make their own alcohol called "moonshine".

Prohibition also boosted crime. Gangs controlled an illegal trade in alcohol despite some police efforts to prevent this. Clashes between gangs led to violence such as the Valentine's Day Massacre of 1929, when rival gang members were murdered by Al Capone's gang. As the police struggled to control the trade in illegal alcohol, violence increased.

Some argued that at the time of the Depression it seemed illogical to spend public money trying to enforce the law of Prohibition and instead the money should be used to create jobs and support the economy.

Recap

Prohibition was meant to address some of the ills in American society, but it proved unworkable as a policy—it did not have public support.

Americans used "speakeasies" (illegal bars) and "moonshine" (home-made alcohol) as ways to get around the ban.

The illegal alcohol trade also caused wider issues, with rival gangs battling each other for control of this lucrative market, and bribing policemen and government officials to overlook illegal business activity.

Exam tip

Prohibition was a failure for many reasons, including the lack of public cooperation, the rise of gang clashes, and the corruption of the police. To answer this question, choose two reasons and explain them.

How were women affected by the changes?

The 1920s brought a revolution in the role of some women. Some became known as flappers. These were often young, wealthy, middle- and upper-class women from the larger towns and cities. These women were the "showy and noisy" minority.

Politics	In 1920 women got the vote in all states. They now made up 50 per cent or more of the electorate.
Work	The number of women in employment increased by 25 per cent to 10 million by 1929, although women continued to be paid less than men for precisely the same work.
	Office work and manufacturing accounted for much of the increase in employment for women. In some new industries, such as electronics, women workers were preferred to men.
Dress	Corsets were abandoned and women began wearing shorter, more lightweight skirts and dresses, and the dresses were often sleeveless. The new fashions and materials, such as rayon, permitted greater movement and self-expression.
Lifestyle	Women began smoking, drinking, and kissing in public. Chaperones were no longer required.
	Women also drove cars. It has been suggested that Henry Ford introduced coloured cars in 1925 as a response to the female market. Previously, all Ford cars had been black.
	Short hair and make-up became symbols of the new freedom.
	Women were acting with more independence. The divorce rate increased from 100 000 in 1914 to 205 000 in 1929.
	Labour-saving devices affected the lives of a minority: only 30 per cent of households owned a vacuum cleaner and 24 per cent owned a washing machine.

Did the changes affect all women?

Not all women were affected by the changes. Compared to women in towns and cities, women from rural areas were less affected, continuing their traditional roles and restricted lives. Many of these women actually opposed the changes.

What was the Wall Street Crash?

What caused the Wall Street Crash?

On the stock market everything depended on confidence in the share prices rising. By the end of the 1920s the American economy was slowing down. On "Black Thursday", 24 October 1929, the fall in share prices turned into panic. Prices plunged and desperate investors sold their shares to try to cut their losses. Thousands were bankrupted as the stock market went into freefall.

Exports

- The United States had limited opportunities for exporting its products.
- Its European customers were impoverished and had still not recovered fully from the financial strains of the First World War.
- American tariffs led to tariffs being set up by potential customers which made it difficult for American exporters to operate in foreign markets.

The action of speculators

Overproduction

- By 1929, American industry was producing more consumer goods than there were consumers to buy them.
- The market had become saturated as Americans with money had now bought their cars, fridges, and other domestic appliances.

The Wall Street Crash

Uneven distribution of income

- Estimates suggest that between 50 and 60 per cent of Americans were too poor to take part in the consumer boom of the 1920s.
- Low wages and unemployment, especially in the farming sector, the traditional industries, and among black people and new immigrants, reduced the potential of the home market.
- By contrast, just 5 per cent of the population was receiving 33 per cent of the income in 1929.
- Too much money was in too few hands. Mass production required mass consumption and that meant higher wages.

Signs of an economic slow-down

- There were signs that the 1920s boom was coming to an end well before October 1929.
- By 1927 fewer new houses were being built, sales of cars were beginning to decline, and wage increases were levelling off.
- Financial experts were aware that stock levels in warehouses were beginning to increase, suggesting that the economy was slowing down.
- All this made investors nervous and anxious to sell their shares at the first sign of serious trouble.

Fig. 10.3 *Causes of the Wall Street Crash*

What impact did the Wall Street Crash have?

- The stock market crash was an economic disaster. The share prices did not stop falling for three years.

- Businesses and banks went bust. Around 11 000 banks stopped trading.

- The economy had to adjust to a general reduction in trade and demand for American goods both at home and abroad.

- Businesses had to reduce their operations by cutting production.

- Workers were dismissed or had their wages reduced.

- Less money in the economy meant that people could not afford to buy goods and business confidence collapsed. Any thought of expansion had to be abandoned.

- By 1933 the economy was producing only 20 per cent of what it had produced in 1929.

Worked Example

Why did Roosevelt feel it was important to deal with the banking crisis? (6)

Roosevelt felt that the collapse of the banks would mean a fall in public confidence. The banks were close to collapse as customers were panicking and withdrawing their savings.

With such uncertainty Roosevelt ordered a national bank holiday to pass his Emergency Banking Act. Unsound banks were closed down. The remainder were helped with government grants and advice. People with savings were asked to return their money to the banks when the banks reopened.

Through these measures Roosevelt felt that he had addressed concern about the banks' possible collapse and that he had helped to support the economy.

Exam tip

In your answer to this question, try to explain the reason behind Roosevelt's actions, but also add some specific detail to support your point.

Fig. 10.4 *A Hooverville in Seattle, 1934*

What was the social impact of the crash?

- By 1933 nearly one in four of the workforce was unemployed.

- There were no welfare benefits for those without an income (but rents and mortgages still had to be paid).

- Many faced eviction from their home, often being reduced to begging, scavenging in rubbish dumps for food scraps, and sleeping on park benches.

- Shanty towns of tents and makeshift huts, constructed from scrap metal and cardboard boxes, grew up on the edges of towns and cities. These "towns" became known as Hoovervilles after the President.

- The unemployed queuing for food from charities or soup kitchens became a common sight.
- In 1932 the government lost support as a result of the way it dealt with the Bonus Marchers, a group of thousands of destitute army veterans. Their peaceful protest ended in tragedy as the government used the army to disperse them, resulting in two veterans being killed and nearly 1000 injured.

Recap
The Wall Street Crash had a devastating effect.
• A cycle of suffering was caused—as businesses were forced to close, jobs were lost so people had less money. This forced more businesses to close and tax revenue to fall.
• By 1933 one in four workers was unemployed.
• There was visible unemployment—it was common to see unemployed workers queuing in the streets for food at soup kitchens or for help from other charity organisations.
• Many people were forced to live in shanty towns.

Apply
Write a fact file that explains the economic and social consequences of the Wall Street Crash.

What did Hoover do to try to combat the Great Depression?

- In 1930 taxes were cut by $130 million to inject more purchasing power into the economy.
- Tariffs were increased by the Hawley-Smoot Act (1930) to protect American-produced food and goods.
- Money was provided to finance a building programme to create more jobs. The most famous project was the Hoover Dam on the Colorado River.
- Employers were encouraged to make voluntary agreements with their employees to maintain wages and production.
- The Reconstruction Finance Corporation (1932) was set up to provide loans, amounting to $1500 million, to businesses facing hard times.
- The Federal Farm Board was set up to buy surplus produce in an attempt to stabilise prices.

Why was Roosevelt elected president in 1932?

	President Herbert Hoover	**Franklin D Roosevelt**
Approach to the crisis	Hoover's approach to the crisis was to "sit it out" until prosperity returned. When he took action it was regarded as too little, too late.	Roosevelt's election campaign was about giving Americans a "new deal".
Social policies	He was against the government providing welfare support as he thought it would undermine the United States' individualism. This gave the impression of being unsympathetic. This was confirmed by his actions against the Bonus Marchers.	He had a reputation for helping those in need when, as Governor of New York, he set up schemes to help the elderly and the unemployed.
Personality	He failed to project himself as a man of vision, giving an impression of being grim-faced and conservative in his approach.	He had an upbeat personality and appeared warm, charming, and optimistic when on the campaign trail. This approach gave confidence to Americans that they would be helped. He had suffered from polio and many Americans admired the way he had coped with this.

Did the New Deal work?

What was the New Deal?

- The term "New Deal" was applied to various measures introduced by Roosevelt between 1933 and 1938 to rescue the United States from the Great Depression.

- The first phase, introduced between March and June 1933, is referred to as Roosevelt's First Hundred Days.

- Roosevelt spoke to the public via radio broadcasts, explaining his policies in an informal and friendly manner.

His first action was to deal with the banking crisis. A main feature of this first phase was the creation of **alphabet agencies**.

Key term

Alphabet agencies— government agencies known for convenience by their initials.

Worked Example

What was Roosevelt's New Deal of 1933? (4)

The "New Deal" was the term used for specific measures taken by Roosevelt between 1933 and 1938. Following the Wall Street Crash, the New Deal was devised in an attempt to rescue the United States from the Great Depression.

Between March and June 1933, Roosevelt's First Hundred Days saw him try to deal with the banking crisis through his creation of alphabet agencies and the passing of the Emergency Banking Act.

Exam tip

The answer to this question should start with a definition of what the New Deal was and include specific issues that Roosevelt was trying to address.

The First Hundred Days

Area for reform	Situation	Government action	Effect
Banks	Banks were close to collapse as customers were panicking and withdrawing their savings.	Roosevelt ordered a four-day national bank holiday while the Emergency Banking Act was passed through Congress. Unsound banks, around 5 per cent of the total, were then closed down while the remainder were helped with government grants and advice.	Those with savings were asked to return their money to the banks when they reopened. Public confidence was restored and the banking system survived.
The unemployed	Unemployment stood at nearly 13 million in 1933, approximately 25 per cent of the workforce.	The Civilian Conservation Corps (CCC) was set up to provide voluntary employment for young men aged 18 to 25. They carried out conservation work, such as planting new forests. The Public Works Administration (PWA) provided jobs by initiating major construction projects such as dams, bridges, railways, schools, hospitals, and houses.	Wages were low but the scheme provided work for over 2 million men during the nine years of its existence. The PWA spent $7 billion between 1933 and 1939 creating millions of jobs for skilled workers.
Farmers	The collapse of food prices after 1929 had left the farming industry in crisis.	The Agricultural Adjustment Agency (AAA) paid farmers to take part of their land out of cultivation and reduce their livestock. Millions of acres of sown land were ploughed up and 6 million animals were slaughtered.	Prices rose, and between 1933 and 1939 farmers' incomes doubled. Farm labourers were not helped by this measure, however, and many found themselves unemployed.

Area for reform	Situation	Government action	Effect
Industry	Wages and production remained low.	The National Industrial Recovery Act set up the National Recovery Administration (NRA) aiming to stabilise production and prices and to improve working conditions and pay. Voluntary codes were drawn up to regulate prices, output, hours, and wages. Businesses that adopted these codes displayed the NRA badge. The public were encouraged to buy from these companies.	The scheme led to an improvement in working conditions and ended price-cutting wars, but it favoured large firms. When the scheme was declared unconstitutional by the Supreme Court in 1935, Roosevelt made no attempt to revive the idea.
The poor	Relief for the poor had been drastically cut, meaning that the employed were also often homeless too.	The Federal Emergency Relief Administration (FERA) had a budget of $500 million to assist those in desperate need.	The money was used to fund soup kitchens, provide clothing and bedding, and set up work schemes and nursery schools.

How was the New Deal changed after 1933?

During 1935, Roosevelt introduced a new phase of reforms that became known as the Second New Deal.

- **The Wagner Act, 1935** confirmed the right of workers to join a trade union and replaced the unconstitutional National Industrial Recovery Act.

- **The Social Security Act, 1935** provided old-age pensions, unemployment benefit, and help for the sick and disabled. It was based on a national insurance scheme.

- **The Works Progress Administration (WPA), 1935** supported efforts to find jobs for the unemployed through a broad range of projects and work programmes.

- **The Resettlement Administration (RA), 1935** aimed to move 500 000 families to areas of better land. While some families benefited, many farm workers remained in poverty.

Why did the New Deal encounter opposition?

There were people who thought that Roosevelt did not go far enough in his reforms, while others thought he was too radical.

Radical opposition came from critics such as the following individuals.

- Father Coughlin became disillusioned as he felt Roosevelt was failing to tackle the problems of the poor. Coughlin broadcast his ideas on radio every Sunday evening to an enormous national audience.

- Dr Francis Townsend campaigned for pension reform through his Townsend Clubs. He claimed that Roosevelt was more interested in preserving society than changing it.

- Huey Long planned a major redistribution of wealth to stimulate the economy. He planned to take money from the very rich and redistribute it among the less affluent.

Conservative opposition came from the following groups.

- Republicans believed that there should be minimal government intervention and low taxation. The New Deal was seen to undermine what were regarded as core American values. They thought that Roosevelt was becoming too powerful and was acting like a dictator.

Apply

Prepare a table of information relating to life for various groups in the United States in the mid-1930s. Complete columns for workers in industry, workers in agriculture, and the unemployed. Include the problems each group faced and what help was available.

- Businessmen resented the level of government interference. They thought it was a form of socialism and un-American. They were unhappy with Roosevelt's support for trade unions.

- The rich thought that it was unfair that they had to pay to help the less fortunate. Many felt that Americans had always believed in self-help. They said that the policy would encourage people to be lazy.

- Some state governors argued that aspects of the New Deal conflicted with the rights of state governments to manage their own affairs.

There was also opposition from the Supreme Court.

- The main role of the Supreme Court was to ensure that any measures introduced were consistent with the American Constitution.

- The nine Republican judges at the Supreme Court disliked the political policies on which the New Deal was based.

- They declared the National Recovery Administration (NRA) and the Agricultural Adjustment Act (AAA) unconstitutional.

- Following his re-election in 1936, Roosevelt wanted to appoint six additional judges who were sympathetic to his policies.

- He was accused of trying to overthrow the Constitution and acting like a dictator.

- He withdrew his plan to appoint new judges who would support the New Deal.

Worked Example

"The New Deal was a failure." How far do you agree with this statement? Explain your answer. (10)

It can be argued that the New Deal failed in many ways, despite the high acclaim and praise it earned.

There were some who thought that the New Deal, and Roosevelt in particular, didn't go far enough in what was achieved. Individuals, such as the outspoken Father Coughlin, thought Roosevelt failed to tackle the problems of the poor. Father Coughlin voiced this view on his weekly radio broadcast. Similarly, Dr Francis Townsend thought that the New Deal didn't reform the situation for the elderly and campaigned for pension reform through his Townsend Clubs.

Roosevelt also faced political opposition from Republicans who believed that there should be minimal government intervention and low taxation—the New Deal seemed to undermine this through increased government intervention in people's lives. Republicans saw Roosevelt as building his own power base and acting like a dictator.

However, the New Deal can be judged a success in many ways. Roosevelt's policies gave many Americans new hope, new confidence, and a sense of purpose. He also managed to address several of the key problems facing the country. Unemployment fell by over 30 per cent between 1933 and 1939, and the introduction of welfare payments and other emergency benefits such as food, clothing, and shelter helped millions who needed it most. Ordinary workers benefited from the support of trade unions, and farmers saw an increase in prices.

Overall, although the New Deal was far from perfect, and certain groups felt it didn't go far enough, it managed to address several grave problems facing the United States at a time of severe crisis.

Exam tip

When answering 10-mark questions remember to examine both sides of the question, as well as offering a summative conclusion to the argument.

Despite the New Deal, why did unemployment continue?

In 1933, when Roosevelt became President, the unemployment figure was 12.8 million. In 1941 this figure was 5.6 million. During the years of the New Deal, unemployment never fell below 5 million. What were the reasons for this?

- The New Deal found work for millions of people, but it was in jobs that were not secure.

- Incomes for many Americans remained low, reducing the money available to spend on American goods.

- There was a worldwide depression so the foreign market was not purchasing American goods. Import tariffs were common practice in Europe as well as the United States.

- Changes in manufacturing required fewer labourers.

Did the fact that the New Deal failed to solve unemployment mean that it was a failure?

	The New Deal as a success	The New Deal as a failure
Unemployment	Unemployment fell by over 30 per cent between 1933 and 1939.	Unemployment never fell below 14 per cent of the workforce between 1933 and 1939.
Industry	Industrial development and prosperity were stimulated by the construction of schools, roads, and hydroelectric dams.	Imposed rules and regulations, the increases in taxation, and the encouragement given to trade unions held back industrial development.
Trade unions	Trade union membership increased to over 7 million. Many strikes were settled in the workers' favour. Working conditions generally improved, as did workers' pay.	Businessmen and industrialists strongly disliked the encouragement given to unions under the Wagner Act. Some companies were prepared to use violence to break up strikes and sit-ins.
Particular groups	Large-scale farmers benefited from the reductions in acreage and livestock and the increase in prices. The introduction of welfare payments and other emergency benefits such as food, clothing, and shelter helped millions who needed it most.	Tenant farmers, labourers, and sharecroppers were forced off the land by government plans to reduce agricultural production. Although some black people made gains in employment and housing, they did not benefit as much as white people—Roosevelt needed the support of Democrats in the south and this prevented him from introducing civil rights laws the southern Democrats would have opposed.
The impact of the New Deal	The impact was huge—Roosevelt's policies gave many Americans new hope, new confidence, and a sense of purpose.	The impact was limited—it was pre-war defence spending and the supplying of armaments to Britain and France that stimulated the economy. Rearmament rather than the New Deal was primarily responsible for the economic revival of 1939 and 1941.

Review

1. What was the main development in the car industry during the 1920s? [4]

2. What problems did farmers face in the 1920s? [4]

3. How significant were Republican policies in causing the boom in the United States in the 1920s? [4]

4. How significant was the impact of the economic boom on the people of America? [4]

5. Describe the activities of the Ku Klux Klan. [4]

6. Describe a Hooverville. [4]

7. Why was the American economy showing signs of weakness by 1929? [6]

8. Why did the government deal harshly with the Bonus Marchers? [6]

9. Why did some industries prosper more than others during the boom in the 1920s? [6]

10. To what extent was intolerance a feature of American society in the 1920s? [10]

11. "The impact of the Ku Klux Klan on American society was greater than that of Prohibition." How far do you agree with this statement? Explain your answer. [10]

12. "Hoover could only blame himself for losing the presidential election of 1932." How far do you agree with this statement? Explain your answer. [10]

13. How significant was speculation as a cause of the Wall Street Crash? [10]

14. How important was Roosevelt's promise of a New Deal in him being elected President in 1932? [10]

15. How significant was the opposition of the Supreme Court in limiting the impact of Roosevelt's New Deal? [10]

For further information, review this section in the Student Book.

Raise your grade ↑

1. What was Prohibition? (4 marks)

Prohibition was the banning of the manufacture, transport, and sale of alcohol in the United States in 1919. It was the 18th Amendment to the American Constitution and lasted 13 years.

The answer correctly explains the facts of prohibition, in terms of what it was and how long it lasted. This is one developed point and another is needed to secure full marks. 2 marks awarded.

Plan your answer

- In the answer aim to write two well-explained points setting out what prohibition was and why it was introduced.
- Prohibition meant that the manufacture, transport, and sale of alcohol was illegal.
- It was introduced in the United States in an attempt to address social issues which many believed were caused by alcohol such as poverty, crime, violence, and ill health.
- Various campaigners wanted prohibition introduced, including the Anti-Saloon League and the Women's Temperance Union.
- Others saw the benefit as improving the work ethic of ordinary Americans who thought a sober society would be a harder-working one.

Mark scheme

1 mark for each relevant point, 1 additional mark for supporting detail; maximum 2 marks per point made.

2. Why was the New Deal criticised? (6 marks)

The New Deal was criticised as it was seen to be too interfering in people's lives and there were groups who resented this. Republicans believed that there should be low taxation and the New Deal was seen to undermine this. Businessmen also resented the level of government interference, as they felt that Roosevelt's support for trade unions undermined their own abilities to run their businesses. The wealthier people in American society also felt it was too much—it was their taxes that were used to support the unemployed and they felt that this government help would encourage people to be lazy.

This is a strong explanation of one reason why some Americans disliked the New Deal. There are different groups covered and it is a well-developed point. To gain the additional mark, another reason needs to be covered. 5 marks awarded.

Plan your answer

- In the answer aim to make two well-developed points explaining different reasons why the New Deal was criticised.
- The New Deal faced political opposition from the Republicans, who thought that it represented too much interference in people's lives and gave Roosevelt too much power.
- It was also opposed by the Supreme Court, who ruled that the National Recovery Administration (NRA) and the Agricultural Adjustment Act (AAA) were unconstitutional.
- Additionally, different elements of society disliked it—some of the rich thought that it was unfair that they had to pay to help the less fortunate, while others such as Father Coughlin felt that Roosevelt was failing to tackle the problems of the poor.

Mark scheme

Level 1:	general answer lacking specific contextual knowledge (1 mark)
Level 2:	identifies AND/OR describes reasons (2–3 marks)
Level 3:	explains ONE reason (4–5 marks)
Level 4:	explains TWO reasons (6 marks)

3. "The roles of women changed little during the 1920s." How far do you agree with this statement?   (10 marks)

Evidence seems to suggest that for women, roles changed a great deal during the 1920s. In 1920 women got the vote in all states. The opportunity for employment also increased and the number of women working increased by 25 per cent to 10 million by 1929.

Their roles in the home also changed, as labour-saving devices such as vacuum cleaners and washing machines came onto the market.

Women also drove cars and their appearance started to change, as short hair and make-up became symbols of the new freedom. This new independence saw an increase in the divorce rate from 100 000 in 1914 to 205 000 in 1929.

Many reasons why women's roles changed are identified here, covering a range of areas. However, the student doesn't explain the points made or offer a counter argument. 3 marks awarded.

Plan your answer

- You need to evaluate the argument in the question by considering the evidence that the roles of women changed very little in the 1920s. Then you need to present evidence that supports the opposite view.

- Women continued to be paid less for work.

- The much heralded labour-saving devices were only used in a minority of homes.

- It is worth noting that women from rural areas were less affected by the changes. They continued in their traditional roles and were less influenced by the changes in the larger towns and cities.

- However, there were significant developments—women could now vote, many more jobs were created, and a more relaxed attitude to fashions and lifestyles developed.

Mark scheme

Level 1:	general answer lacking specific contextual knowledge (1 mark)
Level 2:	identifies AND/OR describes reasons (2–3 marks)
Level 3:	gives a one-sided explanation (4–5 marks) or one explanation of both sides (4–6 marks)
Level 4:	explains both sides (7–9 marks)
Level 5:	explains with evaluation (10 marks)

You need to know

- How the Nazis gained control of Europe in 1940
- The German invasion of the Soviet Union, including the impact of Operation Barbarossa and the Battle of Stalingrad
- Reasons for the initial Japanese military successes at Pearl Harbor and the Battle of Midway
- How bombing affected the lives of people in Europe
- How strict rules from Japan impacted people's lives
- How Nazi control affected occupied Europe, especially Poland, and the Holocaust
- How effective the resistance movements in Malaya and France were
- What happened at the end of the war to Germany and Japan, including war crimes trials
- How the Second World War in the Asia-Pacific developed
- What the impact of war was on civilian populations in Europe and the Asia-Pacific
- How the Allies achieved victory over the Axis powers

Background

The Second World War was a global conflict that lasted from 1939 to 1945, involving many of the world's nations. Tensions both in Europe and Asia developed over a long period of time. The Treaty of Versailles had imposed harsh terms on Germany after the First World War, which led to economic hardships and resentment, contributing to the rise of Adolf Hitler and the Nazi Party.

Hitler's nationalistic aims and aggressive rhetoric soon led to increased likelihood of war. Germany, Italy, and Japan pursued aggressive expansionist policies. Germany invaded Poland in 1939, marking the beginning of the war in Europe. Japan invaded Manchuria in 1931 and later expanded into other parts of Asia.

Initially, the western powers adopted a policy of appeasement, hoping to avoid another conflict. However, Hitler's continued aggression eventually led to the Allies standing firm.

How had the Nazis gained control of Europe in 1940?

By 1940, Nazi Germany had achieved a significant level of control over Europe through a series of military victories and strategic manoeuvres. The main events that marked Germany's dominance in Europe during this period were:

11–13 March 1938: Germany absorbs Austria. This is known as the Anschluss.

29 September 1938: German demands for Czech territory lead to the Munich Agreement. Italy, Britain, and France sign the terms, which means Czechoslovakia must cede control of the Sudetenland to Germany.

14–15 March 1939: The Slovaks declare their independence and form a Slovak Republic. Germany occupies the remaining Czech lands in violation of the Munich Agreement and absorb them into a Greater Germany.

1 September 1939: Germany invades Poland, which forces the beginning of the Second World War in Europe.

9 April 1940: Germany invades Denmark and Norway, with Denmark surrendering on the day of the attack.

10 May 1940: Luxembourg is occupied by German forces.

14 May 1940: The Netherlands surrenders.

28 May 1940: Belgium surrenders.

9 June 1940: Norway surrenders.

Fig. 11.1 *Timeline of countries conquered by Germany, 1938–May 1940*

Fig. 11.2 *Areas under Nazi control, 8 November 1942*

Dunkirk and the attempt to invade Britain

What happened at Dunkirk?

- In May 1940, during the early stages of the Second World War, German forces launched a rapid and successful invasion of France. The German Blitzkrieg tactics, characterised by fast-moving armoured units and air support, overwhelmed the Allied defences.

- As German forces advanced through France, they encircled a large portion of the British Expeditionary Force (BEF) and other Allied troops, along with French soldiers, in the region around Dunkirk, a port town on the northern coast of France.

- The situation for the trapped Allied forces became increasingly dire. With German forces closing in and the likelihood of complete annihilation or capture, the decision was made to attempt a large-scale evacuation by sea.

- Operation Dynamo was the codename for the evacuation of Allied troops from Dunkirk. It involved the coordinated effort to rescue as many soldiers as possible using a combination of naval vessels and civilian boats.

- From 26 May to 4 June 1940, a vast array of vessels, including Royal Navy ships, civilian boats, fishing boats, and pleasure crafts, participated in the evacuation. The operation took place under constant threat from German air raids and artillery fire.

- Over the course of the evacuation, around 338 000 Allied soldiers were successfully rescued and brought across the English Channel to Britain. The operation surpassed expectations, as planners initially hoped to rescue only a fraction of that number.

- While the evacuation was a success, it came at a significant cost. Many Allied soldiers were captured or killed during the fighting and a substantial amount of military equipment and vehicles had to be abandoned.

- Despite the losses, the successful evacuation of a large portion of the British Expeditionary Force became a symbol of resilience and determination. British Prime Minister Winston Churchill's famous "We shall fight on the beaches" speech acknowledged the difficulties but emphasised the resolve to continue the war.

Fig. 11.3 *Thousands of British and French troops wait on the beaches of Dunkirk for rescue, June 1940*

Battle of Britain:
The German Luftwaffe faced determined resistance from the Royal Air Force (RAF), preventing Germany from gaining air superiority. The RAF's success in defending British airspace made a cross-Channel invasion, codenamed Operation Sealion, a risky proposition for Germany.

Strategic bombing campaign:
Britain initiated a strategic bombing campaign against German military and industrial targets. This disrupted German war production, diverted resources, and shifted the focus away from preparing for the invasion of Britain.

Why Germany was unable to conquer Britain

Strategic errors:
Hitler shifted the focus of German attacks from military targets to civilian populations during the Blitz. This decision reduced pressure on British military installations. Additionally, Hitler hesitated to commit fully to Operation Sealion despite the Luftwaffe's failure to secure air dominance.

Logistical challenges:
The logistical challenges of a cross-Channel invasion, given the state of German naval capabilities and the strength of the Royal Navy, were formidable. Germany lacked sufficient landing craft and the risk of being cut off or attacked during the sea crossing was a serious concern.

Royal Navy control:
The Royal Navy maintained control of the English Channel, making it challenging for Germany to launch an amphibious invasion. The potential for the Royal Navy to disrupt German troop movements across the Channel posed a significant obstacle.

Fig. 11.4 *Reasons why Germany was unable to conquer Britain*

Worked Example

What was the importance of the Battle of Britain in the early stages of the Second World War? (4)

The Battle of Britain was a major air campaign fought between the Royal Air Force (RAF) of Britain and the German Luftwaffe during the Second World War, primarily in the summer and autumn of 1940. It was significant because it was the first major military campaign fought entirely by air forces. The Battle of Britain was crucial for preventing Nazi Germany from gaining air superiority over Britain, which would have made a German invasion (Operation Sealion) much more likely. The RAF's successful defence against the Luftwaffe marked a turning point in the war and boosted Allied morale. It also forced Hitler to postpone his invasion plans, shifting the momentum of the war in favour of the Allies.

Exam tip

The Battle of Britain was a comparatively short period of time, but crucial in allowing Britain to prevent German domination of the air, which could then allow Germany to launch an invasion of Britain.

The German invasion of the Soviet Union

Operation Barbarossa, launched on 22 June 1941, became a turning point in the Second World War, shaping the course of the conflict on the Eastern Front and contributing to the eventual defeat of Nazi Germany.

Hitler launched the invasion of the Soviet Union in 1941 for a combination of ideological, strategic, and economic reasons. Key motivations included:

- **Ideological beliefs:** Hitler sought to eliminate communism and Bolshevism, viewing the Soviet Union as a stronghold of these ideologies. The invasion aimed to destroy the Soviet state and further Hitler's vision of expanding German territory eastward.

- *Lebensraum:* Hitler's concept of *Lebensraum*, or living space, played a crucial role. He believed in the superiority of the "Aryan race" and sought to acquire vast territories in the east for German settlement and resources.

- **Strategic considerations:** Hitler aimed to pre-emptively strike the Soviet Union to prevent it from becoming a future threat to Germany. He wanted to cripple the Soviet military and secure resources, particularly oil, to fuel Germany's war machine.

- **Economic resources:** The Soviet Union's abundant resources, including oil, minerals, and agricultural land, were a significant attraction for Hitler. Conquering the Soviet Union would provide Germany with access to these resources and address economic challenges.

Key fact

Hitler outlined his foreign policy aims and beliefs in an Aryan Race in *Mein Kampf*—an autographical book written in the 1920s. His desire for Germany to become the dominant state in Europe and the need for the seizure of large amounts of land to the east were a common theme of the book.

Barbarossa and Stalingrad

Event	Operation **Barbarossa (22 June 1941)**	Battle of Stalingrad (23 August 1942– 2 February 1943)
Aim	Hitler's invasion of the Soviet Union aimed to achieve a swift victory and eliminate the perceived threat of communism. The operation sought to secure vast territories for German colonisation and access to crucial resources.	Stalingrad, a major industrial city on the Volga River, held immense strategic importance for both sides. Controlling the city would secure the southern flank of the Eastern Front for Germany and protect vital Soviet oil fields.
Tactics	Germany employed Blitzkrieg tactics, characterised by rapid and coordinated movements of infantry, tanks, and air support. This approach led to early successes as German forces quickly advanced into Soviet territory. The Germans encircled and captured large numbers of Soviet troops, leading to substantial territorial gains in the initial phase of the operation.	The battle turned into brutal street-to-street and house-to-house combat. The Soviets, under General Vasily Chuikov, resisted fiercely, turning Stalingrad into a symbol of Soviet determination. The Soviets launched a counteroffensive in November 1942, encircling the German Sixth Army. The harsh winter, lack of supplies, and fierce Soviet resistance led to the surrender of the German forces in February 1943.
Impact	German forces captured important cities such as Kiev, Smolensk, and Minsk, causing significant damage to the Soviet military. The Red Army suffered substantial losses in terms of manpower, equipment, and territory. The rapid German advance created a dire situation for the Soviet Union.	The Battle of Stalingrad was one of the bloodiest battles in history, resulting in enormous casualties on both sides. The German defeat marked a turning point in the Eastern Front. Stalingrad shattered the myth of invincibility surrounding the German military. It marked the first significant defeat for Germany in the war and led to a loss of strategic initiative on the Eastern Front.

Worked Example

"The weather was responsible for Germany's defeat in the Soviet Union." How far do you agree with this statement? Explain your answer. (10)

I partially agree with the statement that "the weather was responsible for Germany's defeat in the Soviet Union", although it was not the sole factor. While weather conditions played a significant role in hindering the German advance, other factors also contributed to their defeat. The harsh Russian winter, particularly during the infamous Russian winters of 1941 and 1942, severely impacted the German military operations. The extreme cold, snow, and lack of adequate winter clothing for German troops led to logistical challenges, frostbite, and decreased mobility. These adverse weather conditions slowed down the German advance, strained their supply lines, and reduced the effectiveness of their military equipment.

However, attributing Germany's defeat solely to the weather overlooks other crucial factors. Military strategy and planning, logistical issues, Soviet resistance, and the vastness of the Soviet territory all played significant roles. The Soviet Union's ability to mobilise its vast resources, including manpower and industrial capacity, ultimately contributed to repelling the German invasion. Additionally, strategic errors by the German High Command, such as the decision to divert resources to multiple fronts simultaneously and the failure to adequately prepare for the winter conditions, also undermined their campaign in the Soviet Union.

In conclusion, while the weather indeed posed formidable challenges for the German military during their campaign in the Soviet Union, it was not the sole reason for their defeat. A combination of factors, including strategic mistakes, Soviet resilience, and logistical shortcomings collectively contributed to Germany's failure on the Eastern Front.

Exam tip

This is an interesting question, which could be fully explored to look at the wider factor of "winter" and not just the weather itself. Look at conditions, but also be aware of other factors such as greater Soviet manpower and industrial capacity.

The development of the Second World War in Asia-Pacific

Tensions between the United States and Japan had been growing for a while. The deterioration of US–Japanese relations was characterised by a series of confrontations over Japan's expansionist policies in Asia, its alignment with the Axis powers, and the imposition of economic sanctions by the United States. These tensions reached a climax with the dramatic surprise attack on the US naval base of Pearl Harbor.

The attack on Pearl Harbor occurred on 7 December 1941, when the Imperial Japanese Navy launched a surprise military strike against the United States Pacific Fleet, stationed at Pearl Harbor in Hawaii. The attack marked the entry of the United States into the Second World War and was a turning point in the conflict.

Fig. 11.5 *Three stricken US battleships after the Japanese attack on Pearl Harbor*

Date: The attack took place on the morning of Sunday, 7 December 1941.

Objective: The primary objective of the Japanese attack was to incapacitate the US Pacific Fleet, particularly its battleships, to prevent the United States from interfering with Japan's military expansion in South East Asia.

Aggressors: Japanese forces launched two waves of air attacks against the US naval base at Pearl Harbor. The attack involved six aircraft carriers, with a total of 353 aircraft, including fighters, bombers, and torpedo planes.

Targets: The main targets were the eight battleships of the Pacific Fleet, which were anchored at Battleship Row. These were the USS *Arizona*, USS *Oklahoma*, USS *California*, USS *West Virginia*, USS *Nevada*, USS *Utah*, USS *Maryland*, and USS *Pennsylvania*. Other targets included cruisers, destroyers, airfields, and aircraft on the ground.

Casualties: The attack resulted in significant casualties and damage. The Japanese achieved surprise, catching the US forces off guard. Eight American battleships were either sunk or heavily damaged, and numerous other ships were also damaged or destroyed. Approximately 2403 Americans were killed and over 1000 were wounded. The attack had a devastating impact on the US Pacific Fleet's capabilities.

Significance: The attack prompted the United States to declare war on Japan on 8 December 1941. On 11 December 1941, Germany and Italy declared war on the United States, and the United States reciprocated by declaring war on them.

Fig. 11.6 *Fact file of Pearl Harbor events*

Worked Example

Why did the United States enter the Second World War? (6)

The United States entered the Second World War primarily in response to the Japanese attack on Pearl Harbor on 7 December 1941. Prior to this event, the United States had maintained a policy of neutrality, providing aid to Allied nations through programmes like Lend–Lease. However, the attack on Pearl Harbor resulted in the deaths of over 2400 Americans and prompted the United States to declare war on Japan the following day. Additionally, Adolf Hitler's declaration of war on the United States shortly thereafter, based on Germany's alliance with Japan, further solidified America's entry into the conflict. The attack on Pearl Harbor unified the American public and government behind the war effort, leading to the mobilisation of the nation's resources and eventual involvement in both the European and Pacific theatres of the war.

Exam tip

You need two reasons here. Pearl Harbor and the desire for revenge from the United States is one, but find another too. It might be wise to point out Hitler's declaration of war that followed the attack.

Key term

Lend–Lease—From 1941, the United States lent, leased, and sold military equipment to countries fighting Germany, Italy, or Japan.

Early Japanese successes

After the successful surprise attack on Pearl Harbor on 7 December 1941, Japan launched a series of military offensives across the Asia-Pacific region.

- **Malaya (8 December 1941–31 January 1942):** Japanese forces quickly advanced through Malaya, defeating British, Indian, Australian, and local forces. The campaign culminated in the fall of Singapore, a major British stronghold, on 15 February 1942.

- **Philippines (8 December 1941–8 May 1942):** Japan invaded the Philippines shortly after the attack on Pearl Harbor. Despite determined resistance, including the defence of Bataan and Corregidor, the Philippines fell to Japanese forces in May 1942.

- **Burma (January 1942–May 1942):** Japanese forces invaded British Burma, quickly advancing and capturing the capital, Rangoon, in early March 1942. The campaign aimed to secure a land route to connect with Japanese forces in South East Asia.
- **Wake Island (23 December 1941–23 December 1943):** Japan attacked and occupied Wake Island, a US territory in the Pacific. The capture of Wake Island provided Japan with a strategic outpost.

The importance of Midway

The Battle of Midway, fought from 4 June to 7 June 1942, was a crucial turning point in the Pacific for several different reasons.

> **Apply**
>
> Create a mind map of reasons why the Battle of Midway was a crucial turning point in the Pacific.

> **Recap**
>
> The attack on Pearl Harbor changed the US attitude to the war. Where previously there had been no appetite to involve themselves in the conflict, the attack on Pearl Harbor galvanised the American public and shifted the nation's stance from neutrality to active involvement in the war. It led to a united national effort to support the war, including the mobilisation of resources, the draft, and widespread support for military operations in the Pacific and European theatres.

Factor	Explanation
Strategic importance	Midway Atoll, located north-west of Hawaii, held strategic importance in the control of the central Pacific. Japan sought to eliminate the US Pacific Fleet as a major threat and secure dominance in the region.
Codebreaking	American codebreakers, led by the efforts at Station HYPO under Commander Joseph Rochefort, were able to decrypt Japanese communications. The USA learned of Japan's plans to attack Midway and used this intelligence to prepare a defensive strategy.
Ambush and surprise	The US Pacific Fleet, under Admiral Chester W. Nimitz, set up an ambush for the Japanese fleet. US carriers were positioned to surprise the Japanese forces, who believed they were attacking an under-prepared enemy.
Japanese losses	Japan lost four aircraft carriers—*Akagi*, *Kaga*, *Soryu*, and *Hiryu*—during the battle. The loss of these carriers significantly diminished Japan's carrier fleet and its ability to project power in the Pacific.
Shift in naval power	The Battle of Midway shifted the balance of naval power in the Pacific. The United States, despite losing one carrier (USS *Yorktown*), inflicted a decisive blow on the Japanese navy, halting its expansion and aggressive momentum.
	The victory at Midway gave the United States the strategic initiative in the Pacific. It marked the first significant defeat for the Japanese navy, boosting Allied morale and setting the stage for the Allies to go on the offensive.
	The loss at Midway forced Japan to revise its overall strategy in the Pacific. It marked the end of Japanese naval expansion and the beginning of a defensive posture.

What the impact of war was on civilian populations in Europe and the Asia-Pacific

The Blitz was the German bombing campaign against British cities, particularly London, from 7 September 1940 to 11 May 1941. The Blitz was characterised by nightly bombing raids, particularly targeting major cities. London bore the brunt of the attacks, but other cities, including Coventry, Liverpool, and Birmingham, also faced heavy bombing. Strict blackout regulations were enforced to minimise the visibility of cities at night and make it difficult for German bombers to identify targets. Windows had to be

> **Key fact**
>
> The term Blitz is derived from the German word Blitzkrieg, meaning "lightning war".

covered and all external lights extinguished during blackout hours. Civil defence organisations were established to coordinate emergency response efforts. Air raid wardens patrolled the streets to enforce blackout measures and firefighting units worked tirelessly to extinguish fires caused by bombing.

What was the impact on the people?

The three Ss: Shelters, shortages, and safety!

1. **Shelters:** People sought refuge in public air-raid shelters, which were often located in basements, underground stations, or purpose-built structures. The most famous of these was the London Underground, which provided shelter for thousands.

   Many families had Anderson shelters—small, corrugated iron structures erected in gardens to provide protection from bomb blasts. These were meant for outdoor use. Indoor shelters, known as Morrison shelters, were also issued to households. These were tables with a metal frame and a steel mesh top, providing protection in case of a collapse.

2. **Safety:** To protect children from the bombing raids, the British government implemented evacuation programmes. Children were sent to live with host families in rural areas that were deemed safer than urban areas.

3. **Shortages:** The constant bombing disrupted transportation and supply lines, leading to shortages of various goods. The war effort led to severe rationing of food, clothing, and other essentials in order to make things last. People had to cope with limited supplies and adapt their diets to the available resources.

Allied bombing of Germany

Allied bombing against German cities attempted to weaken the German war machine, disrupt industrial production, and undermine civilian morale.

The Allied powers, particularly the British Royal Air Force (RAF) and the United States Army Air Forces (USAAF), developed a strategic bombing doctrine. The objective was to target key industrial and civilian areas to cripple Germany's ability to wage war.

Fig. 11.7 *The German city of Dresden after Allied bombing*

The early phases of the campaign involved area bombing, where entire cities were targeted to cause widespread destruction and disrupt German industrial production. This tactic aimed to create chaos and hinder the German war effort.

As the war progressed, efforts shifted towards more precision bombing to target specific military and industrial sites. However, challenges with accuracy and weather conditions often led to a combination of area and precision bombing.

Operation Gomorrah, Hamburg (1943)

The bombing of Hamburg in July 1943 marked a shift toward area bombing with the intentional use of incendiary bombs. The resulting firestorm caused massive destruction and civilian casualties.

Operation Thunderclap, Dresden (1945)

The bombing of Dresden in February 1945 remains one of the most controversial episodes of the Allied bombing campaign. The city, which had limited military significance, was subjected to heavy bombing that resulted in widespread destruction and loss of life.

What was it like to live under Japanese control in the occupied countries?

Japan sought to establish the Greater East Asia Co-Prosperity Sphere, expanding its empire across South East Asia and the Pacific. Territories like Singapore, the Philippines, Burma, and the Dutch East Indies fell under Japanese occupation.

- Countries and regions under Japanese control lost their independence and were subjected to Japanese rule. Local governments were often replaced and the Japanese military assumed authority.

- Japanese military officials held significant power in occupied territories and military rule was often characterised by strict control and censorship. Any form of dissent or resistance against Japanese rule was met with harsh measures. Civil liberties were curtailed and individuals who were critical of Japanese policies faced severe consequences.

- The Japanese authorities implemented policies of forced labour, conscripting local populations to work in mines, factories, and construction projects for the benefit of the Japanese war effort.

- Resources from occupied territories were exploited to support Japan's military and industrial needs. Local economies were often redirected to serve Japanese interests, leading to economic hardships for the local populations.

- Japanese authorities imposed strict censorship on media, limiting freedom of expression. Newspapers, books, and other forms of communication were closely monitored and controlled. Efforts were made to assimilate local populations into Japanese culture, eroding local traditions and promoting the adoption of Japanese customs and language.

- The Japanese military set up a system of "comfort women", involving the coerced recruitment of women for sexual services. This practice has been widely condemned as a form of wartime sexual slavery.

Case study: Malaya and Singapore

The Japanese occupation of Malaya and Singapore during the Second World War is a significant case study that sheds light on the impact of Japanese control on the lives of the local population.

- **Impact on the economy and daily life:** The Japanese occupation led to economic instability, with hyperinflation affecting the value of currency. Local currencies, including the Straits Dollar, became virtually worthless. Essential goods such as food, fuel, and clothing were rationed. The scarcity of these items led to widespread shortages, impacting the daily lives of Malaysians.

- **Forced resettlement and displacement:** The Japanese government implemented forced resettlement programmes, displacing communities for strategic reasons or to consolidate control. This disrupted traditional ways of life and had long-term social and economic consequences.

- **Cultural suppression:** Japanese authorities imposed strict censorship on media, suppressing any content deemed critical of the occupation. Newspapers, books, and cultural expressions were tightly controlled. Japan sought to assimilate the local population into Japanese culture. Teaching of the Japanese language and cultural practices was encouraged, eroding local traditions.

- **Resistance and guerrilla warfare:** British-led special forces, known as Force 136, operated in Malaya, engaging in guerrilla warfare against the Japanese forces. Local Malaysians also participated in resistance efforts. In response to resistance activities, Japan carried out harsh reprisals, including executions and mass punishments. Villages suspected of harbouring resistance fighters were subjected to punitive measures.

Area	Malaya	Singapore
Japanese military administration	Japan established the Malaya (later renamed Syonan-to) Military Administration to govern the occupied territory. Local institutions were restructured to serve Japanese interests, with Japanese military officials holding key administrative positions. To create an appearance of local governance, Japan installed puppet governments. These governments had limited autonomy and were subject to Japanese directives.	Japan established the Syonan-to Military Administration to govern Singapore. Local institutions were restructured and Japanese military officials assumed key administrative roles. Similar to other occupied territories, Japan installed puppet governments in Singapore. These governments had limited authority and were subservient to Japanese directives.
Economic exploitation	Malaya was a significant producer of rubber and tin. Japan redirected these resources to meet their military and industrial needs. Rubber plantations and tin mines were placed under Japanese control. Japan employed a large number of locals for forced labour in various projects, including the construction of the Thai–Burma Railway. The harsh conditions and treatment led to significant suffering and loss of life among the labourers.	Singapore, a major British naval base, was strategically important. Japan redirected resources and facilities for their war effort, including the use of the naval base to support their operations in South East Asia. Japan employed forced labour to build military infrastructure and support their occupation. Civilians were conscripted for labour and conditions were harsh.

Case study: The Vichy government

The Vichy government refers to the French government that collaborated with Nazi Germany during the war. The government was based in the town of Vichy, and its leader was Marshal Philippe Pétain, a highly decorated French military officer from the First World War. Facing a rapid German advance, Pétain, who had become Prime Minister in June 1940, sought an armistice with Germany. On 22 June 1940 an armistice was signed, leading to the establishment of the Vichy government.

The Vichy government collaborated with Nazi Germany and became a puppet regime. Under the terms of the armistice, Germany occupied northern and western France, while the Vichy regime retained control over the southern unoccupied zone and the French overseas territories. Pétain's government quickly established an authoritarian regime. The Vichy government implemented laws that restricted civil liberties, curtailed freedom of the press, and targeted political opponents. The regime promoted conservative social values and emphasised traditional notions of authority.

The Vichy government implemented anti-Semitic policies, including the enactment of laws that discriminated against Jewish citizens. These laws were passed independently of direct German pressure, reflecting the collaborationist nature of the Vichy regime. While the Vichy government initially enacted discriminatory laws, it later actively collaborated with Nazi authorities in the deportation of Jewish individuals.

Not all French citizens accepted the Vichy regime and resistance movements emerged both in France and among the Free French forces abroad, led by General Charles de Gaulle. The Free French rejected the Vichy government's collaboration with the Axis powers and continued the fight against Nazi Germany.

Case study: Poland and the Holocaust

The Nazi occupation of Poland was marked by severe repression, exploitation, and systematic brutality. In coordination with the Molotov-Ribbentrop Pact, the Soviet Union invaded Poland from the east on 17 September 1939, leading to the division of Poland between Nazi Germany and the Soviet Union.

Recap

The Vichy government was the part of France that openly collaborated with Nazi Germany. It was established in the unoccupied zone of France after the fall of the French Third Republic in 1940. It implemented Nazi policy within the Vichy region and therefore was allowed greater freedom and control over the country.

Apply

Create a fact file about the Vichy government.

- **Occupation policies:** The German-occupied territory of Poland was divided, with the central and western regions incorporated into the German Reich, and the eastern regions forming the General Government, an area directly administered by Germany.

- **Suppression of Polish identity:** The Nazis sought to eradicate Polish culture and identity. They closed schools, suppressed cultural institutions, and censored Polish publications. Germanisation policies aimed to assimilate Poles into German culture, while also suppressing any expressions of Polish national pride.

- **Forced labour and economic exploitation:** Millions of Poles were subjected to forced labour in Germany and occupied territories. They were often exposed to harsh conditions and faced discrimination and brutality. German authorities seized Polish industries and resources for the German war effort, contributing to widespread poverty and deprivation among the Polish population.

The Holocaust

- **Nuremberg Laws:** The Nuremberg Laws were applied in occupied Poland, institutionalising anti-Semitic policies. Jews were subjected to discriminatory laws, forced labour, and systematic persecution.

- **Deportations:** The systematic deportation of Jews from ghettos to extermination camps, such as Auschwitz and Treblinka, resulted in mass extermination as part of the Holocaust.

- **Auschwitz and extermination camps:** Auschwitz, located in occupied Poland, became a symbol of the Holocaust. It played a central role in the mass extermination of Jews and other targeted groups.

- **Warsaw Uprising (1944):** The Warsaw Uprising, an attempt by the Polish Home Army to liberate Warsaw from German occupation, resulted in the near-total destruction of the city and widespread civilian casualties.

> **Key fact**
>
> The Nuremberg Laws were a set of anti-Semitic laws enacted by Nazi Germany in 1935. The laws were a key step in the institutionalisation of anti-Jewish discrimination and persecution in Germany. The Nuremberg Laws laid the foundation for further persecution of Jews in Nazi Germany. They marked a legal and social turning point, as they institutionalised discrimination and set the stage for more repressive measures, including the eventual implementation of the Holocaust.

The resistance movements in Europe and the Asia-Pacific

Across the occupied territories, resistance movements emerged among the local population in order to resist the occupying forces. Two areas in particular show how resistance movements operated: Malaya and France.

Where?	Malaya	France
Who?	**British-Led Special Force:** Force 136 was a special operations force created by Britain to carry out intelligence gathering, sabotage, and guerrilla warfare against Japan in South East Asia, including Malaya. Force 136 cooperated with local resistance groups and provided training, weapons, and support.	**The French Resistance:** This included members of political parties, intellectuals, communists, ordinary citizens, and even some who had initially collaborated with the Vichy regime. Charles de Gaulle, the leader of the Free French Forces, was a central figure in organising and unifying various resistance groups under the banner of Free France.
	Malayan People's Anti-Japanese Army (MPAJA): The MPAJA was a communist-led resistance force formed by the Malayan Communist Party (MCP). MPAJA engaged in guerrilla warfare against Japanese forces.	In urban areas, clandestine resistance networks operated. These networks were involved in intelligence gathering, producing and distributing underground newspapers, and carrying out acts of sabotage. Notable urban resistance networks included the Combat, Libération-Sud, and Francs-Tireurs et Partisans (FTP).
	Independent Malay and Chinese Groups: Apart from organised resistance movements, individuals and small groups also took part in acts of resistance. Some operated independently, carrying out sabotage, intelligence gathering, and spreading anti-Japanese propaganda.	**Maquisards:** The Maquis were rural guerrilla bands that operated in the French countryside. Composed of both locals and escaped Allied soldiers, they engaged in guerrilla warfare against German forces and their collaborators.

Where?	Malaya	France
Methods of resistance	**Intelligence networks:** Resistance groups focused on gathering intelligence on Japanese movements and activities. This information was often passed on to Allied forces or used to plan acts of sabotage. **Sabotage operations:** Acts of sabotage targeted Japanese infrastructure, transportation, and communication facilities. Railways, bridges, and telecommunication lines were common targets. **Urban sabotage and espionage:** In urban areas, individuals engaged in acts of sabotage, including damaging Japanese military vehicles and equipment. Some individuals worked as spies, providing valuable information about Japanese military movements and plans.	The Maquis operated using hit-and-run tactics, ambushing German convoys, destroying infrastructure, and disrupting communication and supply lines. The Special Operations Executive (SOE) from Britain supported French resistance efforts. They provided training, equipment, and coordination for intelligence and sabotage missions. Resistance members engaged in espionage, gathering crucial information on German military activities. Sabotage operations targeted railways, bridges, and communication networks. Resistance members targeted transportation infrastructure, particularly railways used by the German forces. Sabotage of train tracks and locomotives disrupted German logistics.
Reprisals and brutality	Japan responded to resistance activities with brutal reprisals. Villages suspected of harbouring resistance fighters were often subjected to mass punishments, including executions and the burning of homes. Resistance members who were captured faced torture and execution. Despite the risks, many continued to resist.	Resistance members found support among sympathetic civilians who provided safe houses, food, and information. Some civilians actively participated in resistance activities. The civilian population faced severe consequences if caught collaborating with the Resistance, including arrest, torture, and execution by German forces.
Impact	The resistance efforts in Malaya played a role in the broader Allied strategy against Japan. The resistance movements contributed to the disruption of Japanese plans and military activities.	The Resistance played a vital role in supporting the Allied invasion on D-Day (6 June 1944) by carrying out acts of sabotage and disrupting German communications.

Allied victory over the Axis powers

Italy

The Allied invasion of Sicily, codenamed Operation Husky, was a major step in the Allies' efforts to liberate southern Europe from Axis control.

- **9 July 1943:** Invasion launched, with airborne and amphibious landings along the southern coast of Sicily. The Allies faced initial resistance from German and Italian forces.

- **17 August:** Allied forces successfully captured the island. German and Italian forces, under the command of General Alfredo Guzzoni, resisted the Allied advance. However, facing the prospect of being trapped on the island, the Axis forces decided to evacuate Sicily.

- **3 September:** With Sicily secured, the Allies prepared to invade mainland Italy. The invasion began with landings at Calabria.

- **8 September:** The Italian government, realising the precarious position of its alliance with Nazi Germany, surrendered to the Allies.

- **4 June 1944:** The Allied advance through Italy progressed slowly, but by June 1944 Rome was liberated by the Allies.

The Allied advance through Italy during the Second World War was a strategically significant campaign that had several important implications for the overall war effort. While the Italian campaign did not result in a swift victory, it played a crucial role in the overall strategy of the Allies, contributing to the erosion of Axis strength in Europe and paving the way for subsequent offensives that would ultimately lead to the defeat of Nazi Germany.

> **Key fact**
>
> The Italian surrender led to a complex situation. While some Italian forces joined the Allies, others continued to fight alongside the Germans. Germany swiftly occupied Italy, disarming Italian troops and establishing a defensive line called the Gustav Line.

> **Recap**
>
> The Allied advance through Italy faced challenging terrain and determined German resistance. Battles such as Salerno, Anzio, and Monte Cassino demonstrated the difficulties of the campaign.

Benefits for the Allies	Problems for the Axis powers
Italian surrender and change of sides: The fall of Italy in 1943 after the Allied invasion led to the Italian surrender. Italy then switched sides and joined the Allies. The change in allegiance provided the Allies with valuable bases in the Mediterranean.	**Pressure on Axis forces:** The campaign in Italy diverted significant German and Italian resources and attention away from other theatres, particularly the Eastern Front and the Western Front in France.
Strategic positioning for future operations: The capture of key ports and airfields, such as Naples and Foggia, provided the Allies with strategic bases for launching further offensives in Europe.	**Opening a new front:** The Italian campaign opened up a new front in southern Europe, which required the Axis powers to defend a broader geographical area. This diversion of resources and attention weakened their ability to concentrate forces on other fronts, such as the Eastern Front against the Soviet Union.
Preparation for the Normandy invasion: The Italian campaign served as a valuable training ground for Allied forces, providing them with experience in amphibious operations and mountain warfare. This experience proved useful in planning and executing the larger and more complex amphibious assault on Normandy in June 1944.	**Softening the Axis defences:** The Allied advance through Italy helped to weaken the Axis defences in southern Europe. It forced Germany to spread its forces thinly along the Italian peninsula, making it more challenging for them to mount a cohesive defence.

Germany

Why was the Nazi war machine on the verge of collapse by April 1945?

Nazi Germany was on the verge of collapse by April 1945 due to a combination of military defeats, strategic mistakes, economic exhaustion, and internal unrest. Here are some key factors that contributed to the imminent collapse of Nazi Germany in April 1945:

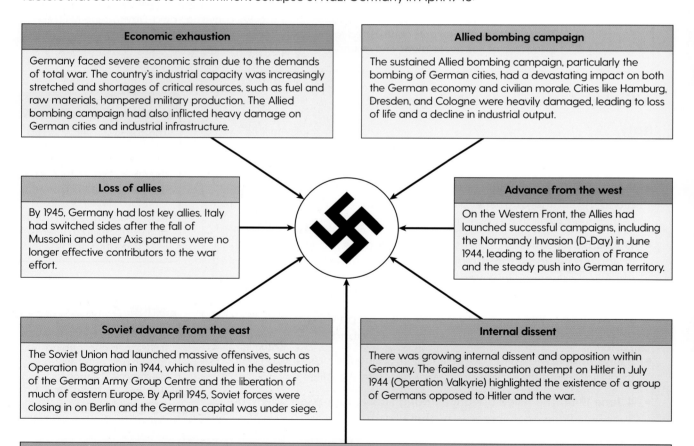

Economic exhaustion

Germany faced severe economic strain due to the demands of total war. The country's industrial capacity was increasingly stretched and shortages of critical resources, such as fuel and raw materials, hampered military production. The Allied bombing campaign had also inflicted heavy damage on German cities and industrial infrastructure.

Allied bombing campaign

The sustained Allied bombing campaign, particularly the bombing of German cities, had a devastating impact on both the German economy and civilian morale. Cities like Hamburg, Dresden, and Cologne were heavily damaged, leading to loss of life and a decline in industrial output.

Loss of allies

By 1945, Germany had lost key allies. Italy had switched sides after the fall of Mussolini and other Axis partners were no longer effective contributors to the war effort.

Advance from the west

On the Western Front, the Allies had launched successful campaigns, including the Normandy Invasion (D-Day) in June 1944, leading to the liberation of France and the steady push into German territory.

Soviet advance from the east

The Soviet Union had launched massive offensives, such as Operation Bagration in 1944, which resulted in the destruction of the German Army Group Centre and the liberation of much of eastern Europe. By April 1945, Soviet forces were closing in on Berlin and the German capital was under siege.

Internal dissent

There was growing internal dissent and opposition within Germany. The failed assassination attempt on Hitler in July 1944 (Operation Valkyrie) highlighted the existence of a group of Germans opposed to Hitler and the war.

Lack of resources

Germany's resources were stretched thin and there was a shortage of manpower. The German military was relying on inexperienced and underage soldiers in its ranks and conscription could not replenish the losses suffered in battles.

Fig. 11.8 *Threats to the Nazi regime in 1945*

Hitler committed suicide on 30 April 1945 as Soviet forces closed in on Berlin, and Germany surrendered on 7–8 May 1945. This marked the end of the Second World War in Europe.

Worked Example

What was the purpose of the D-Day invasion? (4)

The D-Day invasion, also known as the Normandy Landings, was a military operation by Allied forces during the Second World War. It took place on 6 June 1944, when Allied troops landed on the beaches of Normandy in German-occupied France. The purpose of the D-Day invasion was to open a new front in Europe, liberate France from German control, and ultimately defeat Nazi Germany. It was a significant turning point in the war as it marked the beginning of the end for Nazi Germany's domination in Europe. The successful invasion allowed Allied forces to gain a foothold in continental Europe, leading to the eventual defeat of Nazi Germany in May 1945.

> **Exam tip**
>
> Be sure not to fall into the trap of explaining what D-Day was. Focus on the purpose and why the invasion was launched.

Japan

- **Island-hopping campaign:** The United States pursued an "island-hopping" strategy, bypassing heavily fortified Japanese-held islands and capturing strategically important ones. This approach allowed the Allies to move closer to Japan while avoiding some of the most heavily defended positions.

- **Strategic bombing campaign:** The United States conducted a relentless strategic bombing campaign against Japan, targeting industrial and urban areas. This campaign inflicted significant damage on Japan's war-making capabilities and eroded the country's ability to sustain the war effort.

- **Soviet entry into the war:** The Soviet Union declared war on Japan in August 1945, just days before Japan's surrender. The Red Army swiftly invaded Japanese-occupied territories in Manchuria and Korea. The Soviet entry into the war contributed to Japan's decision to surrender, as it faced the prospect of fighting a two-front war.

- **Economic strain:** Japan faced severe economic strain due to resource shortages. The Allied blockade and submarine warfare disrupted Japan's supply lines and isolated the country from essential raw materials, such as oil, rubber, and metals.

> **Key fact**
>
> D-Day, or Operation Overlord, was the largest seaborne invasion in history and a pivotal event during the Second World War. It took place on 6 June 1944 and marked the beginning of the end for Nazi Germany in western Europe.

Two key battles

	Battle of Guadalcanal (August 1942–February 1943)	Battle of Okinawa (April–June 1945)
Strategic importance	The Battle of Guadalcanal was a turning point in the Pacific War. The Allies, primarily the United States, sought to capture and secure the strategically important island of Guadalcanal in the Solomon Islands. Guadalcanal was vital for controlling sea routes between the United States and Australia, and served as an airbase for potential threats to Australia.	The Battle of Okinawa was the largest amphibious assault in the Pacific War and the last major battle before the planned invasion of Japan. Okinawa, located close to the Japanese home islands, was seen as a stepping stone for the planned invasion of Japan.
Japanese resistance	The campaign involved intense fighting on land, at sea, and in the air. Both sides suffered heavy losses in naval battles around the island.	Japanese forces defended Okinawa vigorously, leading to one of the bloodiest battles of the Pacific War. Both sides suffered heavy casualties.
Allied victory	After months of bitter fighting, the Allies, particularly the United States, successfully captured Guadalcanal. The victory marked the first time the Allies had taken the offensive against Japan in the Pacific.	Despite the tenacious Japanese defence, the Allies, primarily the United States, ultimately prevailed. The Battle of Okinawa demonstrated the high human cost of an invasion of the Japanese home islands.

The atomic bomb

In July 1945, the Allied leaders issued the Potsdam Declaration, which called for Japan's unconditional surrender. The declaration warned of "prompt and utter destruction" if Japan refused to surrender. This, coupled with the dropping of atomic bombs, played a role in Japan's decision to end the war.

The United States dropped atomic bombs on the cities of Hiroshima on 6 August 1945 and Nagasaki on 9 August 1945. The devastating impact of these bombings, coupled with the fear of further nuclear attacks, influenced Japan's leadership to seek an immediate end to the war.

Emperor Hirohito's unprecedented intervention in Japan's political affairs played a crucial role. His decision to break with tradition and accept the Potsdam Declaration facilitated the surrender process and spared Japan from further destruction. Japan formally surrendered on 2 September 1945, aboard the USS *Missouri*, marking the end of the Second World War.

What happened at the end of the war to Germany and Japan?

After the unconditional surrender of Germany and Japan in 1945, the Allies undertook a comprehensive effort to consolidate victory, stabilise the defeated nations, and prevent a resurgence of militarism.

Area	Germany	Japan
Allied decision making	The Potsdam Conference, held in July–August 1945, laid the foundation for the Allied occupation of Germany. The conference established zones of occupation for the United States, the Soviet Union, the United Kingdom, and France.	Japan was placed under Allied occupation, led by General Douglas MacArthur, who became the Supreme Commander for the Allied Powers (SCAP). The occupation aimed to demilitarise Japan, dismantle its war industries, and establish democratic institutions.
Political reform	The Allies initiated a denazification process to remove Nazi influence from German society. War criminals were prosecuted during the Nuremberg Trials and Nazi organisations were disbanded.	Under MacArthur's direction, Japan underwent significant constitutional reforms. The new constitution, known as the Postwar Constitution or the Constitution of Japan, renounced war as a sovereign right and established a parliamentary democracy.
Economic reconstruction	The Marshall Plan, initiated in 1948, provided economic assistance to western European countries, including Germany, to aid in post-war reconstruction. This helped stabilise the German economy and contributed to the formation of the Federal Republic of Germany (West Germany) in 1949.	The Allies implemented economic reforms to decentralise industry, break up large conglomerates (zaibatsu), and promote land reforms. These measures contributed to Japan's post-war economic recovery.
Occupation and reform	Germany was divided into four occupation zones, each controlled by one of the Allied powers. Berlin, located in the Soviet zone, was also divided among the Allies. The division of Germany deepened, resulting in the establishment of two separate German states: the Federal Republic of Germany (West Germany) and the German Democratic Republic (East Germany). This division persisted until German reunification in 1990.	The occupation authorities demilitarised Japan, disbanding its military and strictly controlling arms production. The new constitution prohibited Japan from maintaining a military for aggressive purposes. The Allies sought to reintegrate Japan into the international community. The signing of the Treaty of San Francisco in 1951 formally ended the occupation and restored Japanese sovereignty.

Area	Germany	Japan
War crimes	The Nuremberg Trials were a series of military tribunals held after the war to prosecute major war criminals of Nazi Germany. Created during the Potsdam Conference in 1945 by Allied powers, the trials addressed war crimes, crimes against peace, and crimes against humanity committed by Nazi Germany. Twenty-four high-ranking Nazis, including Göring, Hess, and Ribbentrop, were tried with evidence presented by the prosecution and defences offered by the defendants. The tribunal delivered judgements on 1 October 1946. Several defendants were found guilty and sentences included death by hanging, imprisonment, or acquittal. Twelve of the major defendants were sentenced to death and three were acquitted.	The Tokyo War Crimes Trials, known as the International Military Tribunal for the Far East (IMTFE), were held from 1946 to 1948 to prosecute high-ranking Japanese political and military leaders for war crimes. The trials took place in Tokyo and were established by the Allied powers. The major defendants included figures like General Hideki Tojo. The verdicts were delivered on 12 November 1948, with several defendants found guilty. Seven individuals, including Tojo, were sentenced to death by hanging, while others received prison sentences.

Fig. 11.9 *Defendants in the dock at the Nuremburg Trials: Hermann Göring is seated in the front row, far left, with Ribbentrop seated third in the same row*

Review

1. Describe the main features of the Vichy government. [4]

2. What happened at the Battle of Midway? [4]

3. What was the Manhattan Project? [4]

4. What were the D-Day landings? [4]

5. Why was the Battle of Stalingrad so crucial? [6]

6. Why did President Truman choose to use atomic weapons against Japan? [6]

7. Why did Hitler invade the Soviet Union? [6]

8. "Dunkirk was a triumph, not a disaster for Britain." How far do you agree with this statement? Explain your answer. [10]

9. How are far do you agree with the statement "Resistance movements in Europe and the Asia-Pacific failed in their aims". Explain your answer. [10]

10. How far do you agree that the Battle of Britain was a key turning point in the conflict in Europe during the Second World War? [10]

For further information, review this section in the Student Book.

Raise your grade ↑

1. What was Operation Sealion? (4 marks)

Operation Sealion was the code name for Nazi Germany's planned invasion of the United Kingdom during the Second World War. It was devised in 1940, shortly after the fall of France, as Adolf Hitler sought to eliminate Britain as a potential threat to German domination in Europe. The plan involved a massive amphibious assault on the British Isles, with the German army crossing the English Channel.

However, Operation Sealion never materialised into a full-scale invasion. The German air force, the Luftwaffe, was unable to gain air superiority over the Royal Air Force (RAF) during the Battle of Britain. It became apparent that Germany lacked the necessary resources and logistical capabilities for a large-scale invasion of Britain, especially considering the challenges of supplying a distant front. As a result, Operation Sealion was postponed indefinitely in September 1940, and the invasion of Britain never took place.

The student has done well and provided two detailed features of the planned operation. 4 marks awarded.

Plan your answer

- To answer this 4-mark question you need to provide two specific features of Operation Sealion. Make sure you explain the features and do not just identify them.

- Sealion was a planned invasion of Britain by Nazi Germany.

- It would have to be an amphibious assault, hence its name, and would mean large numbers of German forces crossing the English Channel.

- The success of the operation would depend upon first defeating the RAF to ensure that the German forces could cross the English Channel without being attacked from the air.

Mark scheme

1 mark for each relevant point, 1 additional mark for supporting detail.
Maximum 2 marks per point made.

2. Why did Japan attack Pearl Harbor? (6 marks)

Japan attacked Pearl Harbor on 7 December 1941 for several key reasons. Japan sought to expand its empire in Asia and the Pacific. Japan also faced resource shortages, particularly oil, rubber, and iron ore. These resources were vital for its military and industrial capabilities. Lastly, the United States had imposed economic sanctions on Japan in response to its aggression in Asia, including an embargo on oil and scrap metal. This further exacerbated Japan's resource crisis and pushed it toward a more confrontational stance.

The student has done well to identify a range of reasons. But unfortunately, only explains fully the final reason regarding economic sanctions. The student identifies Japan's desire to expand its empire and also the need to addresses shortages, but fails to develop the explanation. 4 marks were awarded.

Plan your answer

- To answer this 6-mark question you need two reasons for the Japanese attack on Pearl Harbor.

- The attacks came after growing tensions between the United States and Japan.

- Japan had significant territorial desires in the Pacific, and knew that if they could limit the United States' ability to resist they would be more successful.

- Japan also had a growing need for economic resources.

Mark scheme

Level 1:	general answer lacking specific contextual knowledge (1 mark)
Level 2:	identifies AND/OR describes reasons (2–3 marks)
Level 3:	explains ONE reason (4–5 marks)
Level 4:	explains TWO reasons (6 marks)

3. How far do you agree with the view that it was the invasion of the Soviet Union that was the key turning point in the Second World War? Explain your answer. (10 marks)

The invasion of the Soviet Union in June 1941 marked a significant escalation of the war on the Eastern Front and therefore should be seen as a key turning point in the Second World War. It opened up a massive new theatre of conflict and diverted a substantial portion of Nazi Germany's military resources to the east. This diversion weakened the German military's overall capacity to wage war on multiple fronts. Initially, the German invasion of the Soviet Union appeared highly successful, with rapid advances and the capture of large territories. However, as the harsh Russian winter set in and the Red Army's resistance stiffened, the German advance slowed and eventually stalled. The Battle of Stalingrad in 1942–43 marked a critical turning point where Germany suffered a decisive defeat, losing a substantial part of its army. The Red Army's determination, coupled with the vastness of the Soviet territory and resources, allowed it to regroup, rebuild, and eventually launch successful offensives that pushed the German forces back. By defeating and inflicting such suffering on the previously all-conquering Nazi war machine, the invasion of the Soviet Union had ultimately led to the beginning of the end of German dominance in Europe.

The student has done really well here to give a good paragraph about why the invasion of the Soviet Union was a key turning point. They explain the demands it placed on the Nazi war machine and the damage that defeat did at Stalingrad. However, the student fails to present a balanced argument. There needs to be the other side of the question, where there is an evaluation of whether other events were more important. There is also a lack of a conclusion. As it only addresses one side of the argument, it would only score 6 marks.

Plan your answer

- The Soviet invasion opened up a whole new front for Germany and placed a huge strain on their military.

- Defeat at Stalingrad meant a huge loss of troops and supplies, but was also a psychological blow for Germany, which had previously largely only enjoyed success.

- However, other events could be seen to be as crucial—the entry of the United States into the war after the attack on Pearl Harbor and the defeat at El Alamein are just two examples.

Mark scheme

Level 1:	general answer lacking specific contextual knowledge (1 mark)
Level 2:	identifies AND/OR describes reasons (2–3 marks)
Level 3:	gives a one-sided explanation (4–5 marks) or one explanation of both sides (4–6 marks)
Level 4:	explains both sides (7–9 marks)
Level 5:	explains with evaluation (10 marks)

Glossary

Alphabet agencies Government agencies known for convenience by their initials.

Anschluss The term given to the unification of Germany with its neighbour, Austria.

Anti-Semitism Hostility to, prejudice, or discrimination against Jews, Judaism, and Jewishness.

The British Expeditionary Force (BEF) The British Army sent to fight in the Low Countries alongside France against Germany prior to the First Battle of Ypres on 22 November 1914. Unlike the conscripted forces of Germany and France, the BEF consisted of volunteer troops, who were renowned for their shooting skills.

Coalition government A government formed by multiple political parties promising to cooperate for the common good, reducing the dominance of an absolute party within that coalition. The usual reason for this arrangement is that no single party can achieve a majority in the parliament.

Collectivisation A policy pursued between 1928 and 1933 to consolidate individual land and labour into state farms.

COMECON The Council for Mutual Economic Assistance—an economic organisation that comprised of the countries of the eastern bloc under the leadership of the Soviet Union between 1949–91, along with a number of communist states elsewhere in the world.

Congress The main law-making institution in the United States.

Containment The United States' government policy under Truman, based on the principle that communist governments would eventually collapse provided they were prevented from expanding their influence.

Enfilade fire First World War tactic of firing across the longest line of soldiers to create a "beaten zone" of fire which would entrap enemy troops as they attempted to progress forward.

Lebensraum The territory which a group, state, or nation believes is needed for its natural development—particularly relating to the post-First World War German concept of settler colonialism into eastern Europe.

Lend–Lease From 1941, the United States lent, leased, and sold military equipment to countries fighting Germany, Italy, or Japan.

Morning hate All sides in the First World War would attempt to prevent a surprise dawn raid by firing rifles and throwing grenades in the direction of the enemy; this was frequently repeated at dusk.

Mustard gas Chemical weapon used by Germany for the first time at Ypres in 1917, its sulphuric compound created blisters, burning the eyes, skin, and lungs.

NATO The North Atlantic Treaty Organization—a military alliance of countries founded on 4 April 1949 to strengthen international ties between member states, especially the United States and Europe, and to serve as a collective defence against an external attack. It remains in existence today.

November Criminals The term was often used to criticise and vilify the politicians involved in the armistice, accusing them of betraying the country. It became a catchphrase employed by nationalist and right-wing groups, contributing to the broader atmosphere of discontent and anger that eventually played a role in the rise of extremist movements, including the Nazi Party led by Adolf Hitler. The term was a propaganda tool, rather than an accurate historical characterisation. The politicians involved in the armistice negotiations and the establishment of the Weimar Republic were acting within the context of the challenges and pressures of the time. The label reflects the divisive and polarised political climate in post-First World War Germany, rather than an objective assessment of the actions of those individuals.

Operation Michael A German offensive launched in 1918 to push troops into France; also referred to as the Ludendorff Offensive or Spring Offensive.

Plebiscite A vote on a single issue in the manner of a referendum. Plebiscites were held after 1918 in areas of uncertain nationality to establish which country the populations wished to be governed by.

Race to the sea The attempt by both sides to capture the Channel ports and outflank each other from the middle of September until the middle of October 1914.

The Ruhr The heavily industrialised area of western Germany named after the river that flows through the region. It was a huge centre for the coal, iron, and steel industry.

Soviet A council made up of workers.

Unrestricted submarine warfare A German naval strategy in the First World War which declared the waters around Great Britain to be a war zone; all shipping in that zone could be targeted, without warning.

Vietminh A communist-dominated nationalist movement, formed in 1941, that fought for Vietnamese independence from French rule.

Vietnamisation Support given by the United States to strengthen the South Vietnamese army to allow the gradual withdrawal of American combat troops from the Vietnam War.

Wall Street Crash The collapse of the New York Stock Exchange on 29 October 1929. The crash started the Great Depression and stock prices did not return to a similar level until late 1954.

The Warsaw Pact A collective defence treaty signed between the Soviet Union and seven Soviet satellite states of central and eastern Europe in Warsaw, Poland in May 1955, during the Cold War. Its members were the Soviet Union, Albania, Poland, Romania, Hungary, East Germany, Czechoslovakia, and Bulgaria.

Index